Mystery of Relationships through the Lens of Scriptures

Mystery of Relationships through the Lens of Scriptures

Marriage, Sex, and Intimacy

Dr. Elizabeth Thambiraj

MYSTERY OF RELATIONSHIPS THROUGH THE LENS OF SCRIPTURES MARRIAGE, SEX, AND INTIMACY

Copyright © 2015 Dr. Elizabeth Thambiraj.

All rights reserved. No part of this book may be used or reproduced by any means, graphic, electronic, or mechanical, including photocopying, recording, taping or by any information storage retrieval system without the written permission of the publisher except in the case of brief quotations embodied in critical articles and reviews.

Unless otherwise noted, scripture quotations are taken from the Holy Bible, King James Version (KJV), Copyright 1994, 1997 by World Bible Publishers, Inc. Italics in scripture have been added by the author for emphasis.

Scripture quotations marked NASB are taken from the New American Standard Bible®, Copyright © 1960, 1962, 1963, 1968, 1971, 1972, 1973, 1975, 1977, 1995 by The Lockman Foundation. Used by permission.

Scripture quotations marked AMP are from The Amplified Bible, Old Testament copyright © 1965, 1987 by the Zondervan Corporation. The Amplified Bible, New Testament copyright © 1954, 1958, 1987 by The Lockman Foundation. Used by permission. All rights reserved.

This is the first publication of this book in 2015 and compiled by the author.

The author has published a book on a biblical approach to nonorganic illnesses.

The author is the writer for the website www.inerrantword.blogspot.com as well. Many of the writings were adopted from that website, compiled later, and edited by the same author.

iUniverse books may be ordered through booksellers or by contacting:

iUniverse
1663 Liberty Drive
Bloomington, IN 47403
www.iuniverse.com
1-800-Authors (1-800-288-4677)

Because of the dynamic nature of the Internet, any web addresses or links contained in this book may have changed since publication and may no longer be valid. The views expressed in this work are solely those of the author and do not necessarily reflect the views of the publisher, and the publisher hereby disclaims any responsibility for them.

Any people depicted in stock imagery provided by Thinkstock are models, and such images are being used for illustrative purposes only. Certain stock imagery © Thinkstock.

ISBN: 978-1-4917-7125-9 (sc)
ISBN: 978-1-4917-7124-2 (e)

Library of Congress Control Number: 2015910736

Print information available on the last page.

iUniverse rev. date: 08/07/2015

In loving memory of my uncle, the late Professor Chandra Sen

It is important to understand and realize the following. "**My beloved is mine, and I am his.**" (Song 2:16a) and "**I am my beloved's, and my beloved is mine.**" (Song 6:3a) The only means of our "owning" the Lord is to be owned by Him. "**We love Him because He first loved us.**" (1 John 4:19) This is the common order of love between a husband and wife. The fair lady is easy to love, but the rough and rugged gentleman is less lovely. But the love of a man for his chosen bride will win the lady if it is sincere, genuine, and unrelenting. We cannot love that which we have not known. We cannot know the Lord until He has loved us. He loved and knew His elect before they were yet conceived in their mother's womb.

—Dr. Jerry Levon Ogles, Presiding Bishop,
Anglican Orthodox Communion Worldwide

Contents

Author Biography xi

Foreword xiii

Part I. Introduction to Relationships
- Preface 3
- The Creation of Man and Woman and the Building of Relationship: Genesis 1–2 7
- The Fall and Destruction of That Beautiful Relationship: Genesis 3 10
- Cain and Abel and the First Murder: Genesis 4 14
- The Birth of Jesus Christ and the Gospel: Luke 2:8–20 17
- Relationship with Other Believers: Ephesians 4–6 19
- The Marriage Supper of the Lamb 26
- New Heavens and New Earth 29
- Instructions for Marriage 32
- Faithful Marriage 34
- Obedience in Love 36

Part II. Articles on Relationships
- Preface 41
- A Litmus Test for Relationship with God 42
- How Can I Be a Loving Neighbor? 47
- Male and Female: Divine Comedy or Brilliance? 52
- Marriage 58
- Triggers of Conflict in Marriages 61
- A Little Glimpse into Marriages beyond the Fall 69
- Tongues 76
- Love … in All the Wrong Places? 81
- Faithfulness 85
- Religion or the Gospel 89
- Whom Am I Living For? 92
- How Great Is Our God! 95
- As the Deer Panteth for the Water … 98
- Holding Loose … 101
- Emotional Abuse in a Nutshell 105

- Misplaced Priorities..124
- True Love 131
- A Scriptural View of Marriage 141
- Gender Roles: A Glimpse...................................147

Part III. Diagrams on Relationships

Part IV. Prayers for Relationships
- Preface...173
- A Prayer for Healing Strained Relationships with Parents 176
- Mending Broken Relationships 178
- A Prayer for Conflict between Husband and Wife.........181
- Physical and Emotional Abuse 184
- A Prayer for an Unsaved Spouse 189

Professional Comment from the Author 191
Notes 197
Selected Bibliography 257
Suggestions for Further Reading 261

Author Biography

Elizabeth Thambiraj is the author of *Biblical approach to non-organic illnesses* (Doss Publications, 2014).

The author's degrees and certifications include a BSc (chemistry), a MSc (chemistry), a CDip AF, an MBA, a DBA, an MDiv (biblical counseling), and NANC certification (Association of Certified Biblical Counselors).

She has worked as a lecturer in chemistry, as a company administrator, and as a company president and director. Now she practices as an NANC counselor and former adjunct professor at Taylor Seminary in Edmonton, Canada. The passion of her heart is to bring the truth to people through God's Word.

She is a member of the Anglican Orthodox Church, USA, and worships at Southgate Alliance Church in Edmonton, Canada.

Brought up in a godly home, the author has been married to her husband, a surgeon, for the past thirty-two years. She is the mother of two girls and a boy and the grandmother of three boys. She has always cherished being nourished by God's Word in different settings, even while a student. She has a thankful heart for God weaving her in Christ in His unfailing love on the cross—in the past and today. She lives in Edmonton, Alberta, Canada, with her husband, with a thankful heart for her family. She enjoys reading, writing, teaching and music.

Foreword

Janet Annan wife of former Senior Pastor of
Bay View Glen Church, Toronto.

Relationships are of upmost important in our world. In North America many individuals have successfully accumulated things, but have not been successful in relationships. Broken relationships are strewn everywhere, leaving unseen, but very painful wounds. Loneliness lies heavy, even if unacknowledged, in many lives.

In this book, Elizabeth clearly offers ways to move beyond hurts of the past.

7Blessed is the man that trusteth in the Lord, and whose hope the Lord is.

8For he shall be as a tree planted by the waters, and that spreadeth out her roots by the river, and shall not see when heat cometh, but her leaf shall be green; and shall not be careful in the year of drought, neither shall cease from yielding fruit. Jeremiah 17:7-8King James Version (KJV)

Elizabeth is one who trusts in the Lord, both in the good seasons and in the droughts of life. I have known Elizabeth for more than a decade and witnessed her personal walk with God.

God has given Elizabeth a good mind and she has studied hard in numerous fields in order to use that intellect to God's glory. Her studies have covered a wide spectrum. Elizabeth has earned degrees in science, in business and in counseling.

What has most consistently stood out over the years I have known her, is her heart for prayer. Elizabeth is always willing to pray one-on-one; she is willing to pray before large crowds; and also has led a prayer ministry.

Dr. Elizabeth Thambiraj

When it comes to problem solving, her incisive, logical mind moves easily toward understanding the root of various problems and then presenting solid solutions. I remember in one prayer committee meeting, Elizabeth drew a chart that clarified the problem we had been discussing. Now her analytical mind is demonstrated in her writing.

Elizabeth is also always willing to listen and to help friends; sometimes at great cost to her personally. She is a thoughtful and generous friend; a faithful friend that you can trust with confidences. I believe as you read Elizabeth's book you will gain understanding that will strengthen your relationship with God and with others.

Elizabeth is one of the most accomplished and dedicated Christian mothers and workers I have known. She has been the mother of two daughters and one son. These three children have been raised up by their mother in the nurture and counsel of the Word of God. She has ever been a most conscientious mother. The character and reputation of her children stand in strong testimony to that fact. She is one of the finest examples of motherhood of which I am familiar. She always seeks to learn from any challenge she faces and improve her ability to address the needs of others, always serving others and taking particular notice of their needs in counseling.

She has also proven to be a dear and loyal friend over an extended period of time. I could recommend no one with greater assurance and confidence.

On marriage, she has given one of the most biblically insightful explanations of the drastic change in the marriage relationship that resulted from the Fall at Eden and provides excellent guidance on ways that the marriage covenant can be maintained through feeding our better angels with forgiveness, understanding, patience, and forbearance. If we feed our lustful tendencies, we have committed adultery long before the physical act itself.

I will incorporate the counsel of this message in my counseling of marriage prospects in the future.

—Dr. Jerry L. Ogles, Presiding Bishop, Anglican Orthodox Church

Mystery of Relationships through the Lens of Scriptures

On "Religion or the Gospel":

Thank you again for another enlightening post. Your emphasis on the way our acceptance by God through Christ changes us is an important message. You state that we no longer feel the need to win arguments and that He releases us from the spiral of bitterness, self-recrimination, and despair. Excellent points. The new life in Christ is not simply a matter of being forgiven; it affects the entire being, including our mental/emotional state.

On "True Love":

This post is solid, biblical counsel that will help all who read it. Not only love but all of the good things of this world fail to ultimately satisfy us, because they are not God.

—Dr. Bishop Dennis Campbell, Anglican Orthodox Church, USA

Relationships

Pastor Tim Cook

Hi, my name is Tim Cook and looking back over the last 34 years, one of the most wonderful things in my life was discovering that special woman that God had been preparing for me to meet at Canadian Bible College (CBC) in Regina, Saskatchewan. Her name was Sandy Fowler; she had an older brother, came from a Christian family in Calgary, attended First Alliance Church and was in her first year of studies at CBC.

My parents were Alliance missionaries and served in the countries of Costa Rica, Colombia, Argentina and Peru. I have 3 brothers and one sister and we grew up in those wonderful countries. I along with 2 of my brothers attended, for a few years, a boarding school called the Alliance Academy in Quito, Ecuador.

I returned to Canada and was in my second year at Bible College when I met Sandy in the gymnasium on the basketball court shooting baskets. After 2 years of engagement and finishing my Bachelor of Theology degree, we were married in Toronto, where both our parents had recently moved.

We began our marriage in December 1982 with the blessing of both sets of our parents who loved the Lord. They have modelled for us, not perfect marriages but God centered relationships. It has been our privilege to have recently celebrated the 60th and 62nd wedding anniversaries with our parents!

Sandy and I are looking forward to celebrating our 32nd Anniversary this December. We also are entering our 28th year of pastoral ministry with the Christian and Missionary Alliance. God has been very gracious and good to us for which we continue to praise him!

God has blessed us with 3 children who are now married. We prayed for their future spouses as they were growing up and God has blessed

Dr. Elizabeth Thambiraj

them and us with wonderful Christian spouses that fit them just right! Our son has been married for 6 years and they have a beautiful 10 month old son. Our oldest daughter has been married for a year and our youngest daughter has been married for 3 years. They live in the same city as we do; Edmonton, Alberta and we are blessed to see them often!

As a Pastor, it has been my privilege to participate in many weddings. A wedding is a joyful occasion that marks the beginning of a marriage. I think that it is significant that Jesus marked the beginning of his public ministry by attending a wedding with his mother Mary! John 2.

In spite of what our society seems to say about marriage today, marriage is still commendable and honorable in the sight of God, who after all was the one who instituted marriage in the first place! Genesis 2:23, 24. God has not changed His mind about marriage and is still committed to helping us build solid marriages and families! The fact of the matter is that we desperately need strong marriages and families to strengthen and form the foundational fabric of our Canadian society and nation!

I like the story of the school teacher who once stood in front of a group of grade 3 high powered over achievers and said, "Okay, it's time for a quiz!" She pulled a 1 gallon wide-mouth mason jar and set it on the table in front of her. Then she produced 12 fist size rocks and carefully placed them one by one, into the jar. When the jar was filled to the top and no more rocks would fit inside, she asked "Is the jar full?"

Everyone in the class answered yes! "Really," she asked as she reached under the table and pulled out a bucket of gravel. She dumped some gravel in the jar and shook it causing pieces of gravel to work themselves between the big rocks. Again she asked the class "Is the jar full?" "Probably not," replied one student! "Good," she replied as she yet again reached under the table for a bucket of sand. She poured sand into the jar filling the spaces between the rocks and the gravel and asked, "Is the jar full? No," the whole class shouted!

Mystery of Relationships through the Lens of Scriptures

The teacher then pulled out a pitcher of water. She poured water into the jar until it was filled to the brim. Then, she looked at the class and asked, "What is the point of this illustration?" One eager student raised his hand and said, "The point is, no matter how full your schedule is, if you try really hard, you can always fit more things into it!"

"No," replied the teacher, "that's not the point. The truth this illustration brings to life is this, "If you don't put the big rocks of life in first, you'll never get them in at all!" There are many aspects and qualities to a marriage that we could touch on. I would like to mention just a few of those key rocks of marriage that I've found helpful in building our marriage over the last 31 ½ years.

First, a tenacious faithful commitment to each other is vital to our marriage!

There is no back door that we will step out of our marriage. "We are all in!" We live in an age where commitment seems to be a lost or endangered quality in people's lives! But I have noticed that when we see commitment in action, we highly admire and esteem that quality! We often hear common phrases like, "If it's too hard, just quit!" or "If it doesn't fit your time schedule, your needs or expectations, just walk away!"

In order for a marriage to last and grow over time, we must both be committed to each other and willing to work at building your relationship daily! Let's let our love and faithfulness to each other be seen as a testimony of our commitment to our marriage. Most of our popular songs today seem to focus on love as simply a feeling! Love is clearly not just an emotion like "a quiver in my liver" that may come and go as our feelings dictate but rather love is also a strong action verb!

We read the Apostle Paul's words in 1 Corinthians 13: 4-8 which describe love like this*!*

4 Charity suffereth long, and is kind; charity envieth not; charity vaunteth not itself, is not puffed up, 5 Doth not behave itself unseemly,

Dr. Elizabeth Thambiraj

seeketh not her own, is not easily provoked, thinketh no evil; *⁶ Rejoiceth not in iniquity, but rejoiceth in the truth;* *⁷ Beareth all things, believeth all things, hopeth all things, endureth all things.* *⁸ Charity never faileth: but whether there be prophecies, they shall fail; whether there be tongues, they shall cease; whether there be knowledge, it shall vanish away.* 1 Corinthians 13:4-8.

Secondly, we have discovered that we need to continue to work at developing an open and growing communication in our marriage.

I find as a husband and father that I can tend to be a very poor listener! Developing clear communication skills is vital to encouraging and nurturing growth in our marriage and family! I heard of an old Alberta farmer who said to his wife on their wedding day, "Honey, I'm telling you today that I love you and if I change my mind, you'll be the first to know!"

Communication on a "need to know" basis only, is not the greatest way to build our marriage! Communication is hard work to both share our thoughts and feelings and then in turn listen to our partner's thoughts and feelings! I like how well a little kid described a key component of communication when he said; "Listening is really wanting to hear the other person!"

All too often we are busy preparing our rebuttal to what our spouse or children are saying to us that we are not really hearing what they are telling us! Many times it takes a conscious effort to turn off the T.V., cell phones, personal electronic devices and any other distractions in order to sit down and talk and pray about what is happening in our lives!

Thirdly, we need to work at keeping a loving consideration that puts the needs of our spouse and children first!

Oh may the tone of our relationships be such that those who know us would see a loving attitude and actions that put others first! I have found this to not a very easy thing to do, as we usually find that our closest three friends in life can often be; me, myself and I!

Mystery of Relationships through the Lens of Scriptures

Have you noticed that if we're not careful, time can have a strong eroding effect on this characteristic of consideration; that of put our spouse and children's needs first! It takes daily work to look for practical ways to continue to say and do things that will build up, encourage, add courage into our relationships not, discourage, suck courage out and tearing down our relationships!

When we do blow it, we should be quick to say, "I'm sorry, please forgive me," even saying the word, "period" at the end. We all have a natural tendency to try to justify your mistakes or wrong doing by adding on reasons for our actions! "I'm sorry but ..."

I have found a real "Booster Juice" shot in our marriage and family life is when we are quick and willing to humble ourselves and often practice giving and receiving forgiveness to each other! *And be ye kind one to another, tender hearted, forgiving one another, even as God for Christ's sake hath forgiven you;* Ephesians 4:32.

Sandy and I have found that it is an impossible to task to try to build our marriage and family characterized by the key rocks of;

A tenacious commitment and faithfulness to each other!

A willingness to work at clear communication!

A loving consideration of putting your partner first!

The truth of the matter is that we can't do all these things in our own strength! We need God's daily help as we walk and talk with the Holy Spirit to help us grow our marriages and families! We have found it helpful that as we start each day, walk throughout our day and as we wrap up our day to have a continued conversation with the Lord.

[20] Now unto him that is able to do exceeding abundantly above all that we ask or think, according to the power that worketh in us,

[21] Unto him be glory in the church by Christ Jesus throughout all ages, world without end. Amen. Ephesians 3:20, 21.

xxi

To Love and to Cherish ...

Viola M. Brooks

Almost fifty-six years ago my husband and I stood before family and friends and vowed to God to "have and to hold from this day forward, for better or for worse, for richer, for poorer, in sickness and in health, to love and to cherish, until death do us part." As the years have passed, both "love" and "cherish" have taken on a much fuller meaning than we understood on that day.

The dictionary defines "**love**" as: a tender feeling, a strong or passionate affection; "**cherish**" as: hold dear; treat with tenderness; aid or protect; cling to; keep or guard carefully. My husband's definition of "cherish" is: engulfing a person into your bosom – being part of your being. It implies treasuring and watching over with loving care.

Since we believe that God is an integral part of our marriage, I also believe that the Bible gives us much insight into how "love" is defined. 1 John chapters 3 and 4 are especially rich in describing love. 1 John 4:7 says, " ...love comes from God" and verse 8 goes even further: "God is love." There are hundreds of other verses that clearly show us God's definition of Biblical love. Although most of them are not specifically about married love, the principles still apply, and a marriage based on God's word and God's principles cannot help but be a marriage that will bring more fulfillment than a marriage based only on secular principles.

What does "to love and to cherish" mean? In our experience, some of the components of loving and cherishing one another are: commitment, honoring one another, trust, sharing in all of life's experiences and laughing together.

In today's world, **commitment** to one's spouse all too often does not mean "until death do us part." Recently, upon hearing of the death of Mickey Rooney and the fact that he had been married eight times, my husband said, "He didn't have much of a life as I see it." Increasingly,

Dr. Elizabeth Thambiraj

we see couples, even Christian couples, who are not willing to put aside their own desires or plans and to stick with their marriages, but feel that life apart is a better option for them.

We did not promise to "have and to hold" only in the good times, but also when times were "worse" instead of better, if we were "poor" instead of rich, or when we suffered "sickness" instead of health. Those "worse" things come in many shapes and forms, and are not the same in every marriage. It is so inspiring to see a person whose spouse is suffering a disability or illness, to patiently and lovingly help their spouse even when it means putting their own needs aside and to show what it means to *[3] "Let nothing be done through strife or vainglory; but in lowliness of mind let each esteem other better than themselves. [4] Look not every man on his own things, but every man also on the things of others"* Philippians.2:3, 4. Commitment means putting your spouse's needs above your own whatever your circumstances.

Commitment is possible only when we **honor** our spouse. Honor is defined as: respect highly; think highly of. A synonym is "deference": respect shown to a person by putting his wishes or opinions before one's own. It involves listening and understanding the other's points of view, and discussing calmly and prayerfully issues where your opinions differ.

Colossians 3: 18 & 19 give specific rules for Christian households: *[18]Wives, submit yourselves unto your own husbands, as it is fit in the Lord. [19]Husbands, love your wives, and be not bitter against them;* Colossians 3:18-19.

Ephesians 5:22 – 33 expands on this, especially the duties of the husband. The concept of a wife submitting to her husband is not very popular in today's world, but God had a purpose for putting that rule in place as it clearly establishes that there is a head in the family, and that is to be the husband. In all of our years of marriage, I have never found submitting to my husband to be onerous, because my husband has followed the directives to husbands in that passage: " … love your wives, just as Christ loved the church and gave himself up for her" v.25; and comparing a husband's love to that of Christ for

Mystery of Relationships through the Lens of Scriptures

the church, *²⁸ So ought men to love their wives as their own bodies. He that loveth his wife loveth himself. ²⁹ For no man ever yet hated his own flesh; but nourisheth and cherisheth it, even as the Lord the church: ³⁰ For we are members of his body, of his flesh, and of his bones.³¹ For this cause shall a man leave his father and mother, and shall be joined unto his wife, and they two shall be one flesh;* v.28-31. Verse 33 sums up the passage by saying: *³³ Nevertheless let every one of you in particular so love his wife even as himself; and the wife see that she reverence her husband.* 1 Peter 3:1-7 is another passage that adds more details of the duties of husbands and wives, and especially emphasizes the influence a godly wife can have on her husband by her inner beauty which is only possible by allowing the Holy Spirit to give her *"the unfading beauty of a gentle and quiet spirit;"* v.4b.

"To love and to cherish" also entails **trust** – complete trust- between husband and wife, in every area of their lives. This involves an honesty and transparency which is deeper than in any other relationship. If we cannot trust our spouse unreservedly, there will be jealousies, uncertainties, and questions that can so easily start little rifts that can grow into major chasms in a marriage. This kind of deep trust can come only from God. A favorite passage of mine is Proverbs 3: 5 & 6: *"⁵ Trust in the LORD with all thine heart; and lean not unto thine own understanding. ⁶ In all thy ways acknowledge him, and he shall direct thy paths."* This, to me, is an excellent example of how a principle from God's Word, although not directly applying to marriage, can help to make a marriage stronger.

"To love and to cherish" also means **sharing**. This means companionship – whether it is enjoying travel, recreation, a meal out, or sitting quietly in our living room, content that we are sharing the same space, and (as we grow older), even the same thoughts! Although time spent with family and friends are always special and important, we have found that doing things together as a couple always has special meaning and rewards. Sharing also means working together to accomplish something that would be a much bigger job for one alone. Painting is a mundane task, but with my husband manning the paint roller while I did the brush work, the task took much less time and also gave us many opportunities to talk.

Dr. Elizabeth Thambiraj

Sharing responsibilities at home or in raising our children also provided opportunities for growth in our relationship. Sharing the same values in the area of finances is also very important in maintaining marital harmony. For us this has never been an issue, as we were born into the post-depression era when we both learned at an early age the importance of prudent financial management. Related to this has been our practice to discuss all major purchases before going ahead. Not only does this lead to consensus in our decisions, but the knowledge that it matters to our spouse what we think about an issue.

Finally, we have learned the value of having a good **sense of humor**. Not only have we enjoyed laughing together over all the humorous situations we encounter daily, but we have also learned that being able to lighten a situation that could cause dissention by staying calm instead of heating up the situation with harsh words is a much better approach to resolving differences in opinions. Again, a principle from the Bible applies: *[15]A soft answer turneth away wrath: but grievous words stir up anger*; Proverbs 15:1.

How much better to share a laugh than to be "right."

"To love and to cherish" has so many facets. It encompasses everything we think, or say or do as a married couple from the moment we say "I do" until one of us draws his last breath. The well-known "love chapter," 1 Corinthians 13, contains a passage which I believe is an excellent summary of the meaning of "to love and to cherish":

[4]Charity suffereth long, and is kind; charity envieth not; charity vaunteth not itself, is not puffed up,

[5]Doth not behave itself unseemly, seeketh not her own, is not easily provoked, thinketh no evil;

[6]Rejoiceth not in iniquity, but rejoiceth in the truth;

[7]Beareth all things, believeth all things, hopeth all things, endureth all things.

1 Corinthians 13:4-8.

Part I

Introduction to Relationships

Preface

I had the blessing of being brought up in a Christian family, and my early education was in mission schools and universities. I professed at age thirteen my desire to follow Jesus Christ, and I believe God's hand was with me while I was studying the scriptures. Well, professing publicly in front of people in my home church was my humble beginning of a new life and my walk with Jesus Christ. When I moved out for further education, Proverbs and Psalms became my daily food, and my mother constantly had a hand on me even though I was away from her. Walking with Jesus Christ gave me happiness but not without challenges, and God proved to be faithful time and again. His word strengthened me in different trials.

Now that I am a mother and grandmother, when I turn back and look, I see God weaving me in Christ with His unseen hand from a very tender age—even before I professed publicly. If anyone asks, I can say that I am beginning to explore His love, which is beyond my understanding, and in my human mind, I am unable to fathom His precious love. Each time I think of Him dying on the cross for humanity, I stop for a minute from my work, because I cannot fully comprehend His unconditional love. My heart explodes with a great passion and deep desire to know my Lord and Savior, Jesus Christ, more and more with each passing moment. I want to live for Him each moment and do not want a single minute to pass by without giving my best for Him. I am trying to fathom what Apostle Paul meant by saying, "For to me to live is Christ, and to die is gain. But if I live in the flesh, this is the fruit of my labour: yet what I shall choose I wot not" (Phil. 1:21–22).

I have been married to Joshua, a surgeon, for the last thirty-two years, and I live in Edmonton, Alberta, Canada. Married life is not without trials, and it took lots of time and energy and prayer to bring up godly children and to train them in the path of righteousness and truth. For me, it is a choice one has to make whether to follow Jesus Christ wholeheartedly or to follow the pattern of the world. The choice one makes affects every decision in marriage, especially when there are conflicting views, and often I revel to see the hand of the mighty God in my marriage. I have a son and two daughters who love the

Dr. Elizabeth Thambiraj

Lord, and two of my three children are in the medical profession. My other daughter is a neuropsychology graduate. She did her masters in a seminary and is married to a pastor in Iowa. She has three sons, a three-year-old, an eighteen-month-old, and a newborn. I love my family, and my heart's desire is that each member will stand firm in Jesus Christ and His unfailing love all the time, bringing glory to God.

The Garden of Eden was full of relationships—a relationship between God the Father and the male, between God the Father and the female, and between the male and the female. We know what happened to that beautiful relationship at the Fall in Genesis 3. We lost it all, and now marriage comes in a package of good and bad things and families are dysfunctional. How we handle bad times biblically will be the theme of this book, and where we should focus our hope runs through it. Where do we find nourishment in marriage? Where do we find help? Where do we find true love, wisdom, and discernment? These questions will be the foundation of this book.

Throughout centuries, well-meaning professionals have come out with various models to help people and families with marital problems. Different psychodynamic models, such as existential therapy, person-centered therapy, Gestalt therapy, behavior therapy, cognitive behavior therapy, and family-systems therapy have come out to help families and individuals who need help and emotional support. These models indeed have helped dysfunctional families to a certain extent, and below are a few examples that will help us to understand the good intentions of many psychodynamic models to resolve the issues and conflicts people face.

Psychoanalytic therapy focuses on making the unconscious conscious and reconstructing the personality. Therapists with this philosophy try to assist clients in reliving earlier experiences and working through repressed conflicts in their emotions. In this process, they aim to achieve intellectual awareness.

Family systems therapies aim at helping family members gain awareness of patterns of relationships that are not working well and create new ways of interacting to relieve their distress. Sometimes

Mystery of Relationships through the Lens of Scriptures

they work to resolve specific problems, and that may force the family to come to therapy.

In general, most of the models share common goals. These include restructuring the personality, uncovering the unconscious, creating social interest, trying to find meaning in life, curing any emotional scars and disturbances, examining old decisions and trying to make new decisions based on new awareness, developing trust in oneself, becoming more self-actualizing, reducing severe anxiety, throwing away maladaptive behaviors and learning new behavior patterns—and, through the whole process, gaining effective control of one's life.

The above models are beautiful and beneficial to an extent, but if they are unable to help the people in truth and point them to Calvary, then there is a real cause for concern. It is unfortunate that there are strong teachings that fundamental problems of marriage stem from low self-esteem, deep yearning for relationship, the search for significance, unmet needs, wounds, trauma, and so forth. Obviously, this destroys our hope in Jesus Christ, and it is in total contrast to what God's Word teaches us. The Word of God says that the fundamental problems of humanity stem from sin and that sin takes deep root in the active desires of our hearts—the patterns and processes of our thoughts and the intentions of our hearts. Who is able to fathom fully that God chose to send Jesus, His only Son, away from the security and comfort of heaven to be nailed to the cross in order to save humanity? Who else can love us more than God, who formed us in His image and does not want our souls to perish?

Many of us do not want to agree that our relationships serve as an important gauge of our walks with God. In other words, if our relationships with God are mature and sincere, this will be evident in our relationships with our spouses and with godly men and women in the body of Christ. A pattern of strained relationships points to an area in our lives that needs attention and further work and maturing. Our relationships with God are directly proportional to our relationships with spouses or other friends, and I am focusing on a Christian setting.

Dr. Elizabeth Thambiraj

We observe that emotions are, in fact, internal signals that let us know there is a situation that may need attention in our life or marriage. A person who possesses emotional intelligence (i.e., is emotionally mature) will heed these signals, and I believe that this is God's way of showing to us that something is wrong in our system and needs attention. This is applicable in a marriage, and we are called to listen to what God's Word says regarding this first divine institution in the Garden of Eden. Please come with me on the journey of building strong relationships.

I want to thank many people who have walked with me in my journey; their brief notes and views on marriage are enclosed in this book. I want to thank God for their godly input in my life in many different ways. I am glad these men and women of God who walked with me brought a good biblical flavor to this book, and I am thankful for their godly lives.

As I write this book, I am praying that our triune God—God the Father; God the Son, Jesus Christ; and God the Holy Spirit—will help each one of us to understand what I have written. Psalm 45:1 says, "My heart is inditing a good matter: I speak of the things which I have made touching the king: my tongue is the pen of a ready writer." May the Lord open the eyes of our understanding of this true love, which differs from what the world portrays as true love. Blessings!

Readers may visit my website and blog at www.livinghopecounseling. net and www.inerrantword.blogspot.com.

The Creation of Man and Woman and the Building of Relationship: Genesis 1–2

Scripture tells us that after surveying and naming all living creatures, Adam could not find a suitable helper. So God put him to sleep, removed a rib, and made woman, a suitable helper, and he named her Eve: "So God created man in his own image, in the image of God created he him; male and female created he them. And God blessed them, and God said unto them, Be fruitful, and multiply, and replenish the earth, and subdue it: and have dominion over the fish of the sea, and over the fowl of the air, and over every living thing that moveth upon the earth" (Gen. 1:27–28).

God purposely designed a void in Adam's life that could be filled only by a wife. "And the Lord God said, It is not good that the man should be alone; I will make him an help meet for him.

"And Adam said, This is now bone of my bones, and flesh of my flesh: she shall be called Woman, because she was taken out of Man. Therefore shall a man leave his father and his mother, and shall cleave unto his wife: and they shall be one flesh" (Gen 2: 18, 23–24).

We observe here something very special: God, in His omniscience, withheld His blessing from Adam till He gave Eve to be his wife, and this proves that God has ordained the family as His primary means of blessing. It is reasonable to believe one need not be married with children in order to be the recipient of God's blessing. Single people and childless couples are equally loved and accepted in God's eyes. At the same time, there is something about family unity, because every individual has a longing in his or her heart for the safety and nurture only a family can offer. The Creator put this longing inside, and it is fulfilled initially in marriage through the intimacy of couples.

Problems at home affect an individual in all areas and every facet of life. For example, if there is a problem in a couple, it invariably affects their child, especially in his or her performance at school. Very often, I have observed if the parents quarrel, invariably the child tries to find love

Dr. Elizabeth Thambiraj

outside home and gets into some wrong relationship with someone, and this dramatically affects his or her grades at school. It is unfortunate that we cannot run away from problems in our lives, but if the family unit is the first divine institution God planned, it is reasonable to assume that God wants to be personally involved in that unit.

Our family experiences relate to our spiritual lives. I have heard the saying, "A family that prays together will stay together," and I believe there is truth in this saying. In a very mysterious way, a healthy, loving family points us to a far deeper understanding of the love shared between God the Father, God the Son, and God the Holy Spirit. "Now therefore ye are no more strangers and foreigners, but fellow citizens with the saints, and of the household of God," it says in the book of Ephesians chapter 2, telling us that family connections describe our membership in the Kingdom of God. The phrase used in the New King James version of Bible is "household of God."

If one has an abusive earthly father, this can very much distort the perception of a loving heavenly Father. Our view of normal sibling relationships can very much color the way we relate to our brothers and sisters in Christ. In general, our family relationships can provide the simple framework by which we work out our salvation, and for this, prayer becomes the backbone in the family. Healthy family relationships are important to God, and He wants very much to be involved in our earthly relationships. If there is an obstacle or a mountain in the family, this is important to God, and He wants to remove it. God works in such a way to bring the family members closer to Him using that obstacle or mountain.

Simone Paget is a freelance writer, and she writes in Sun Life; below is the link for her article, and I have given some related links for further reading. <a href="http://polldaddy.com/poll/7873193/">Are humans meant to be monogamous? </a>

Modern love: Is monogamy really the best answer?
"However, I like to think that one of the bi-products of our evolution is personal choice. Instead of trying to slot ourselves into a set of binary categories, we should

Mystery of Relationships through the Lens of Scriptures

choose the relationship style that feels best to us at any given point in our lives - whether that's monogamy, polyamory or something in between."
Love and sex: by <u>Simone Paget</u>, Special to QMI Agency

Throughout this book, I brought the theme that the first divine institution between male and female was glorious before sin entered in (Genesis 3). The above links will give us a guide to understand how much we have fallen. In our total depravity, we even tend to question marriage. Various studies have proved time and again that humans are not wired to face the world alone, and that is true. That is why after the creation of man God said it was not good for a man to be alone. God gave a companion comparable to him yet wired differently. Johnson is a psychology professor at the University of Ottawa, and he says that couples in monogamous relationships have more fulfilling intimacy in their sex lives. Johnson, after decades of neuroscience research into human emotion, claims that just like the bond parents have with their offspring, monogamous love makes sense as a survival code. When we look around, we also observe that many polyamorous people argue that their sex lives are as fulfilling and meaningful as those of people in monogamous relationships. It looks like God did not think through these different relationships when He created the first divine institution in the Garden of Eden! We will explore sin and its effects in different sections of this book.

Related Stories

- <u>Multiple relationships can fulfill needs</u>
- <u>Is wife open to 'open' marriage?</u>
- <u>Should you have a threesome with your partner?</u>

Above are a few related links for further reading. From such articles, we infer that we are in a world where people need love, and they want to run out and find that somehow totally apart from God. So what is our true responsibility as believers while we are residing in this part of heaven (the earth)?

The Fall and Destruction of That Beautiful Relationship: Genesis 3

Genesis 3 explains the Fall in the following way:

- In verses 1–5, the serpent deceives Eve.
- Adam and Eve transgress the divine command and fall into sin and misery in verses 6–8.
- God calls upon Adam and Eve to answer in verses 9–13.
- In verses 14–15, God curses the serpent.
- The punishment of humankind takes place in verses 16–19.
- Adam and Eve fashion the first clothing in verses 20–21.
- God drives Adam and Eve out from paradise in verses 22–24.

If we read carefully Genesis chapter 3, we notice that Satan was a murderer, a liar, and a thief from the very beginning. When Eve was alone, he tempted her, assaulted her, and enticed her into sin. She took the forbidden fruit, and it was her own act and deed. Satan put a seed of doubt in her heart, made her question the words of God, and made her believe what he was saying was true. He told her a mixture of truth and lies. She fell into his trap, and this was fatal to humanity. By eating of the tree of knowledge, which was forbidden, Adam plainly showed contempt for what God had bestowed on him and a desire for what God had not seen fit to give him.

The tempter was the devil from the beginning, though he was in the shape of a serpent, and his scheme was to entice and lure our first parents into sin and separate them from the living God and their communion with God. We wonder why the devil is such a mischief-maker from the beginning, and we see that around us! It makes reasonable sense to believe from God's Word that male and female were wired in the likeness and image of God, and God enjoyed communing with our first parents in the cool of the day before the Fall.

Genesis 3:14–15 says, "And the Lord God said unto the serpent, Because thou hast done this, thou art cursed above all cattle, and

Mystery of Relationships through the Lens of Scriptures

above every beast of the field; upon thy belly shalt thou go, and dust shalt thou eat all the days of thy life: And I will put enmity between thee and the woman, and between thy seed and her seed; it shall bruise thy head, and thou shalt bruise his heel." We see here that God passes the great sentence, and that is the judgment for humanity for disobedience. This great judgment begins where the sin began, with the serpent, the deceiver from the beginning. We can safely say that when we become the devil's instruments, we have to share in the punishments, because we have taken part in his schemes. Adam and Eve failed to realize that under the cover of the serpent, Satan was sentenced to be degraded and accursed of God, and he became the enemy of God. The enemy will be detested and abhorred by all humanity eventually through the birth of Jesus Christ. Now war is proclaimed between the seed of the woman and the seed of the serpent, the enemy and the mischief-maker. The fruit of this enmity can be seen in the world around us, because there is continual warfare between grace and corruption even in the hearts of God's people.

Satan, the enemy of God, continuously corrupts, buffets, and sifts God's people and seeks to devour them. There continues to be war between the godly and the wicked. There is no relationship between light and darkness, and according to Mathew Henry, heaven and hell cannot reconcile to this truth, because Satan is not a sanctified soul and he is God's enemy. The only way of escape from this war is through a true deliverer, and that is our mighty warrior, Jesus Christ. God, in His graciousness, provided the remedy, and the good news is that the revelation of the savior came unasked. This is the great revelation of mercy, giving hope of forgiveness, and anyone can come to this mercy seat. A convinced sinner has hope and forgiveness without sinking into despair. In this promise of faith, our first parents and the patriarchs before the flood were justified and saved. Here our focus is on Jesus Christ, the mighty warrior who crushes the serpent's head to redeem humanity. Mathew Henry comments as follows regarding the Fall and the redemption through Jesus Christ for humanity.

1. His incarnation, or coming in the flesh, speaks great encouragement to sinners. Their Savior is the seed of the woman, bone of our bone, as it says in Hebrews 2:11 and 14.

Dr. Elizabeth Thambiraj

2. His sufferings and death are pointed at in Satan bruising his heel—that is, his human nature. And Christ's sufferings are continued in the sufferings of the saints for his name. The devil tempts, persecutes, and slays them and so bruises the heel of Christ, who is afflicted in their afflictions. But while the heel is bruised on earth, the head is in heaven.

3. In this way, Christ gains victory over Satan. Christ baffles Satan's temptations and rescues souls out of his hands. By His death, he gave a fatal blow to the devil's kingdom, a wound to the head of this serpent that cannot be healed. As the Gospel gains ground, Satan falls.[1] Mathew Henry Commentary on Genesis 3:14, 15.

This is what generally happens to us when we sin and refuse to confess before a Holy God genuinely. We seem to worry about our fame and credit before human beings more than before God, so we have a hard time confessing and our hearts are hardened. We try to give many excuses and try to lessen the effect of sin, and in our carnal minds, we do not see that as vain and frivolous. This is similar to the story in Genesis 3. Adam and Eve covered themselves with fig leaves and did not see that the situation was getting worse and not better. This is a constant reminder to all of us that we, in our fallen state, are capable of covering our transgressions like Adam and Eve.

Before Adam and Eve sinned, they enjoyed communing with God, and then suddenly God became a terror for them. The effects of the Fall cut off communion with God, and they became a terror to themselves and totally depraved in body, mind, and spirit. They were confused. Satan had promised them they would be safe, and this was a huge lie to humanity. He robbed our parents of their thinking capacity. In fact, the perfect companionship between Adam and Eve was lost, and they became miserable companions to each other. This shows the falsehood of the tempter and the fraud of his temptations continuously operating in this world to lure people away from God. This is a very serious thing to consider.

God sent the first man and the woman away from the garden because of their disobedience. This eventually shut Adam and his future generations out of that communion with God that was the bliss and

Mystery of Relationships through the Lens of Scriptures

glory of paradise. He had to till the ground from which he came. God sent Adam to toil but not for torment; and our first parents were shut out from the privileges of their state of innocence, yet they were not left to despair.

The way to the tree of life was shut. It was henceforward vain for him and his to expect righteousness, life, and happiness by the covenant of works; for the command of that covenant having been broken, the curse of it is in full force: we are all undone if we are judged by that covenant. God revealed this to Adam not to drive him to despair but to quicken him to look for life and happiness in the promised seed, by whom a new and living way into the holiest is laid open for us.[2]
Mathew Henry Commentary on Genesis 3:22–24

Cain and Abel and the First Murder: Genesis 4

In Genesis 4, we see continued destruction and increased corruption on the face of earth.

Genesis chapter 4 covers the following topics:

- Verses 1–7 describe the birth, employment, and religion of Cain and Abel.
- In verses 8–15, Cain murders Abel and receives his curse.
- Verses 16–18 describe the conduct of Cain and his family.
- We learn about Lamech and his wives and the skill of Cain's descendants in verses 19–24.
- Verses 25 and 26 cover the birth of another son and grandson of Adam.

There was deep malice in the heart of Cain, and he ended up murdering his younger brother, Abel. Cain never thought for a minute that he should have protected Abel instead of being angry with a younger brother who had done no wrong against him. These were the fatal effects of our first parents' sin, and one can imagine how much Adam and Eve's hearts must have been in turmoil and anguish. Here we observe the pride, jealousy, anger, unbelief, and impenitence of Cain. Worse, Cain denied the sin he had committed and thought he could conceal it from God. Cain tried to cover a deliberate murder with a deliberate lie, and murder is a crying sin. God said to Cain, "Your brother Abel's blood is crying out to God."

Blood calls for blood! Here the blood of the murdered is crying out to God for the blood of the murderer. At this point, no one—and this includes Cain—knew the extent and weight of the divine curse that would follow the murder. The world did not understand how far this reaches, how deep it pierces. Only in Christ are believers saved from the curse, and only in him do they inherit the blessing. Cain was cursed on the face of the earth. Cain found his punishment

Mystery of Relationships through the Lens of Scriptures

there where he had chosen his portion and had set his heart, and God placed a mark on his forehead.

All creatures including humans are to us what God makes them, a comfort or a cross, a blessing or a curse. The wickedness of the wicked brings a curse upon all they do. Whatever they do, they do not flourish, and they must toil in the earth. Even here, Cain does not repent of his sin, but he is worried only about his punishment. It shows the hardness of his heart, and obviously this points us to the effect of the Fall and total depravity on humanity.

When we look around, sometimes we find wicked people flourishing, and their lives are long. Here it is wise to trust the omniscience of God. God has wise and holy ends in prolonging the lives even of very wicked people, and we often wonder about the mark set upon Cain. The heinous guilt of murder teaches us that Abel, though dead, still spoke, and the righteous can expect persecution from the wicked in this world.

From God's Word it was doubtless known both as a brand of infamy on Cain and a token from God that they should not kill him. Abel, being dead, yet speaks. He tells the heinous guilt of murder, and warns us to stifle the first risings of wrath, and teaches us that the righteous must expect persecution.

Also, this passage reminds us that there is a future state and an eternal recompense to be enjoyed through faith in Christ and his atoning sacrifice. He also tells us the excellence of faith in the atoning sacrifice and blood of the Lamb of God. Cain slew his brother because his own works were evil and his brother's righteous (1 John 3:12). In consequence of the enmity between the seed of the woman and the seed of the serpent, the war broke out which has been waged ever since. In this war, we are all concerned. None are neutral; our Captain has declared, "He that is not with me is against me." Let us decidedly, yet in meekness, support the cause of truth and righteousness against Satan.[3] Mathew Henry's Commentary on Genesis 4:8–15.

This is a warning for all of us who read this, because Cain lost all godly reverence and fear and failed to walk in God's ordinances. It

15

Dr. Elizabeth Thambiraj

is even possible to know many scriptures and fail to know the God of the Bible. Hypocritical professors of God's Word who dissemble and trifle with God very often do something scandalous, because the Word of God does not descend to their hearts to be fruitful. Very often in this world, we see such people throw off that form of godliness, because they have reproached and finally end up denying the power of God. Cain went away from God, lost all his comfort, and dwelt in the land called Nod, which means "trembling" or "shaking." It is possible that Cain in this state was conflicted, confounded, confused, and confronted. Cain was restless and uneasy in his spirit, and this will be the fate of anyone who chooses to depart from God and do things on his or her own.

Conflict, turmoil, and wickedness continue to increase on the face of the earth. The first person recorded in the Bible who broke the law of marriage was found in the generation of Cain. Cain's wicked descendant Lamech took for himself two wives, breaking the first divine institution and its law, and brought tremendous disgrace to God. Wicked people set their hearts on the things of the world, and they are very industrious about doing those things, because they are carnal. In today's context, people want their children to be educated and get high-income jobs, but only very few are keen on educating their children in the laws and the ordinances of the Lord Most High.

When Seth was born, Adam and Eve were comforted; the name Seth means "settled" or "placed." It was from Seth's generation that the Messiah, Jesus Christ, was born. It is awe inspiring to note that Cain was a wanderer and was apostate while Seth walked with God just like his murdered brother, Abel, and from him came the true church. God allowed Adam and Eve to see the true revival of religion in their family. In Christ and His church are true religion and true settlement. We have a choice to follow the path of Cain or of Seth. Where is our true settlement?

The Birth of Jesus Christ and the Gospel: Luke 2:8–20

People began to worship God, and some of them openly professed true religion and protested against the wickedness. A distinction arose between those who genuinely professed and those who were profane just as we see around us today.

> And there were in the same country shepherds abiding in the field, keeping watch over their flock by night. And, lo, the angel of the Lord came upon them, and the glory of the Lord shone round about them: and they were sore afraid. And the angel said unto them, Fear not: for, behold, I bring you good tidings of great joy, which shall be to all people. For unto you is born this day in the city of David a Saviour, which is Christ the Lord. And this shall be a sign unto you; Ye shall find the babe wrapped in swaddling clothes, lying in a manger. And suddenly there was with the angel a multitude of the heavenly host praising God, and saying, Glory to God in the highest, and on earth peace, good will toward men. And it came to pass, as the angels were gone away from them into heaven, the shepherds said one to another, Let us now go even unto Bethlehem, and see this thing which is come to pass, which the Lord hath made known unto us. And they came with haste, and found Mary, and Joseph, and the babe lying in a manger. And when they had seen it, they made known abroad the saying which was told them concerning this child. And all they that heard it wondered at those things which were told them by the shepherds. But Mary kept all these things, and pondered them in her heart. And the shepherds returned, glorifying and praising God for all the things that they had heard and seen, as it was told unto them. (Luke 2:8-20)

The time had now come when God would send forth his Son from a woman and under the law. The circumstances of his birth were very mean. Christ was born at an inn; he came into the world to sojourn here for a while as at an inn and to teach us to do likewise. Because of sin, we have become like outcast infants, helpless and forlorn, and such a one was Christ. He well knew how unwilling we are to be meanly lodged, clothed, or fed; how we desire to have our children

Dr. Elizabeth Thambiraj

decorated and indulged; how apt the poor are to envy the rich and how prone the rich to disdain the poor. But when we, by faith, view the Son of God being made man and lying in a manger, our vanity, ambition, and envy are checked. We cannot, with this object rightly before us, seek great things for ourselves or our children. Matthew Henry's Concise Commentary on the Bible.

We are talking about the Fall of our parents Adam and Eve and how it affects each one of us and humanity at large. After getting deceived by the devil and losing all the glory they had with God, they made for themselves aprons of fig leaves, covering too narrow for them to wrap themselves in: "For the bed is shorter than that a man can stretch himself on it: and the covering narrower than that he can wrap himself in it" (Isaiah 28:20). This shows such are all the rags of our own righteousness. But God did really care for them, and He made them coats of skin, large, durable, and well fitting. This points to the righteousness of Christ, and this call is for all people. We are to adorn ourselves with the righteousness of Christ by accepting Jesus Christ as Lord and Savior, and this is good news, which is the Gospel.

Relationship with Other Believers: Ephesians 4–6

With the birth of Jesus, there is hope and restoration for strained and broken relationships with God and human beings. Here the focus shifts toward fellowship with others and especially with a community of believers. Ephesians 4–6 talks about unity in the body of Christ, new life in Christ, walking in love, husbands and wives, children and parents, bondservants and masters, and putting on the whole armor of God.

Ephesians chapter 4 can be divided into the following sections:

- Verses 1–6 consist of exhortations to mutual forbearance and walking in unity.
- In verses 7–16, Paul encourages the appropriate use of spiritual gifts and graces.
- Verses 17–24 call for purity and holiness and discuss the concept of the new man.
- Verses 25–32 tell us to take heed of the sins practiced among the heathens and command us not to grieve the Holy Spirit.

Walking in lowliness and meekness, which is an excellent disposition of the soul, brings the unity of the Spirit in the bond of peace. When one walks humbly in meekness in the Lord, one is not easily provoked or offended. God the Father dwells in all believers as in His holy temple by His Spirit and special grace.

Christ gives believers spiritual gifts, so we use them for the edification of the church, which is the body of believers. There is fullness in Christ, and this fullness and perfection come when we come to heaven; but till then, God's children are growing. As Ephesians 4:15 says, when we speak the truth in love, this is a tremendous opportunity for believers to grow up in all things into Him who is the head and is Christ. In Christ the whole body is knitted, and every part does its share.

Dr. Elizabeth Thambiraj

Satan always looks for an opportunity in the life of every person just as he did in the Garden of Eden. The tempter promises many things, and sinful desires are deceitful lusts; they promise people happiness but render them more miserable and bring them to destruction if not subdued and mortified. These, therefore, must be put off as an old garment, a filthy garment; they must be subdued and mortified. One has to become a new man in Christ, and Ephesians 4:17–24 calls us to put off our former conduct, which is corrupt. The Word of God calls us to put on the new man in Christ, which God created with the power of Christ in true righteousness and holiness.

One of the greatest discernments we need today is to distinguish the truth from the counterfeit truth. By lying and by being angry toward a brother without cause, we are providing a foothold for the tempter. We are called to be honest in all of our dealings and watch the words that proceed from our mouths. In other words, Christians are not called to become rich by deceitful practices, fraud, or oppression but in true honesty and by hard work.

For example, filthy words can corrupt the mind of the person who speaks and the one who hears. There is a sure connection between the heart and mind, and this has the capacity to destroy our souls slowly but surely. Our behavior toward our fellows can grieve the Holy Spirit. We are called to be kind to one another, and corrupt passions of bitterness, wrath, anger, clamor, evil speaking, and malice will grieve the Holy Spirit. One may ask a question: This is hard, and how is this possible when we face trials and conflicts? Yes, I understand this is not possible with our human effort, but it is possible when God becomes a part of us in our journey toward holiness. God enables us to accomplish what He wants us to in Jesus Christ.

Ephesians chapter 5 addresses the following subjects:

- Verses 1 and 2 exhort us to brotherly love and to walking in love.
- Verses 3–14 caution against several sins and tell us to walk in light.
- In verses 15–21, we find directions to a contrary behavior and to relative duties as well as a call to walk in wisdom.

Mystery of Relationships through the Lens of Scriptures

- Verses 22 and 23 emphasize the duties of wives and husbands by analogy with the spiritual relationship between Christ and the church.

As Christians, we are called to walk in love, to walk in light rather than darkness, and to walk in wisdom. The focus here is marriage, which points to Christ and the church as the model. When we desire to follow the ordinances of God through Christ in Jesus, He is able to keep believers from sinning against Him. He is able to help us walk in submission to each other (verse 21), and doing so promotes His glory. In that process, we are able to fulfill our duties to each other.

If we observe the Word of God in Ephesians 21–33, we see that marriage is a mystery. There is a definite correlation between a wife honoring a husband and a husband loving a wife. A wife is expected to honor her husband from a principle of love. The duty of husbands is to love their wives, and this is very much related to the love of Christ for the church. If we look a little bit closer, we see that Christ died for the church so that He might sanctify the world, so that He might bestow on all His members the principle of holiness and deliver them from the bondage of guilt, pollution, and the dominion of sin. Verse 29 goes an extra mile to show how one never hates one's body but nourishes and cherishes it just as the Lord does the church. Verse 30 says that we are members of His body and of His bones, and verse 31 continues, "For this reason a man shall leave his father and mother and be joined to his wife and the two shall become one flesh." This is indeed a mystery, and God wants it to be a mystery. He is comparing this relationship to that of Christ and the church.

We constantly see reminders that we are in a fallen world, so the perfection of Christ's love for the church is beyond our comprehension and is hard to attain. There will be failures and defects in husbands and wives in the present state of human nature, but that does not alter God's intention for marriage, the first divine institution. If we are able to follow God's ordinances for marriage, we will be able to avoid many heartaches, illnesses, and painful effects. Even from the angle of sociological issues, God's order for marriage is beautiful and relatively painless. We learn to love in good times and bad times and bring glory to God.

Dr. Elizabeth Thambiraj

Ephesians 6 covers the following topics:

- Verses 1–4 address the duties of children and parents.
- Verses 5–9 discuss the relationship between servants and masters.
- All Christians are to put on spiritual armor against the enemies of their souls, according to verses 10–18.
- The apostle desires the Ephesians' prayers and ends with his apostolic blessing in verses 19–24.

The first part of the chapter talks about the relationship between children and parents. Children are to obey and revere their parents in the fear of the Lord: "Honour thy father and mother; (which is the first commandment with promise) That it may be well with thee, and thou mayest live long on the earth. And, ye fathers, provoke not your children to wrath: but bring them up in the nurture and admonition of the Lord" (Ephesians 6:2–4). Parents are not to provoke them to anger but to deal with them reasonably. It is important to teach children the fear of the Lord, and family becomes an important mission field in which parents are to be witnesses and teach the true Gospel. Very often, we forget this and think that our children should have high-status jobs but completely neglect, as parents, to care for their souls from a young age. We fail to realize the possible impact of sin in the tender souls of our children if we do not teach them Christ's love and teachings.

The next section is about the relationship between servants and their masters. Servants are to respect their masters sincerely. They are to obey and serve faithfully, knowing that one day they will have to give an account of their doings to God. Steady faithfulness to Jesus Christ makes people faithful and sincere in all stations of life. Masters are called to show good will and concern to their servants, understanding that they also have a master in heaven. The relationship between masters and servants will be better if they both understand they have to give an account to God of their behavior, and thus families and workplaces will be more orderly and happy.

Verses 10–19 talk about the whole armor of God and how we should be ready at all times. We are called to be strong in the Lord and in

22

Mystery of Relationships through the Lens of Scriptures

the power of His might. This passage reminds us that Christian life is warfare and the combat is not against human enemies but an enemy who has a thousand ways of beguiling unstable souls. We must guard constantly our hearts and minds. The different parts of the armor guard different parts of the body from the fiercest assaults of the enemy.

Full Armor of God

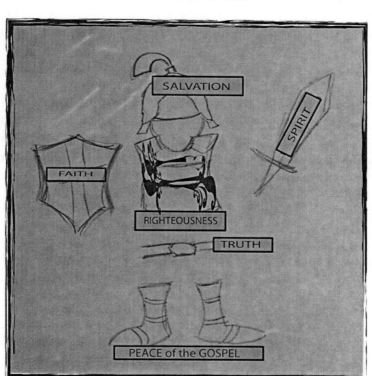

Why is it important to protect yourself with the full armor of God?

Christians today are taking the ideas and practices of our culture and forming their Christian beliefs around them. "We are being taught by society to be "tolerant" of anti-Bible actions and practices. We must hold firm to Christ's teachings and commandments".[4]

[4]*Full **Armor of God***

www.christianarsenal.com/Christian_Arsenal/Full_**Armor_of_God**.html

Dr. Elizabeth Thambiraj

It is important that as believers and warriors of Christ we buckle around our waists the belt of truth. When we read the book of Colossians, we understand that it is easy for the culture around us to infiltrate the teachings of the church and water down the truth. Moral and philosophical relativism allows people to have the idea that what is true for one may not be true for another. As we struggle in the world with the idea of moral and philosophical relativism, we need to remember that there is only one truth. The Word of God is inerrant and is the only standard for truth, and we have to stand on truth.

When Paul was writing this particular passage, he was thinking of a Roman soldier dressed in armor. Truth in all dealings becomes the foundation of all the different pieces of armor: the belt of truth, the breastplate of righteousness, the Gospel of peace for our feet, the shield of faith, the helmet of salvation, and the sword of the Spirit. Wearing these, we are to pray always and be watchful in our walks with God:

> Finally, my brethren, be strong in the Lord, and in the power of his might. Put on the whole armour of God that ye may be able to stand against the wiles of the devil. For we wrestle not against flesh and blood, but against principalities, against powers, against the rulers of the darkness of this world, against spiritual wickedness in high places. Wherefore take unto you the whole armour of God that ye may be able to withstand in the evil day, and having done all, to stand. Stand therefore, having your loins girt about with truth, and having on the breastplate of righteousness; And your feet shod with the preparation of the gospel of peace; Above all, taking the shield of faith, wherewith ye shall be able to quench all the fiery darts of the wicked. And take the helmet of salvation, and the sword of the Spirit, which is the word of God: Praying always with all prayer and supplication in the Spirit, and watching thereunto with all perseverance and supplication for all saints; And for me, that utterance may be given unto me, that I may open my mouth boldly, to make known the mystery of the gospel, For which I am an ambassador in bonds: that therein I may speak boldly, as I ought to speak. (Ephesians 6:10–20)

Mystery of Relationships through the Lens of Scriptures

Prayer is a powerful weapon and hedge against the enemy, and as warriors of Christ, we are called to be vigilant just like a Roman soldier. As I have mentioned before, there is a tremendous connection between the heart and the mind, and a vain heart will lead to vain prayer. We can pray privately, publicly, socially, and on our own, confessing sins of commission and omission and always thanking God for received petitions. This is a serious thought for our walks with God, and we must do this with the help of the Holy Spirit, who enables us to fulfill what He has called us to do.

Education is not the whole answer to changing the world. If we educate the devil, we get a cleverer devil. Satan is slicker than the world's greatest criminal lawyer. He certainly can fool our intellects if that is what we rely on. Our minds have accumulated good and evil, true and false information. Even after the baptism of the Holy Spirit, it takes time to change. The intellect is wonderful, however, when submitted to God and renewed by the Holy Spirit. We must bring every thought process into obedience to Christ. Scriptural references for further reading are Romans 12:2, Philippians 2:5, and 2 Corinthians 10:5.

The Marriage Supper of the Lamb

Now we are moving toward the final book of the Bible, and that is the book of Revelation. This is important, because the Bible starts with marriage, and the finale is the wedding of the Lamb and the marriage supper. When we begin to understand the marriage supper of the Lamb, we get a biblical perspective of the first divine institution in the Garden of Eden. We also begin to understand that the only perfect marriage is the marriage of the Lamb, and it is a call for every believer to be a part of that marriage supper. My heartrending cry and prayer is that God will give us grace upon grace in our lives so that we may understand this mystery.

Revelations chapter 19 has the following sections:

- Verses 1–10 show the church in heaven and on earth triumphing and praise the Lord for his righteous judgments.
- A vision of Christ going forth to destroy the beast and his armies appears in verses 11–21.

> Let us be glad and rejoice, and give honour to him: for the marriage of the Lamb is come, and his wife hath made herself ready. And to her was granted that she should be arrayed in fine linen, clean and white: for the fine linen is the righteousness of saints. And he saith unto me, Write, Blessed are they which are called unto the marriage supper of the Lamb. And he saith unto me, These are the true sayings of God. And I fell at his feet to worship him. And he said unto me, See thou do it not: I am thy fellow servant, and of thy brethren that have the testimony of Jesus: worship God: for the testimony of Jesus is the spirit of prophecy. (Revelation 19:7–10)

Christ is the bridegroom of the church, and the second union will come to completion in heaven, where Christ will reign and his subjects will exist in a state of happiness. This is the celebration of His nuptials on earth. The bride of Christ, the church, appears in fine linen, clean and white. The church is robed in the righteousness of Christ, justified and sanctified. This is the marriage of the Lamb, and blessed are those who are invited to the marriage supper of the

Mystery of Relationships through the Lens of Scriptures

Lamb. There is tremendous hope for believers on this earth who are waiting for this union, the true and perfect marriage, the marriage of the Lamb.

"Then the church of Christ, purified from errors, divisions, and corruptions in doctrine, discipline, worship, and practice will be made ready to be publicly owned by Him as His delight and His beloved".[5] Matthew Henry- Mathew Henry Commentary on Revelations 19:1-10

"The promises of the Gospel, the true sayings of God, opened, applied, and sealed by the Spirit of God in holy ordinances, are the marriage feast. This seems to refer to the abundant grace and consolation Christians will receive in the happy days that are to come".[6] The Matthew Henry Study Bible. King James Version

God is faithful and true to His promises, and He is righteous in all His judicial acts. The army He commands is a very large one, and angels and saints follow His conduct and resemble Him. Believers who have a relationship with Him and follow His statues and ordinances are in this army of God. Those who molested the church, who walked in vanity and in lusts and pleasures, not following the ordinances of God, are thrown in the lake of fire.

Christ, the glorious head of the church, rides on a white horse, the emblem of justice and holiness. He has many crowns, for he is King of kings and Lord of lords. He is arrayed in vesture dipped in his own blood, by which he purchased his power as mediator, and in the blood of his enemies, over whom he always prevails. His name is the Word of God, a name none fully knows but himself. Only this we know: that this Word was God manifest in the flesh, but no creature can fully understand his perfections. Angels and saints follow and are like Christ in their armor of purity and righteousness. He is going to execute the threats of the written word on his enemies. The ensigns of his authority are in his name, asserting his authority and power, warning the most powerful princes to submit or fall before him.

The powers of earth and hell make their utmost effort. These verses declare important events foretold by the prophets. These persons were not excused because they did what their leaders bade them. How

Dr. Elizabeth Thambiraj

vain will be the plea of many sinners on the great day! "We followed our guides; we did as we saw others do!" God has given a rule to walk by in His word; neither the example of most nor of the chief must influence us contrary thereto: if we do as most do, we must go where most go, even into the burning lake. Mathew Henry Commentary on Revelations: 19:11–21.

New Heavens and New Earth

Revelation chapter 21 has the following themes:

- Verses 1–8 describe a new heaven and a new earth, the New Jerusalem where God dwells and banishes all sorrow from his people.
- In verses 9–12, we learn of its heavenly origin, glory, and secure defense.
- Verses 22–27 describe its perfect happiness, its enlightenment in the presence of God and the Lamb, and the free access of multitudes made holy.

By new heaven and new earth, one may understand a new state for the bodies of human beings as well as heaven for their souls. The old world where we are now, with all its commotions, trouble, and conflict, will vanish away. The New Jerusalem is the church of God in its perfect state of beauty, wisdom, and holiness. This will be ready for its bridegroom, who is our Lord, Jesus Christ. So, in a nutshell, Revelation chapter 21 talks of the church of God, the bride, and the bridegroom, who is Jesus Christ. Ephesians 5, remember, tells us that marriage is related very much to the relationship between the church and Christ.

The presence of God with His church is the glory of the church. One may wonder how a holy God can dwell with the children of men. The presence of God in the new heaven and new earth with human beings will be continuous, and their souls will be assimilated with Him, filled with His love, honor, and delight in God. These are the people of God who have gone through many trials and tribulations on the old earth and have been bought and redeemed with the precious blood of Jesus Christ.

In this new and blessed state, people will be free from trouble, sorrow, and pain. God will do away with the effects of former trouble and wipe away their tears, and they will have no memory of their pain and sorrow anymore. Those who inherit the new heaven and new earth where there is no more sorrow receive the title true and faithful.

Dr. Elizabeth Thambiraj

God is the author and finisher of our lives, and He is the Alpha and Omega. He brings those who have been thirsting for this sinless perfection and the uninterrupted enjoyment of God to this place according to their desiring hearts.

The multitudes who are sealed on this earth by His precious blood, the saved souls, are the inhabitants of this city, New Jerusalem, and they represent people of all nations. These saints will have no impure things residing in them, and no impure person will be admitted to this place. In the physical church in today's context on this earth, there are impure people who profane the ordinances of God and prostitute the church for worldly ends. Those who come to the New Jerusalem are reserved, chosen, and faithful, and their names are written in the Lamb's book of life and are visible in this church.

Revelation 22:20–21 reads, "He which testifieth these things saith, Surely I come quickly. Amen. Even so, come, Lord Jesus. The grace of our Lord Jesus Christ be with you all. Amen." This is Christ's farewell to His church, and he parts with them in great kindness and assures them that it shall not be long before He comes again to them. We should desire nothing more than that the grace of Christ may be with us in this world to prepare us for the glory of Christ in the new heavens and the new earth.

The Bible starts with a definite first divine institution in the Garden of Eden, which became imperfect and corrupted because of the tempter and the wilful yielding in Adam and Eve's choice. Again in the New Testament, God's Word definitely gives us instructions for this mysterious relationship of marriage and relates it to Christ and the church. Apostle Paul calls this a mystery. The Bible finishes with a perfect marriage, the wedding of the Lamb where the saved souls are in union with Christ, which is a huge mystery again. May the God of glory give us His peace and understanding as we read the scriptures, and may He not withhold any good thing from those who walk uprightly.

May God help us to understand scriptures the way they were written, inspired by the Holy Spirit. The Bible is useful for knowing what is right (teaching), pointing out what is not right (rebuke), making

Mystery of Relationships through the Lens of Scriptures

things right (correction), and helping us to stay right (training in righteousness), according to 2 Timothy 3:16–17. The Word of God, by the Spirit and power of God, will help us build a healthy worldview so that we see circumstances from a perspective the world may not teach and see. May the God of the universe, who made the first divine institution, give us the necessary grace to view marriage in general as well as our own marriages through the lens of the Scriptures.

Instructions for Marriage

"Marriage is a union which binds a man and his wife together in such a bond of life and communion in every aspect of their life that they cease to be two and become one flesh. Marriage as an unbreakable bond is rooted in God's creation, whether the marriage of believers or unbelievers, whether performed in the church or by civil authority". *By Rev. Thomas Miersma, Missionary Pastor.*

Jesus said, "Wherefore they are no more twain, but one flesh, What therefore God hath joined together, let not man put asunder" (Matthew 19:6).

In Matthew 19:3, the leaders of the day during Jesus's earthly ministry came with a question about divorce: "Is it lawful for a man to put away his wife for every cause?" The leaders had great struggles about the fundamental doctrine concerning marriage and human sexuality, because they wanted to teach that divorce was acceptable for any reason. They failed to realize and understand that God made human beings male and female and ordained that a man should desire and cleave to his wife. God ordained for this to happen, and it is a command mainly for the well-being for the new relationship.

Jesus pointed out to the religious leaders that, as written in Genesis 2:24, a man should leave his father and mother and cleave to his wife and that God ordained that a man should dwell with a woman and that they should be one flesh (Matthew 19:5). This was the first wedding in the Garden of Eden, and today it is still God who joins a man and a woman in a holy matrimony. Marriage is a beautiful and good gift from God. Since God is the bride giver, God alone has the ability and authority to separate them, and eventually God does this through the death of one of the spouses. God has made this union to be beautiful, glorious, and lawful between a man and a woman. Any other sexuality outside of this union is sin, and it comes from total depravity and is a corruption of a good gift of God. Jesus, in His earthly ministry, taught that marriage is a permanent and unbreakable bond in the sight of a holy God who ordained it in the

Mystery of Relationships through the Lens of Scriptures

beginning. God did not give any authority to human beings to tamper with marriage by an unlawful divorce.

Let us think a bit about divorce and remarriage. In Luke 16:18, Jesus says, "Whosoever putteth away his wife, and marrieth another, committeth adultery: and whosoever marrieth her that is put away from her husband committeth adultery." Jesus makes it very clear that remarrying is committing adultery, because divorce does not terminate the original marriage relationship. Do we view marriage the way Jesus does, knowing that he calls us to be obedient to His word? "Marriage is honourable in all, and the bed undefiled: but whoremongers and adulterers God will judge" (Hebrews 13:4).

Faithful Marriage

"A faithful marriage is impossible in man's strength. Promise-keeping concerning one's vows in marriage is by grace alone. To trust in one's own ability to keep the promised vows of marriage is a form of living out of salvation by one's own strength and works. Do you know that all-sufficient grace?" *By Rev. Thomas Miersma, Missionary Pastor*

"Neither do I condemn thee: go, and sin no more" (John 8:11). These are the words of Jesus for the woman caught in adultery when the people around her wanted her to be stoned to death. "So when they continued asking him, he lifted up himself, and said unto them, He that is without sin among you, let him first cast a stone at her." He says in John 8:7. This verse definitely affirms that all of us have sin rooted in our hearts, because the Word of God says that all of us have sinned and fall short of the glory of God.

"Ye have heard that it was said by them of old time, Thou shalt not commit adultery: But I say unto you, That whosoever looketh on a woman to lust after her hath committed adultery with her already in his heart" (Matthew 5:28). True repentance requires a forsaking of these sins; we must go and sin no more as Jesus told the crowd in John 8:11. "Jesus calls us to true faithfulness to that lifelong bond of marriage under all circumstances". *By Rev. Thomas Miersma, Missionary Pastor*

"Jesus said, 'If ye love me, keep my commandments'" (John 14:15). One of those commandments appears in Mark 8:34 and Luke 9:23: "Whosoever will come after me, let him deny himself, and take up his cross, and follow me." Marriage is a huge privilege and a gift from God, and a believer may enjoy single life and be a eunuch for the Kingdom of Heaven's sake (Matthew 19:12); but that does not negate the first divine institution or the fact that God said it was not good for a man to be alone. Even to the victim of divorce, if he or she is a believer, there is one calling: "let her remain unmarried or be reconciled to her husband" (1 Corinthians 7:11). This is the doctrine of Jesus concerning marriage. "All men cannot receive this saying, save they to whom it is given" (Matthew 19:11).

Mystery of Relationships through the Lens of Scriptures

Marriage is to be honored, because it was the first divine institution. Spouses learn in marriage that no one is perfect, and we love each other because we have the privilege of seeing the dirt and ugliness as well and pray for the weaker spouse.

Obedience in Love

"Does obedience to Christ rule your life because He is your Lord? Does your church reprove sin and seek those who wander in sin to their own hurt, or does anything go"?

By Rev. Thomas Miersma, Missionary Pastor.

"Jesus said: 'If ye love me, keep my commandments'" (John 14:15). It is important that the church teach the saving love of Christ through the death and resurrection, which works in an obedient love for Christ. Eventually, the love of Christ bears fruit in the life of the church by the grace of believers being new people in Christ and rooted and planted in Christ (Matthew 7:17).

A Christian denies his or her own will and follows Christ in obedient love. This is a lifestyle of biblical separation and walking in purity and not compromising with sin. Hypocritical love is not genuine, and it can take one only that far, because one has to have a deep personal relationship with Jesus Christ in order to be genuine and bear fruit eventually. When a tree is planted, it has to be watered and weeded out, and it takes time to yield fruit. Hypocritical love is not love, and the toleration of an unbelieving, humanistic notion of love will permit our neighbors to walk to their eternal ruin. There is a huge difference between love and being nice to people, and as Christians, we are called to love one another!

Is the love we profess for Christ biblical, or is it the human philosophy of tolerance masquerading as Christianity? Jesus came to call sinners to repentance, and He calls the church to admonish, rebuke, discipline, train in righteousness, and take a biblical stand in separation from iniquity and wickedness. "Whosoever therefore shall break one of these least commandments, and shall teach men so, he shall be called the least in the Kingdom of heaven," says Jesus in Matthew 5:19. When we offend someone, the Bible has strict admonishment: "But whoso shall offend one of these little ones which believe in me, it were better for him that millstones were hanged about his neck, and that he were drowned in the depth of the sea" (Matthew 18:6).

Mystery of Relationships through the Lens of Scriptures

A believer who genuinely loves the Lord and knows what Jesus has done for us will genuinely want to love his neighbor and share the love of Jesus. Jesus says, "Moreover if thy brother shall trespass against thee, go and tell him his fault between thee and him alone: if he shall hear thee, thou hast gained thy brother. But if he will not hear thee, then take with thee one or two more, that in the mouth of two or three witnesses, every word may be established. And if he neglect to hear them, tell it unto the church: but if he neglect to hear the church, let him be unto thee as a heathen man and a publican" (Matthew 18:15–17).

Part II

Articles on Relationships

Preface

Building relationships does not come naturally for a fallen person. We have to keep in mind that in our fallen states, we are totally depraved mentally, spiritually, and emotionally. We also cannot forget our aging bodies, which grow in weakness, according to God's Word.

> Remember now thy Creator in the days of thy youth, while the evil days come not, nor the years draw nigh, when thou shalt say, I have no pleasure in them; While the sun, or the light, or the moon, or the stars, be not darkened, nor the clouds return after the rain: In the day when the keepers of the house shall tremble, and the strong men shall bow themselves, and the grinders cease because they are few, and those that look out of the windows be darkened, And the doors shall be shut in the streets, when the sound of the grinding is low, and he shall rise up at the voice of the bird, and all the daughters of musick shall be brought low; Also when they shall be afraid of that which is high, and fears shall be in the way, and the almond tree shall flourish, and the grasshopper shall be a burden, and desire shall fail: because man goeth to his long home, and the mourners go about the streets: Or ever the silver cord be loosed, or the golden bowl be broken, or the pitcher be broken at the fountain, or the wheel broken at the cistern. Then shall the dust return to the earth as it was: and the spirit shall return unto God who gave it. Vanity of vanities, saith the preacher; all is vanity. (Ecclesiastes 12:1–8)

We have a call to think of God sooner than later, and it is absurd and useless to spend our days without thinking about where we are going to spend eternal life. In part I, we examined the theology of relationship with God's Word as the foundation. In part II, we are going to see how to build relationships in a practical way biblically.

A Litmus Test for Relationship with God

The Bing dictionary defines *litmus test* as a "test determined by single factor: a test in which a single factor determines the outcome," or a "test to identify acid or base: a test in which litmus is used to find out if something is an acid or a base." Its synonyms include *acid test, proof, confirmation, test,* and *measure.*

Prayer is a kind of litmus test of our relationships with God, and often our prayers reveal who and what is most important to us. They also expose our innermost feelings, our thoughts about ourselves and God. For example, Psalm 35 is a plea for protection by David, and it is an appeal to God concerning David's integrity and the justice of his cause. In other words, we can say prayer is raising our minds and hearts to God, and the first part is generally easier for most of us than the second part. What I intended to say here is that prayer involves the whole person—that is the mind, heart, and emotions—in a relationship with God.

Prayer is a heartfelt conversation or communication with God, and believers in Christ Jesus pray to God the Father through Jesus Christ, the only mediator, in the power of the Holy Spirit. It is a deliberate communication to the holy God, and the foundation is relationship with God. It can be done individually or corporately and either privately or publicly, and it is one of the ways of worship and thanksgiving. Different people around the world pray in different languages. Prayer can take the form of a hymn or creed or spontaneous expression.

For an unbeliever, prayer is a deliberate invocation to a deity, which is an object of worship or a spiritual entity. I have lived in different parts of the world including Malaysia, Singapore, and India and have witnessed different forms of prayer and worship to different deities. In India, which is a nation of many religions, prayer takes the form of chants and repeated words or phrases called *mantras.* Hindus offer supplications, praises, and requests to their gods and goddesses in this format. People all over the world pray and worship for different reasons and often for their own benefit and for the blessing of others.

42

Mystery of Relationships through the Lens of Scriptures

"Prayer can be a form of <u>religious practice</u>, may be either individual or communal, and may take place in public or in private. It may involve the use of words or song. There are different forms of prayer, such as <u>petitionary</u> prayer, prayers of <u>supplication</u>, thanksgiving, and <u>worship</u> or praise"[1]. *Prayer <u>- Wikipedia, the free encyclopedia</u>*

*en.wikipedia.org/wiki/**Prayer***

"The Hebrew word for prayer is tefilah. It is derived from the <u>root</u> Pe-Lamed-Lamed and the word l'hitpalel, meaning to judge oneself. This surprising word origin provides insight into the purpose of Jewish prayer. The most important part of any Jewish prayer, whether it be a prayer of petition, of thanksgiving, of praise of <u>G-d</u>, or of confession, is the introspection it provides, the moment that we spend looking inside ourselves, seeing our role in the universe and our relationship to G-d."[2]

*2. Judaism 101: **Prayers** and Blessings*
*www.jewfaq.org/**prayer**.htm*

I want to use an earthly example to make my point regarding our relationship with God. Think of a very close friendship or marriage. We know instinctively that key relationships in our lives are matters of the heart and that the other person in friendship or in marriage is important to us. If this relationship is growing in love, we want to serve the person we are in relationship with, and this comes naturally. Relationships are hard to work with, because they involve time. They will fade if we have no continuing interest in spending time with and connecting with the other person. In marriage, intimacy in the bedroom is an important but smaller part of the relationship bond. If the spouses' hearts are not connecting in relationship, intimacy in the bedroom will suffer as a result. We see that communication is the mark of relationship. According to God's Word husbands and wives should stay together on the earth in the natural sense, till death separates them. They are called to love and cherish and nurture their life together to exhibit the highest level of relationship.

What do we understand by the conversation between Abraham and God in Genesis 18:16–33?

Dr. Elizabeth Thambiraj

And the men rose up from thence, and looked toward Sodom: and Abraham went with them to bring them on the way. And the Lord said, Shall I hide from Abraham that thing which I do; Seeing that Abraham shall surely become a great and mighty nation, and all the nations of the earth shall be blessed in him? For I know him, that he will command his children and his household after him, and they shall keep the way of the Lord, to do justice and judgment; that the Lord may bring upon Abraham that which he hath spoken of him. And the Lord said, Because the cry of Sodom and Gomorrah is great, and because their sin is very grievous; I will go down now, and see whether they have done altogether according to the cry of it, which is come unto me; and if not, I will know. And the men turned their faces from thence, and went toward Sodom: but Abraham stood yet before the Lord. And Abraham drew near, and said, Wilt thou also destroy the righteous with the wicked? Peradventure there be fifty righteous within the city: wilt thou also destroy and not spare the place for the fifty righteous that are therein? That be far from thee to do after this manner, to slay the righteous with the wicked: and that the righteous should be as the wicked that be far from thee: Shall not the Judge of all the earth do right? And the Lord said, If I find in Sodom fifty righteous within the city, then I will spare all the place for their sakes. And Abraham answered and said, Behold now, I have taken upon me to speak unto the Lord, which am but dust and ashes: Peradventure there shall lack five of the fifty righteous: wilt thou destroy all the city for lack of five? And he said, If I find there forty and five, I will not destroy it. And he spake unto him yet again, and said, Peradventure there shall be forty found there. And he said, I will not do it for forty's sake. And he said unto him, Oh let not the Lord be angry, and I will speak: Peradventure there shall thirty be found there. And he said, I will not do it, if I find thirty there. And he said, Behold now, I have taken upon me to speak unto the Lord: Peradventure there shall be twenty found there. And he said, I will not destroy it for twenty's sake. And he said, Oh let not the Lord be angry, and I will speak yet but this once: Peradventure ten shall be found there. And he said, I will not destroy it for ten's sake. And the Lord went his way, as soon as he had left communing with Abraham: and Abraham returned unto his place.

Mystery of Relationships through the Lens of Scriptures

The above conversation definitely talks about Abraham's deep relationship with God. Abraham considers God as his best friend and keeps on talking and bargaining as if God is his friend. As Christians, we are privileged people: we can pray to communicate with God. When we pray, we are building relationship with God and begin to understand Him. Apostle Paul mentions that praying consists of two components: praying with understanding and praying with spirit (1 Corinthians 14:2, 14–15, 18). This means our 'whole being' is involved in prayer. Prayer directly engages a Christian's renewed spirit from the Holy Spirit of God. This is not possible without a relationship with God, and there is a definite connection of minds and hearts when we pray genuinely.

How could prayer be a relationship with God if it only remains a lifting of our minds to God? We need very special times of intimacy with God, but we must prepare for and build up to those times. To enrich a relationship with God, we have to engage our hearts, and we have to learn to love Him with all of our heart, mind, soul, and strength. This does not come naturally to a fallen person, because we want to do it on our own, and this relationship of intimacy is a process and a lifelong journey. The more we talk to Him, depend on Him, and involve Him in our lives, the more we begin to understand who He is. Eventually, we will be able to trust Him despite our situations. That involves finding intimacy with God in the midst of the everyday business of our lives. It also involves God in other important relationships in our lives.

If the above article stirs a desire for that kind of deep relationship with God, one place to begin is to let God tell us about how much He loves us. We will never know what God is telling us unless we read His Word. God says, "You are precious in my eyes and I love you" (Isaiah 43:4). If we are open to God's expressions of affection toward us that can open our hearts to stir up affection in the form of grateful response. Remember that it only takes a spark to get the fire going, and we need to take ongoing care to keep the fire from going out if that relationship is to continue. The Word of God, the Holy Spirit, and the people of God will help us to build that lasting relationship

Dr. Elizabeth Thambiraj

with God and to improve our prayer life. Our journey is very personal to Jesus Christ, and prayer is indeed a litmus test that assesses our relationships with Him. With special care, it can become a warm and comforting lifelong relationship.

How Can I Be a Loving Neighbor?

What makes a neighbor is a huge topic for discussion. Does it include geographical proximity, race, religion, or shared social or economic status? The question "Who is my neighbor?" caused endless debate among the Jews in biblical days, and they considered the heathen and the Samaritans strangers and enemies. When people live in the same nation, how do we make the distinction? Is it based on social class, or culture or ethnicity groups, or value system or religion?

Who is my neighbor? Dictionary.com defines a neighbor as "a person who lives near another" or "a person who shows kindliness or helpfulness toward his or her fellow humans." [1]

[1]*Neighbor | Define Neighbor at Dictionary.com*
dictionary.reference.com/browse/neighbor

Greek word for neighbor

[*Ουσ.* γείτονας//

ο πλησίον (μτφ.)//

γειτονικός/

Ρημ. γειτνιάζω, γειτονεύω, συνορεύω][2]

[2] *What is the Greek word for 'neighbor'? | ChaCha*
www.chacha.com/question/what-is-the-greek-word-for-%27neighbor%27

We understand that one of the greatest commandments is to love our neighbors as ourselves. In Luke 13:25–37, Jesus teaches the parable of the good Samaritan, and this gives us a wiser understanding of this topic as we explore the Scriptures and meditate a little deeper.

Dr. Elizabeth Thambiraj

As the story unfolds, we find that the route to Jericho, still visible today, includes long stretches of rocky terrain, and that could have made it a useful base of operations for robbers! The priest and the Levite had an opportunity to help the man who fell into the hands of the robbers, but they passed by. In other words, they were deceived and missed a good opportunity to serve. Here we find that Jesus picked a Samaritan, someone from an ethnic group Jews detested, as the hero of the story (Luke 10: 31–33).

The Samaritan set the injured man on his own animal, brought him to the inn, gave the equivalent of two days' wages to the innkeeper, and continued to care for him. Jesus is making an additional point that loving one's neighbor involves showing compassion and care even to those with whom we do not have any relationship. In this way, He answers the question of the lawyer who wants to "justify himself."

Culturally, it would have been so unthinkable for a Samaritan to help a Jew (John 4:9 and 8:48). The lawyer understood partially that the Old Testament was the definitive, unerring standard of faith and practice as he questioned Jesus, wanting to prove himself. Jesus knew that the man fell far short of following the commandments (Mark 10:19) and corrected his question. The correct question should have been "How can I be a neighbor?" rather than "Who is my neighbor?" There is more to this question and to the motives of our hearts, and we can see that the lawyer had no genuine desire to learn from Jesus.

Satan is a liar by nature, and he always opposes the truth. We can safely say that Satan is a pathological liar (John 8:44). He would lie even if he didn't have to. He is both self-deceived and a deceiver (Revelation 12:9). From the beginning of time, Satan has sought to oppose God and His people by opposing the truth. Consider some of Satan's tactics throughout history as exposed in the Scriptures. He works to keep men from the truth or to keep the truth from men (Mark 4:15 and 2 Corinthians 4:3–4). He denies the truth, usually declaring a 'new truth' in its place (Genesis 3:1–7). He seeks to deceive people about the truth by disseminating his false teaching and doctrines as the truth (1 Timothy 4:1–5). He distorts the truth (Matthew 23:23–24). He works to produce disobedience to the truth. Satan knows that keeping men from obedience to the truth is as good

Mystery of Relationships through the Lens of Scriptures

as keeping them from the truth (1 John 2:4–6). He seeks to fan the flames of humanity's curiosity and ego so that we will forsake God's truth in the pursuit of a supposedly higher truth (1 Corinthians 4:6). He even works among believers to turn them from the truth and to incite them to be untruthful. We can see that in Matthew 24:24 and Acts 20:29–30 and 5:1–11.

"All God's exposure of meaning confronts us with God's will, and this confrontation changes us *noetically*: it is simultaneously an exertion of control. Moreover, God's fellowship with us transforms us: we cannot remain the same when we stand in the presence of the Holy One. We are either destroyed or made holy. Thus, God's presence is always a form of control".[3]

[3]*by Vern Sheridan Poythress*
[Published in Westminster Theological Journal *50/1 (1988): 27-64. Used with permission.]*

If we try to understand the Fall and the consequences of it in Genesis 3 and the redemption story, we can trust that the presence of God in all circumstances is a very good control. It exists to prosper us and not to destroy us.

Noetic means "of or pertaining to the mind" or "originating or apprehended by the reason." It comes from the Greek word for "intelligent."[4]

[4]*Babylon 9 Translation Software and Dictionary Tool*
*www.babylon.com/definition/neighbor/***Greek**

Let us think of a time when we hesitated to respond to someone in need and particularly the thought that kept us from responding to that person's need. How do we feel when we see pictures of starving people on TV and in magazines? Can we place ourselves in the place of the expert in law who can question God's Word to justify our actions like the lawyer and let us pause for a brief moment!

Jesus knew it was impossible for human beings to follow the Ten Commandments using their own strength. Jesus desired to lead the

Dr. Elizabeth Thambiraj

lawyer toward critical research on his own so that he might find the truth. It becomes increasingly clear that we need the tremendous grace of Christ to keep the law. Belief that Christ becomes the propitiation of our sin is necessary and vital. This understanding may enable fallen human beings to love God with their whole hearts so that they may love their neighbors as themselves.

The lawyer also knew that he did not keep all of the Ten Commandments, but instead of confessing his sins and being broken before the Lord, he tried to excuse himself. The lawyer hoped both to parry conviction and to vindicate himself in the eyes of the people, so he came with this question: "Who is my neighbor?" Jesus refused to be drawn into a controversy but answered the lawyer's question with the story of the Good Samaritan. If we apply this story to our lives, where do we fall in our thinking? If our thought patterns have been like those of this learned lawyer so far in our lives, what do we do to correct our thought pattern based on Jesus's teaching? Do we have teachable spirits? Or do we want to justify our positions and think we know everything—and, in doing so, expose our stupidity and allow ourselves to be deceived?

Loving the Lord involves not only having faith in Him but also delighting in Him above all else, and I understand that this does not come naturally to a fallen person! Total devotion of one's entire being must include one's heart (the emotions, will, and deepest convictions); one's soul (the immaterial part of a person's being); one's mind (reasoning); and one's strength, which is how one uses the ability, skills, and power God has given in His infinite mercy.

In our quiet reflection, let us think of a time when we have experienced love from someone expressed in a practical way. How did that make us feel? In what practical ways can we "go and do likewise"? The Samaritan ministered to the injured, suffering robbery victim when the priest and the Levite lost that opportunity to serve. In our families, in our marriages, communities, and society, how do we move with empathy and apply our love to be Samaritans? How do we extend mercy in a deeper way?

Mystery of Relationships through the Lens of Scriptures

In the parable of the Good Samaritan in Luke 10:25–37, Jesus showed that a neighbor does not mean someone who belongs to the church or faith where we are comfortable. It has no reference to color, race, class, or economic distinction; in fact, a neighbor is one who needs help at that point in time. In other words, every soul who has been devastated by adversity, who has been wounded or bruised, may be our neighbor. God created all of humanity, and we belong to Him. The question here is this: How can we be loving neighbors?

Male and Female: Divine Comedy or Brilliance?

When we talk to the most happily married couples or to the best of friends, they will tell us that sometimes they do not understand each other or feel listened to. If this sounds familiar or normal, we do not need to fret, because it is to be expected in a relationship.

"The female and male brains are different, and the two brains process information differently. The good news is that some conscious effort can enhance communication between the brains and lower frustrations".[1]

[1]The **Male/Female** Brain | Brain Health & Brain Fitness Blog
www.fitbrains.com/blog/2008/10/ ... /the-malefemale-brai ... - United StatesCached - Similar

Many of the problems we face are not problems between individual couples but between men and women in general. These problems arise because we are either too lazy or too selfish to get to know our spouses well enough to understand how different from us they really are! Let us look at this article from a biblical perspective. Gender somehow reflects something about God and His glory. A man reflects something about God's character that is different from what a woman reflects. Let me start with a question: Why do we struggle with being men and women?

Satan is God's enemy, and he wishes to destroy God's glory. Since he cannot destroy God, he wishes to destroy God's reflection, men and women. Satan's prime way of attempting to destroy God's glory and image in humanity is to make it too frightening to be truly a man or a woman and to offer counterfeit ways to live out our genders. What does it mean to be a male or a female? What does it mean that God made Adam and Eve to work together? How do we work together as husbands and wives to fulfill the creation mandate to fulfill, subdue, and rule creation?

Mystery of Relationships through the Lens of Scriptures

God created Adam for relationship, and He made a woman from the rib He had taken out of the man and brought her to the man (Genesis 2:18, 21–22). The point here is that God made another person who was neither Adam's master nor his inferior but his equal. According to Matthew Henry, "Eve was not made out of his head to top him, not out of his feet to be trampled upon by him, but out of his side to be equal with him."

God knew that without intimacy with an equal, Adam was lonely, even with the creation and the Creator. God could have filled Adam's heart exclusively, but in His divine brilliance, He did not do that. This was staggering humility on God's part—to make something that would not be fully satisfied by the Creator and His creation. This is incomprehensible for us!

To understand the uniqueness of males and females, we have to ask three exegetical questions.

- Why did God make Adam first and give him the prohibition about the tree of the knowledge of good and evil before He created Eve?
- Why did God have Adam name the animals without Eve and realize in the process that Adam needed a helper suitable for him?
- Why did God bring different curses on man and woman?

Adam had a more direct role in subduing and bearing responsibility for the direction of the Kingdom. This does not mean that Eve was not responsible for her sins or that she had no role in subduing and directing their activities in the garden. Dan B. Allender says, God built Adam with the physical and internal makeup to "enter, create, and shape form out of chaos." The curse given to Adam involved his work, and all his shaping of chaos would be fraught with futility. He would succeed but not without sweat, blood, and sorrow, and even his success would be a trial. God meant the curse to punish and to provide the humbling context for redemption.

A woman's role as a helper does not mean that she is weaker or stronger. She is a helper who is to engage creation jointly and enter

Dr. Elizabeth Thambiraj

into relationship to bring glory to God. Her primary calling is to be a warrior of relationship, a guardian of truth in relationship. She is made to reflect uniquely God's heart for relationship. The curse given to Eve involved relationships; she would bring forth life only with sweat, blood, and sorrow and would be in conflict with her husband (Genesis 3:16).

To extrapolate further, the curse dictated that in her loneliness, the woman would desire to absorb, to swallow the man to fill her emptiness, and he would fail her with base withdrawal or violent assault, and this indeed is a sad reality. Professionally, I do marriage counseling, and I see the above pattern repeated again and again. A normal woman can never flower in a marriage where she is not encouraged and is assaulted verbally on a regular basis. When God created Eve, he wired her differently from Adam, shaping her for relationship. Her internal makeup was to receive and gestate, and she was called to be a nurturer. As Dan B. Allender says, "Eve was created with the physical and internal makeup to receive, gestate, and shape relationships out of the beauty of form." Here again God meant the curse to punish for disobedience and to provide the humbling context for redemption.

"Sexually, a man plants his seed, and a woman slowly incubates the mysterious union of egg and sperm. Together, they create a human being. A man is a planter, a pursuer who is to enter the world with a strength and courage that form a new being. This tells us that human strength is an analogue of God's love of order, righteousness, and wrath". - *Intimate Allies By Dan B. Allender, Tremper Longman, III.*

"A woman is a nurturer who brings creation to life through the tender interconnectedness of her body and soul with the unborn child. This tells us that human tenderness is an analogue of God's love of mystery, tenderness, and mercy. A man courageously creates, and a woman creatively shapes his creation into a lovely, relationally enhancing beauty! One without the other is a grave distortion, male moving to violence and female gravitating to absorption. Order without mercy is authoritarian; mystery without form is hedonism. In other words, male and female operate in a precious balance between life and death". - *Intimate Allies By Dan B. Allender, Tremper Longman, III.*

Mystery of Relationships through the Lens of Scriptures

What does love mean? We are talking about true love here. Here we are discussing about a family home with two sources of love: female love and the masculine love. These loves are complementary, which means God has wired female and male differently so they complement each other.

"Many people are surprised to learn there is not a single word for love in the Bible, there are TWO words! And only two words. The Hebrew word for maleness love means: The 'strong person in the home.' The Hebrew word for femaleness love means: The 'strong person in the home, (with his) Person behold!'"[2]

[2] *Hebrew, letters, love, maleness, femaleness, ahab, ahabah, agape spiritualsprings.org/ss-16.htmCached*

Strong's Number or Single Word Search. Spiritual Springs: File z = 16. Hebrew, letters, love, maleness, femaleness, ahab, ahabah, agape ... This is the Hebrew word for femaleness love. The "strong ... May God bless our relearning of His love.

The above is the true picture of love in the Bible, and 1 Corinthians chapter 13 talks about love. According to God's Word, indeed love suffers long and is patient and kind. We know that *agape* is God's love, and it is the supreme love. The Word of God instructs us to love God with all of our being—heart, soul, mind, and strength—and we are called to love our neighbors. *Agape* is a Greek word translated from *ahab,* the Hebrew word for maleness love. In the Bible, God is a family of members—God the Father, God the Son, and God the Holy Spirit—each expressing distinct and complementary personalities of love. I pray that God will give us understanding as we relearn of His love.

Scientific studies indicate that men are more perverse and violent than women. Sexual abusers are mostly men. Women are most likely to be depressed and struggle with bulimia and codependency. What do all these symptoms point to? Even when it comes to the symptoms of sin, men and women differ greatly.

Dr. Elizabeth Thambiraj

A strong husband generally will draw forth the strong tenderness of his wife, and a tender wife will birth the tender strength of her husband. This is supposed to be so when husbands and wives labor to grow into the likeness of God. They will equally grow and shape one another and, as a result, will fill the earth and subdue the earth to God's character. Together, they bear a splendor that cannot be found in either person alone. Their relationship dispels loneliness and offers the one and only truly equal relationship found on earth.

Psalm 45 describes the splendor of maleness and the beauty of femaleness. Gender is the revelation of God, who also is protected by mystery, and men and women are created in the image of God. The image of God is particularized in gender, and the human bearers of his image cannot capture His character. In other words, each gender typically accentuates certain aspects of God's character. God is King, which highlights strength, but also mother, which emphasizes compassion (Psalm 131 and Isaiah 66:13).

In *Intimate Allies,* Dan Allender and Tremper Longman III writes, "As males and females we are significantly and intriguingly different ... The differences invite fascinating, unending eexploration."[3] They go on to say, "We have a choice: We can either delight in diversity or destroy distinctions."[4]

[3,4]Allender, Dan and Tremper Longman III. *Intimate Allies.*

Marriage is the first divine institution, and God, in His brilliance, made it between a male and a female in order to reveal and accentuate His character. A husband's strength helps him resonate with God's strong qualities, and he can help his wife understand that aspect of God more clearly, even though he does it imperfectly. In a similar fashion, a woman's tenderness and compassion can increase her husband's awareness of God's mercy (1 Peter 3:1–2). An awesome God, great designer of the universe and gender, made us male and female to have communion with Him. Maybe we can try to understand this unfathomable mystery of gender!

God is the author of relationship, and He, in His brilliance, made the genders, male and female, wired differently yet in His image, to revel

Mystery of Relationships through the Lens of Scriptures

in His love. Nothing—absolutely nothing—is more important in this world than to have a beautiful relationship with the Living God and to find our identity in Him and through Him. Divine Comedy is the title of Dante's famous poem, mainly describing Christ triumphing and Christians living in paradise eventually, which was a journey through heaven and hell with a happy ending. What I am mentioning here as Divine Comedy has nothing to do with Dante's poem, but simply a phrase people often use in their puzzle when men and women cannot get along especially in relationships. So in addressing that phrase I narrate that I can never imagine even for a minute that the creation of male and female was Divine Comedy; indeed, it was Divine Brilliance. It is our lack of understanding in our fallen state that leads us to misunderstand gender and speak of it as a Divine Comedy!

For Further Reading

Website References

1. *"Intuition is thinking without thinking. It's what people call gut feelings.*

   http://www.independent.co.uk/life-style/the-hardwired-difference-between-male-and-female-brains-could-explain-why-men-are-better-at-map-reading-8978248.html

   *http://www.independent.co.uk/life-style/the-hardwired-difference-between-male-and-female-brains-could explain-why-men-are-better-at-map-reading-897 HYPERLINK "http://www.independent.co.uk/life-style/the-hardwired-difference-between-male-and-female-brains-could%20explain-why-men-are-better-at-map-reading-897"8248.html^*

2. *The hardwired difference between male and female brains could explain why men are 'better at map ...*

   www.independent.co.uk

   A pioneering study has shown for the first time that the brains of men and women are wired up differently which could explain some of the stereotypical

Marriage

Marriage is the first divine institution. Within this relationship, God alone is the third person who will participate in all that we do. It is a relationship between a man and a woman, and it is the most important relationship in this world. We must honor it. Married couples have to honor it if they want to understand the Gospel. It is a relationship where the individuals move from being two separate human beings to become one flesh, a new unity of soul and body before God. This is an exclusive commitment.

Marriage is a mission field where God gives both the man and the woman opportunities to serve, nurture, cherish, and grow in the knowledge and love of God and at the same time please Him. When two sinners join in holy matrimony, it is always possible for something to go wrong. Through the motives of our hearts and the words we speak to one another, we may hurt our spouses, and our marriages may suffer. If we focus our attention on our hearts' issues, our marriages can have the privilege and opportunity to be living pictures of the Trinity. Then we can reveal God through the way we love our spouses.

Mutual submission is a key factor for a successful marriage. When the spouses care for each other and stay committed to their relationship through the intense heat of the many battles that arise, then the marriage becomes a successful marriage. In this way, marriage is very much like our relationship with God. God does not promise a world without worries once we become Christians, but He does gives us glimpses of joy and incredible bursts of brilliance in the midst of the marital struggle. God's Word gives us the strong foundation for a successful marriage in Ephesians 5:21–22: "Submitting yourselves one to another in the fear of God. Wives, submit yourselves unto your own husbands, as unto the Lord. For the husband is the head of the wife, even as Christ is the head of the church: and he is the savior of the body. Husbands, love your wives, even as Christ also loved the church, and gave himself for it; nevertheless let every one of you in particular so love his wife even as himself; and the wife see that she reverence her husband."

Mystery of Relationships through the Lens of Scriptures

"Married people confront life as a battle. As intimate allies, they push back the chaos."[1] Couples should constantly take effort to avoid the trigger situations but also use the triggers to remind themselves to be more loving and reasonable. Plan ahead to deal with those triggers, letting those triggers serve as reminders to put the plan into action. "A successful marriage is one in which two broken and forgiving people stay committed to one another in a sacrificial relationship in the face of life's chaos."[2]

[1, 2] Allender, Dan and Tremper Longman 111. *Intimate Allies.*

"God created marriages to bring forth a harvest of fruit. The fruit involves not only children but also changes in character, passion, and purpose. The process God instituted to create children and to bring about a change in character is sexual union. Sex changes the heart. It brings forth a chorus of praise, wonder, and joy or a song of sorrow and harm."[3]

[3] *Allender, Dan and Tremper Longman 111. Intimate Allies.*

One of the reasons for marital conflict is the inability of the husband and wife to leave, weave, and cleave. The failure to leave and weave often damages a healthy sexual relationship between husband and wife. These little foxes can destroy the beautiful vineyard, and it is wise to pay attention and keep necessary boundaries. It comes naturally for parents to love our children, but to love our spouses is a constant effort. In order for it to bear fruit, we must regularly nurture our marriages.

The offenses we commit against our spouses constantly challenge our marriages. Forgiveness is the key issue, and we should remember this as much as possible in our relationships with our spouses. God speaks of our relationship with Him as a marriage. This is amazing, but our relationship with God is so intimate that we can understand it only in the light of the passion that is to be shared within a marriage union. Although we cannot fathom the depth of this mystery, there is a deep desire in the heart of God for us to have deep relationship with Him.

Dr. Elizabeth Thambiraj

The above relates to the first divine institution, which is marriage. God created male and female so that they would be companions to each other to nullify loneliness, to communicate, to know each other intimately, and to glorify God. What a glorious thing it is if a couple can join in many things and most of all in prayer, which is a huge weapon against the enemy of our souls!

Marriages should be safe places where spouses communicate without fear. This is God's desire for married couples. In the light of the fear of God, all other fears should fade into insignificance. Indeed, our marriages can become the testing ground where God can win us to Himself!

Triggers of Conflict in Marriages

In this section, we are going to talk about the triggers and conflicts in marriage and also some ways to overcome them biblically. Some of the triggers are trivial, and some are major. Please explore with me in prayer.

Sex

One of the major triggers of conflict in marriage is sex. Sexual intimacy is for marriage alone. God created it that way when He made the first divine institution in the Garden of Eden. Ever since the fall in Genesis 3, sin has eaten away the beauty and joy God intended to be in marriage. Sin not only distorted that beautiful relationship but also tremendously affected sexual intimacy in marriage. In other words, sex can also become a minefield of disaster. Adultery, which is sexual intimacy outside of marriage; lack of desire for sexual intimacy within the boundaries of marriage; and perversion of sex, which has a vicious dimension are other areas that could trigger conflict in marriage.

The sexual revolution of the sixties and seventies called into question traditional morality. The AIDS epidemic has been like a sudden rain at a picnic. Sex, especially outside of a monogamous relationship, has taken on a never-before-thought-of danger. Very often, our culture accepts sex outside of marriage, and we are deviant from what Bible teaches us. God's Word is inerrant and unchanging. Let us see what the Bible says about sex outside marriage.

The Bible's message is that sex is the prerogative and joy of marriage and marriage alone. Hebrews 13:4 says, "Marriage is honorable in all, and the bed undefiled: but whoremongers and adulterers God will judge." Deuteronomy 22:22 says, "If a man be found lying with a woman married to an husband, then they shall both of them die, both the man that lay with the woman, and the woman: so shalt thou put away evil from Israel."

Dr. Elizabeth Thambiraj

Sex is the physical reflection of what takes place in the human soul. Adultery is like the worship of false gods. Adultery is not merely having sex with the wrong person. It is union with someone who will never require us to face our sinfulness, someone who will never draw forth our glory so that we are more and more in awe of God. It is intimacy without commitment, flight from the struggle of intimacy without ever facing our part in the loss. Intimacy without commitment is what the world wants today, and we are treading a dangerous path. Let us look at a biblical scenario regarding adultery and sex outside marriage.

Adultery

David's sexual escapade with Bathsheba sends its destructive shock waves through the rest of his life. Adultery triggers trouble that often dissolves marriage. In 2 Samuel 11:2–5, the Bible tells the story of King David and Bathsheba as follows:

> And it came to pass in an evening tide that David arose from off his bed, and walked upon the roof of the king's house: and from the roof he saw a woman washing herself; and the woman was very beautiful to look upon. And David sent and inquired after the woman. And one said, Is not this Bath-sheba, the daughter of Eliam, the wife of Uriah the Hittite? And David sent messengers, and took her; and she came in unto him, and he lay with her; for she was purified from her uncleanness: and she returned unto her house. And the woman conceived, and sent and told David, and said, I am with child.

Adultery is the main reason marriages dissolve, and the Bible has strong words to admonish against adultery. Adultery does not stop there but spirals down, and eventually it may lead to murder too, because jealousy, bitterness, and other emotions follow to the point of the destruction of life. Following his adultery, David eventually murdered Uriah.

What does wisdom say?

> To deliver thee from the way of the evil man, from the man that speaketh froward things; Who leave the paths of uprightness, to

Mystery of Relationships through the Lens of Scriptures

walk in the ways of darkness; Who rejoice to do evil, and delight in the forwardness of the wicked; Whose ways are crooked, and they froward in their paths: To deliver thee from the strange woman, even from the stranger which flattereth with her words; Which forsaketh the guide of her youth, and forgetteth the covenant of her God. For her house inclineth unto death, and her paths unto the dead. None that go unto her return again, neither take they hold of the paths of life. (Proverbs 2:12–19)

Absence of Sexual Desire

The second evidence of sex gone awry is the absence of sexual desire. Let us see what the Scriptures point out in 1 Corinthians:

Now concerning the things whereof ye wrote unto me: It is good for a man not to touch a woman. Nevertheless, to avoid fornication, let every man have his own wife, and let every woman have her own husband. Let the husband render unto the wife due benevolence: and likewise also the wife unto the husband. The wife hath not power of her own body, but the husband: and likewise also the husband hath not power of his own body, but the wife. Defraud ye not one the other, except it be with consent for a time, that ye may give yourselves to fasting and prayer; and come together again, that Satan tempt you not for your incontinency. But I speak this by permission, and not of commandment. For I would that all men were even as I myself. But every man hath his proper gift of God, one after this manner, and another after that. (1 Corinthians 7:1–7)

In marital sexuality, we gift our spouses with our bodies' power to bring pleasure to them. As marriage partners, we do not own our own bodies; in a way, our bodies belong to our spouses. Paul knows that sex is an important and crucial expression of marital union. Certainly, no one enjoys perfect sex throughout marriage. Our sinfulness and selfishness emerge to keep us from the type of intimate vulnerability involved in the sexual act.

Perversion

Transvestism, bestiality, incest, and homosexuality are some of the other sexual sins that the Bible recognizes and condemns. In Deuteronomy

Dr. Elizabeth Thambiraj

22:5, we read, "The woman shall not wear that which pertaineth unto a man, neither shall a man put on a woman's garment: for all that do so are abomination unto the Lord thy God." Deuteronomy 27:20–22 says, "Cursed be he that lieth with his father's wife; because he uncovereth his father's skirt. And all the people shall say, Amen. Cursed be he that lieth with any manner of beast. And all the people shall say, Amen. Cursed be he that lieth with his sister, the daughter of his father, or the daughter of his mother. And all the people shall say, Amen." In Romans 1:26–27, Apostle Paul writes, "For this cause God gave them up unto vile affections: for even their women did change the natural use into that which is against nature: And likewise also the men, leaving the natural use of the woman, burned in their lust one toward another; men with men working that which is unseemly, and receiving in themselves that recompense of their error which was meet."

Sexual perversion is always a violent assault against the beauty of God's design for sexual pleasure and intimacy. No woman under the sun can flower into glory if her husband sees sex as nothing more than his divine right and prerogative. I am a counselor, and I see time and again women and even men coming to my door crying, and they want to save their marriages. The deeper issues are usually issues of the heart, and sex, as I have mentioned before, is only an outward expression of inward reality. I wanted to be careful and mention, 'unfortunately, in our fallen world, very often husbands see sex as their divine right and prerogative to feel good about themselves, and women become victims in order to save their marriages. It is not surprising to me that many marriages are suffering and that the biblical beauty and glory of sex are turning into nothing but shame. Having said the above, I am not denying there are marriages that are beautiful and authentic, without falsehood and lies'.

Violence

A second major trigger to conflict in marriage is violence. Comparing the violence in our culture with 2 Samuel 13:9–14 will speak for itself. Loneliness and futility can ignite a rage that leads to violence, and the violence can be sexual, physical, or emotional. Biblical records indicate that violent sex invaded the lives and homes of people from all levels of society, and all around the globe.

Mystery of Relationships through the Lens of Scriptures

Let us look at a biblical example of violence in the home:

> And she took a pan, and poured them out before him; but he refused to eat. And Amnon said, Have out all men from me. And they went out every man from him. And Amnon said unto Tamar, Bring the meat into the chamber that I may eat of thine hand. And Tamar took the cakes which she had made, and brought them into the chamber to Amnon her brother. And when she had brought them unto him to eat, he took hold of her, and said unto her, Come lie with me, my sister. And she answered him, Nay, my brother, do not force me; for no such thing ought to be done in Israel: do not thou this folly. And I, whither shall I cause my shame to go? and as for thee, thou shalt be as one of the fools in Israel. Now therefore, I pray thee, speak unto the king; for he will not withhold me from thee. Howbeit he would not hearken unto her voice: but, being stronger than she, forced her, and lay with her. (2 Samuel 13:9–14)

More prevalent are emotionally abusive homes in which family members violate one another with demeaning, hurtful, and shameful words. No one knows, sees, and feels the impact of our sin more than our spouses do. Our homes became a place for emotional abuse with the Fall, and in the worst scenario, the abusers are those who hold the authority.

Often, when our loneliness or fears of failure are exposed in our marriages, we develop a rage that desires to bind and silence our spouses. There is a great temptation to deprive our spouses of their glory when we feel deprived of our own. In those cases, verbal abuse is likely to occur, and the other spouse will experience emotional trauma. It is very sad that this happens in Christian marriages and homes. Dan B. Allender says that physical and sexual abuse in a marriage is a grave sign of degradation that must be dealt with both legally (it is a crime) and spiritually (with church discipline).

Limited Time and Money

Time and money are two resources that most expose our limits, our failures, and even our impending deaths. In our society, they represent power, the ability to do things, and even the ability to

Dr. Elizabeth Thambiraj

influence people. Money is the medium of power. The battle is not about who is trustworthy but about who controls the most palpable means of setting the family agenda. For example, is the husband spending too much time with his colleagues, neglecting his wife, just because he is earning more? This conflict over time and money will really cloud the issue. Quarrels over time and money usually reflect a demand to own our lives than to serve the other with our wealth and existence.

Ecclesiastes 5:10 says, "He that loveth silver shall not be satisfied with silver; nor he that loveth abundance with increase: this is also vanity." Ecclesiastes 9:11–12 adds, "I returned, and saw under the sun, that the race is not to the swift, nor the battle to the strong, neither yet bread to the wise, nor yet riches to men of understanding, nor yet favour to men of skill; but time and chance happeneth to them all. For man also knoweth not his time: as the fishes that are taken in an evil net, and as the birds that are caught in the snare; so are the sons of men snared in an evil time, when it falleth suddenly upon them."

Divided Loyalties

Do we value money or time more than we value our spouses? Are we more committed to something or someone else than we are to our beloveds? The hints of a divided loyalty always bring tension and heartbreak to the surface.

King Solomon's divided loyalty is a biblical example of this phenomenon:

> But king Solomon loved many strange women, together with the daughter of Pharaoh, women of the Moabites, Ammonites, Edomites, Zidonians, and Hittites; *Of the nations concerning which the LORD said unto the children of Israel, Ye shall not go in to them, neither shall they come in unto you: for surely they will turn away your heart after their gods: Solomon clave unto these in love.* And he had seven hundred wives, princesses, and three hundred concubines: and his wives turned away his heart. For it came to pass, when Solomon was old, that his wives turned away his heart after other gods: and his heart was not perfect with the LORD his God, as was the heart of David his father.

Mystery of Relationships through the Lens of Scriptures

> For Solomon went after Ashtoreth the goddess of the Zidonians, and after Milcom the abomination of the Ammonites. And Solomon did evil in the sight of the LORD, and went not fully after the LORD, as did David his father. (1 Kings 11:1–6)

The consequences of his actions were extensive; after his death, the kingdom of Israel split into two parts.

- The concept of divided loyalty also can apply to our worship of God. What is our commitment to the triune God? Is our loyalty divided between the world and God?
- If we truly believe that the triune God is all-powerful, why do many Christians get involved in occult practices in order to exercise power over someone else? Marriages come with a package of struggles along with joy. Divided loyalties and becoming involved in the occult definitely makes the journey of marriage harder. If we explore further our families of origin, we see that any involvement in occult practices definitely affects newly formed family units.
- What is our commitment to our spouses? Are we committed to the first Divine Institution, the marriage God has made, or to something else?

Paul addresses the issue of divided loyalty in the New Testament and warns that intimate relationships must have Christ in common; otherwise, they will fail: "Be ye not unequally yoked together with unbelievers: for what fellowship hath righteousness with unrighteousness? and what communion hath light with darkness? And what concord hath Christ with Belial? or what part hath he that believeth with an infidel? And what agreement hath the temple of God with idols? for ye are the temple of the living God; as God hath said, I will dwell in them, and walk in them; and I will be their God, and they shall be my people" (2 Corinthians 6:14–16).

We must keep our loyalties as husbands and wives in balance with great commitment. Our relationships with our families of origin and in-laws and children are secondary. After relationship with God, a marriage relationship must command the deepest commandment. How is our relationship to God? Do we really believe He is the Alpha

Dr. Elizabeth Thambiraj

and Omega, the Beginning and the End? Do we genuinely believe He is all-powerful? Do we truly believe that Jesus Christ is God's only Son and in Him we are saved? Do we think that there is a marriage of the Lamb and that we (the church) will be His bride? Do we believe that God's Spirit is working very powerfully in the world and that He is a mighty warrior protecting His own? Can we use the Biblical model of marriage to get out of some of the destructive patterns in our marriages? Do we believe that marriage is a gift from God?

A Little Glimpse into Marriages beyond the Fall

Marriages struggle under the freight of the Fall. We struggle with sin in all aspects of our lives, and in marriage, sin has great potential to cause damage. Marriages are a crucible not only for sin to be exposed but also for forgiveness to restore relationship and intensify our hope for heaven. Redemption can never come without war.

The Fall not only affected relationships but also the internal makeup of men and women. God, in His grace, provided to Adam and Eve clothes to cover their nakedness after the Fall. This account of the Fall should remind us the readers that we will never experience the kind of intimacy, passion, and union God intended for husbands and wives! In other words, increased loneliness and a sense of futility came in full into marriages after the Fall.

When someone doubts his or her capacity to deal with the chaos of life, it is easier to snipe at a spouse and blame him or her for a lonely existence. It is easier to blame a spouse than to acknowledge what is wrong in a marriage. Ultimately, there are only two options: either choose to live by pretense or be broken by sin and surrender to the Gospel. After all, we are sinners, every single one of us born of a woman. The following section is based on various passages of the book of Romans. A good confirmation that we are sinners is that our consciences constantly tell us that we are not living up to God's expectation for our lives!

The Nature of Sin

"Sin involves not only what we do; but also what we think and feel."[1]

[1] Allender, Dan and Tremper Longman III. *Intimate Allies.*

Referring to passages in James 2:8–11, it is clear that in God's eyes, the least sin is as major as the grossest sin. Eve ate the fruit, but her dialogue with the serpent took place with Adam next to her. When Eve finished eating it, she handed the fruit to her husband, and he ate

Dr. Elizabeth Thambiraj

it without an argument. Through the lens of Genesis 3, we see clearly that both Adam and Eve are rebellious sinners. The truth of the matter here is that human beings are glorious creatures of God as well as ugly sinners. As men and a women we must try to understand this point clearly before entering into the marital covenant relationship.

Sin has affected all marriages, and we see how sin disrupts and occasionally tears marriages apart. We also see certain triggers that lead to conflict and pain in the marriage relationship. These include sex, violence, limited time and money, and divided loyalty, and I have dealt with these issues through the lens of the scriptures in the previous chapter. God does not leave His people to wallow in sin. Within the context of the Curse at the time of the Fall, God gives us a glimpse of the promise of redemption: "And I will put enmity between thee and the woman, and between thy seed and her seed; it shall bruise thy head, and thou shalt bruise his heel" (Genesis 3:15).

The Pervasiveness of Sin

How pervasive is sin? Romans 3:23 says, "For all have sinned, and come short of the glory of God," reminding us of the effects of the Fall and the intensity of sin. When we rely on anything else but God for sustenance, strength, wisdom, and beauty, we have turned away from worshipping Him. Sin is not only a matter of choosing between right and wrong; in one sentence, sin is the refusal to trust God (Romans 5). Speaking metaphorically, rebellion is in our blood. "Who changed the truth of God into a lie, and worshipped and served the creature more than the Creator, who is blessed for ever, Amen" (Romans 1:25). The consequences of the Fall showed Adam and Eve just how wrong they were.

We do not see the weight of our own sin as the fundamental issue that we must deal with in all relational problems. It means that nothing is free from the impact of our sin, not even our intellect, feelings, choices, or actions. But God did not create us to be sinners; He created us to be His glorious creatures. James pointed out that the law of God is a unity and that by breaking any part of the law, we have broken the entire law. Other biblical passages that address this

Mystery of Relationships through the Lens of Scriptures

same idea are Matthew 5:48, Levi 19:2, Deuteronomy 18:13, James 2:8–11, and Romans 3:9–20.

"Oddly, it will be the 'wounds of marriage' that may propel each partner to look to God in the midst of their heartache."[2]

[2] Allender, Dan and Tremper Longman III. *Intimate Allies.*

This may sound very strange, but when we look at our lives through the lens of the Scriptures, we begin to realize how true the above statement is! We now see just how deep our guilt goes and how hard it is for us to forgive our offenders, especially in marriage. We realize that all of us are desperate for mercy and forgiveness. How many marriages do we see around us that jointly propel both spouses to hunger for forgiveness? Sadly, many couples function with relational and spiritual detachment, and this becomes a norm—but it is not what God wants us to do.

Heartaches of Marriage

In Ecclesiastes 7:26–29, we read,

> And I find more bitter than death the woman, whose heart is snares and nets, and her hands as bands: whoso pleaseth God shall escape from her; but the sinner shall be taken by her. Behold, this have I found, saith the preacher, counting one by one, to find out the account: Which yet my soul seeketh, but I find not: one man among a thousand have I found; but a woman among all those have I not found. Lo, this only have I found, that God hath made man upright; but they have sought out many inventions.

It is unfortunate that the preacher talks about women and men this way, but it is practical wisdom for living. In other words, this means that our great designer God wired men and women differently! In today's context, people marry for varied reasons, and often they believe that marriage will remove their loneliness once and for all. As a counselor, I have seen cases where marriage did not remove people's loneliness; instead, they became more abused, depressed, conflicted, and confused than they had been before they got married.

Dr. Elizabeth Thambiraj

We have to remember what happened to Adam in the Garden of Eden after the Fall. Adam began to blame Eve, and Eve blamed the serpent.

"After sin entered the world, the loneliness that Adam felt before the Fall returned, and this time the loneliness was not a benign sigh but a heartrending cry! We have a hope here! Marriages after the Garden of Eden are not the final solution but the Promised Land that will restore Eden". Intimate Allies by Dan B. Allender.

When we begin to understand the effect of the Fall, we can learn to expect less from marriage. This means we begin to understand that our spouses are weak like us. We can expect intimacy without expecting the total bliss of Eden before the Fall. The teacher in Ecclesiastes recognizes and focuses on the benefits of relationship when he says. "Again, if two lie together, then they have heat: but how can one be warm alone?" (Ecclesiastes 4:11). When one spouse feels unfulfilled by the other spouse, this can lead to violence, and the marriage can become very lonely.

Anger murders relationship. Let us see what the Word of God says about anger:

> Ye have heard that it was said of them of old time, Thou shalt not kill; and whosoever shall kill shall be in danger of the judgment: But I say unto you, That whosoever is angry with his brother without a cause shall be in danger of the judgment: and whosoever shall say to his brother, Raca, shall be in danger of the council: but whosoever shall say, Thou fool, shall be in danger of hell fire. Therefore if thou bring thy gift to the altar, and there rememberest that thy brother hath ought against thee; Leave there thy gift before the altar, and go thy way; first be reconciled to thy brother, and then come and offer thy gift. Agree with thine adversary quickly, whiles thou art in the way with him; lest at any time the adversary deliver thee to the judge, and the judge deliver thee to the officer, and thou be cast into prison. Verily I say unto thee, Thou shalt by no means come out thence, till thou hast paid the uttermost farthing. (Matthew 5:21–26).

Mystery of Relationships through the Lens of Scriptures

The book of Proverbs tells us not to associate with an angry man. Anger is an emotion that follows a real or a perceived attack, and often the weaker person in a relationship becomes the target for that anger. For example, when a person is afraid of losing control or when the situation defies his or her expectations, that person becomes angry. Anger can kill relationship with a spouse, and the results of this are increased loneliness and a sense of futility. It is a sad reality that often a spouse becomes the target of another spouse's anger and hatred. It is not wise to use anger in the wrong way, and we have to be careful. Otherwise, we are giving Satan a way to destroy good relationships. It is extremely evil even to think that someone has to pay for someone else's emptiness, unfairness, and unhappiness or for the cruelty of life in general.

"Anger says, 'If I suffer, then you will suffer too. If I get kicked by life, then I will kick someone who is weaker and smaller in an attempt to bear the rage I feel toward the strong.'" Intimate Allies by Dan B. Allender.

What does God's Word say about lust?

> Ye have heard that it was said by them of old time, Thou shalt not commit adultery: But I say unto you, That whosoever looketh on a woman to lust after her hath committed adultery with her already in his heart. And if thy right eye offend thee, pluck it out, and cast it from thee: for it is profitable for thee that one of thy members should perish, and not that thy whole body should be cast into hell. And if thy right hand offend thee, cut it off, and cast it from thee: for it is profitable for thee that one of thy members should perish, and not that thy whole body should be cast into hell. (Matthew 5:27–30)

Lust of the eye is one of the reasons for major sins like adultery. Often, before adultery becomes a physical act, it starts in the mind and in the heart. What one sees with the mind, of course, descends to the heart including all the twisted and evil passions. The energy of the heart then pushes the heart to perform the evil act of adultery. This evil desire goes out of control, and there is a ravenous demand to fulfill the act. It is sad that I have to mention here that the futility brought on by loneliness in a relationship can lead to lust and even

Dr. Elizabeth Thambiraj

murder, which are twisted passions. Lust also leads to uncontrollable desire to do things like gossiping, indulging in pornography, or even eating food excessively.

What do we understand by loving our enemies? When we read Matthew 5:41–48, we hear a hard reality and to accept it is extremely hard and to put it into practice using our own strength is unimaginable.

> And if any man will sue thee at the law, and take away thy coat, let him have thy cloke also. And whosoever shall compel thee to go a mile, go with him twain. Give to him that asketh thee, and from him that would borrow of thee turn not thou away. Ye have heard that it hath been said, Thou shalt love thy neighbour, and hate thine enemy. But I say unto you, Love your enemies, bless them that curse you, do good to them that hate you, and pray for them which despitefully use you, and persecute you; That ye may be the children of your Father which is in heaven: for he maketh his sun to rise on the evil and on the good, and sendeth rain on the just and on the unjust. For if ye love them which love you, what reward have ye? do not even the publicans the same? And if ye salute your brethren only, what do ye more than others? do not even the publicans so? Be ye therefore perfect, even as your Father which is in heaven is perfect.

The focus of Jesus here is on our thoughts, actions, emotions, and choices we make. We need to bring our focus totally before the Lord God of the universe, knowing that we have to be rooted in Him and in His strength. We begin to understand slowly that we continue to sin in our thoughts, actions, emotions, and the choices we make with our whole being, and because of this, following God's command to love our enemies seems impossible. "Love your neighbor as yourself" is a command; and is it possible with only our own strength, and where is our hope? Where does our help come from, and how do we do this?

Where is our hope of redemption in marriage relationships?

There is biblical hope and redemption for contemporary marriages in this part of eternity. The Lord's Prayer asks God to "forgive us our debts as we forgive our debtors." Forgiveness must be a daily act in a marriage relationship, and this is crucial. Many marriages now

Mystery of Relationships through the Lens of Scriptures

days, even though not abusive, are simply cold and unhappy. Spouses have a hard time providing compassion and support in the everyday battles of life, and relationships are simply loveless. A lifestyle of forgiveness and a deep desire to cancel debt and to love boldly are the basic ingredients for a good flavor in a marriage.

In a marriage relationship, we begin to know not only our spouse's faults but also his or her strengths, and this allows us to pray more effectively for our spouse. We also begin to acknowledge our own faults, failures, and strengths, and this makes us look beyond our relationship to something greater. Opening our faults and failures to our spouse is not a sign of weakness but a strength of maturity, and this vulnerability increases the confidence in a marital relationship. This strengthens the bond of love in a marriage, and the Gospel indeed brings hope and joy in a relationship.

"The Gospel opens our eyes to the Marriage that every one of us desires."[3]

[3]Allender, Dan and Tremper Longman III. Intimate Allies.

A life spent without a deep personal relationship with the Living God through Jesus Christ and His Spirit is the greatest of tragedies. My heart's cry and desire is for all the readers of this book to focus on this relationship first. Fellowship with other believers and especially in marriage will eventually propel us toward this relationship, because through this fellowship, we begin to understand how much God has forgiven us!

Tongues

You may wonder why I am addressing a different topic while still discussing relationships. The word *tongues* immediately brings to mind speaking in tongues, which was a dramatic miracle that helped the Christian church began as recorded in Acts 2. Here I am not going to debate about speaking in tongues; instead, I am going to explore the four different kinds of tongues. Often, in marriages, our tongues play a huge role and have the capacity to either build or to destroy. The real purpose of this article is to magnify the importance of the use and misuse of tongues.

[The Latin word for To Tame is Domito,

Domito is defined as: to tame, subdue, break in.

The word "tame" is from the Greek word damadzo,

Damadzo means: to domesticate, to subdue, to tame, or to bring under control][1].

Synonyms for *tame*

[bridle, check, constrain, contain, curb, govern, hold, inhibit, keep, measure, pull in, regulate, rein (in), restrain, rule, control][2]

[1]*Taming Synonyms, Taming Antonyms | Thesaurus.com*
thesaurus.com/browse/tamin

verb: domesticate, make compliant. Synonyms: break, break in, break the spirit ...
verb: train in new skill. Synonyms: accustom, condition, educate, gentle, get ...

[2]*Synonyms of tame | Infoplease.com - Thesaurus Search Page ...*
thesaurus.infoplease.com/tame

tame: synonyms, definitions, and usage ... Synonyms for tame Verb 1. tame, chasten, subdue, change, alter, modify usage: correct by punishment or discipline

Mystery of Relationships through the Lens of Scriptures

Some examples of an untamed tongue include gossiping, putting others down, bragging, manipulating, false teaching, exaggerating, complaining, flattering, and lying. Examples of a tamed tongue include encouraging others and deciding not to put another person down. Proper speech is not only saying the right words at the right time but also controlling one's desire to say what one should not.

The word *tame (damadzo)* appears in Mark 5:4: "Because that he had been often bound with fetters and chains, and the chains had been plucked asunder by him, and the fetters broken in pieces: neither could any man tame him." This passage talks about the maniac of Gadara. This helps us to establish the proper meaning of the word in the book of James. The word *taming* has nothing to do with domesticating animals or training them to perform. The meaning here is "control or dominion over an animal," and the book of James chapter 3 talks about controlling the tongue. Humanity in general can control every other creature, but no one can control his or her own tongue.

James 3 talks about the dangers of the tongue and compares the damage the tongue can do to a raging fire. Satan uses the tongue to divide people, to set them against each other, and to spread destruction like a raging fire in a forest. James 3:5–12 reads,

> Even so the tongue is a little member, and boasteth great things. Behold, how great a matter a little fire kindleth! And the tongue is a fire, a world of iniquity: so is the tongue among our members, that it defileth the whole body, and setteth on fire the course of nature; and it is set on fire of hell. For every kind of beasts, and of birds, and of serpents, and of things in the sea, is tamed, and hath been tamed of mankind: But the tongue can no man tame; it is an unruly evil, full of deadly poison. Therewith bless we God, even the Father; and therewith curse we men, which are made after the similitude of God. Out of the same mouth proceedeth blessing and cursing. My brethren, these things ought not so to be. Doth a fountain send forth at the same place sweet water and bitter? Can the fig tree, my brethren, bear olive berries? either a vine, figs? so can no fountain both yield salt water and fresh.

Dr. Elizabeth Thambiraj

I would like to classify tongues into four categories, and their meanings are self-explanatory:

1. the caring tongue,
2. the careful tongue,
3. the careless tongue, and
4. the conniving tongue.

Our tongues are a system and a world of iniquity that can set the whole course of a life on fire. Satan often uses our tongues to accomplish whatever the world system and the schemes he wants. The book of James explains that human beings are made in the image of God (Genesis 1:26–27 and 5:1). We have to remind ourselves that to curse people and bless God is inconsistent (James 3:9). The Fall has distorted God's image in human beings, but with the indwelling power of the Holy Spirit and His work in us, we can tame our tongues, one of the smallest organs in our bodies. We can ask ourselves in which of the above categories we fall, and we can work toward perfection for His glory.

James 3:13–18 talks about worldly wisdom and godly wisdom. The wisdom of God is pure and always promotes peace, ending in righteousness (James 3:17–18). As disciples of Jesus Christ, we can learn slowly to control our tongues, and this is a true mark of spiritual maturity. As we read and meditate on His word, we begin to understand the destructive power of the misuse of tongues. Godly wisdom trains us in the path of righteousness and truth, and we learn to use our tongues for the edification of others.

Our contradictory speech often puzzles our inner cores and destabilizes our states of mind. At times, our words are right and please God, but often they are violent, caustic, and destructive. My question is this: Which of the speech patterns reflects our true identity? The tongue—that is, our speech—very often gives a true picture of our basic human nature and our relationship with God. God loves to work in us inside out, and the Holy Spirit is able to purify our hearts and give us the necessary control to speak the right words that please God.

Mystery of Relationships through the Lens of Scriptures

Jeremiah 17:9 says, "The heart is deceitful above all things, and desperately wicked: who can know it?" This confirms that one's speech is a reflection of one's heart, which is inclined to evil. For this reason, with regard to control over one's tongue, the Bible primarily advocates silence. For "In the multitude of words there wanteth not sin: but he that refraineth his lips is wise" (Proverbs 10:19), and "He that hath knowledge spareth his words: and a man of understanding is of an excellent spirit" (Proverbs 17:27).

"This is particularly a challenge to teachers and preachers. Such people I advise to consider how much of their teachings are factually based, to what degree they use the Bible, and how much is their own opinion. Sometimes its best just to cage your speech as you would a wild animal".[3]

[3]*James 3:1-12 Study Guide - BCBSR*

www.bcbsr.com/books/jam3a.html

If we cannot tame our tongues, then we should not speak, and this is considered wise. Paul characterizes the human condition by saying, "Their throat is an open sepulchre; with their tongues they have used deceit; the poison of asps is under their lips" (Romans 3:13). We have to be careful when we think that we have tamed our speech, because leaving it unguarded is like making a house pet out of a wild animal. "No man can tame the tongue," and this is in accordance with God's Word. If anyone can control his or her tongue, he or she is a perfect person. If we are careful and caring in our speech, we can grow in holiness, because careless and conniving speech not only harms others but also harms our heart's disposition greatly.

The Tongue's Antithetical Nature

Let us study the following Scriptures and think about the nature of our tongues in our fallen world. James 3:9–12 says, "Therewith bless we God, even the Father; and therewith curse we men, which are made after the similitude of God. Out of the same mouth proceedeth blessing and cursing. My brethren, these things ought not so to be. Doth a fountain send forth at the same place sweet water and bitter?

79

Dr. Elizabeth Thambiraj

Can the fig tree, my brethren, bear olive berries? either a vine, figs? so can no fountain both yield salt water and fresh."

While it should not be, this is the case due to our dual nature. Paul writes, "This I say then, Walk in the Spirit, and ye shall not fulfil the lust of the flesh. For the flesh lusteth against the Spirit, and the Spirit against the flesh: and these are contrary the one to the other: so that ye cannot do the things that ye would" (Galatians 5:16–17). He also writes, "Let no corrupt communication proceed out of your mouth, but that which is good to the use of edifying, that it may minister grace unto the hearers. And grieve not the Holy Spirit of God, whereby ye are sealed unto the day of redemption. Let all bitterness, and wrath, and anger, and clamour, and evil speaking, be put away from you, with all malice" (Ephesians 4:29–31).

In Ephesians 5:4, he adds, "Neither filthiness, nor foolish talking, nor jesting, which are not convenient: but rather giving of thanks." Even if we do not achieve perfect control of our tongues, we can still learn enough control to reduce the damage our words do. The Holy Spirit is able to give us increased power to monitor and control what we say so that when we are offended, the Spirit will remind us of God's love. When we are reminded of God's love, we will not react in hateful ways when we are criticized, and the Spirit will heal the hurt. We will not lash out with our tongues, which can dishonor God. "For in many things we offend all. If any man offend not in word, the same is a perfect man, and able also to bridle the whole body" (James 3:2).

Love … in All the Wrong Places?

Love is a word we hear around the globe, and it has an intoxicating effect on human emotions. Love seems to be a common denominator in every relationship, and everyone, no matter which culture they come from, wants to be loved. Unfortunately, when someone claims to love someone, very often they do not, partly because they do not know what genuine love is. Humanity in general searches for this love, and often we search in the wrong places!

Unlike Greek, Hebrew has only one word for love.

[*There is only one Hebrew word for love. The noun form is ahava (אהבה) and the verb is ahav (בהא). (You may be thinking of Greek, which has 4 different words for love).*][1]

[1]*What is the Hebrew word for love*

wiki.answers.com › … › Translations › English to HebrewCached

[There are several *Greek words for love*, as the *Greek language* distinguishes how the word is used.

Agápe (ἀγάπη agápē[1]) means "love" (unconditional love) in modern day Greek, such as in the term s'agapo (Σ'αγαπώ), which means "I love you".

Éros (ἔρως érōs[2]) is passionate love, with sensual desire and longing. The Modern Greek word "erotas" means "intimate love;"

Philia (φιλία philía[3]) means friendship or affectionate love in modern Greek.

Storge (στοργή storgē[4]) means "affection" in ancient and modern Greek. It is natural affection, like that felt by parents for offspring.][2]

[2]*Greek words for love - Wikipedia, the free encyclopedia*

en.wikipedia.org/wiki/Greek_words_for_loveCached - Similar

81

Dr. Elizabeth Thambiraj

What is true love, and where do we find it? Expecting something from someone in return for something, fear, lust, jealousy, and possessiveness are not genuine love. Even in parent-child relationships and in marriages, most people on this planet earth never experience that perfect love, and humanity is in search of it. True love is unconditional. To love someone unconditionally means to love the other person in the past, the present, and the future even when he or she disagrees sometimes with your opinion.

Human beings long for something from other human beings that only God can provide, and we all fail to realize this. Much of the dissatisfaction people experience in marriage comes from expecting too much from it. We want to get a major percentage of life's fulfillment from our spouses and fail to realize that they are only human and limited in all aspects—including the ability to love! Here I do not mean to minimize the joy that marriage brings, the sense of fulfillment that spouses gain from sharing with one another their mental, emotional, physical, and spiritual lives! What I am trying to share here is beyond marriage, the joy and happiness that God alone can provide regardless of circumstances. The focus here is on spiritual growth, and marriage simply becomes the context or the vehicle to promote that growth. It exposes both the truth and weaknesses so that spouses may grow in maturity.

"We must never be naïve enough to think of marriage as a safe harbor from the fall ... The deepest struggles of life will occur in the most primary relationship affected by the Fall: marriage."[3]

[3]Allender, Dan and Tremper Longman 111. *Intimate Allies.*

In this fallen world, no one will ever find a spouse in whom the Fall does not have an effect. Husbands and wives are married to sinful spouses who have a limited ability to express their love. They may sin against each other, disappoint each other, or even have physical limitations that could frustrate and sadden a spouse. For example, a husband may have all the best intentions but may lose his temper when he gets back from work; and a wife, despite a strong desire, may not have the energy to accomplish all that she wanted to, that day. This is life and reality, and even in Christian marriages, this

Mystery of Relationships through the Lens of Scriptures

could be the norm. We have to understand marriage and love from God's perspective and not from the perspective of the world or the contemporary Hollywood model.

Contempt breeds when we focus on our spouse's weaknesses and are not able to think about his or her achievements. In Matthew 7:3–5, Jesus says, "And why beholdest thou the mote that is in thy brother's eye, but considerest not the beam that is in thine own eye? Or how wilt thou say to thy brother, Let me pull out the mote out of thine eye; and, behold, a beam is in thine own eye? Thou hypocrite, first cast out the beam out of thine own eye; and then shalt thou see clearly to cast out the mote out of thy brother's eye."

Gary and Betsy Ricucci remind us, "A magnificent marriage begins not with knowing one another but knowing with God."[4]

"From whence [come] wars and fightings among you? [come they] not hence, [even] of your lusts that war in your members? Ye lust, and have not: ye kill, and desire to have, and cannot obtain: ye fight and war, yet ye have not, because ye ask not." This verse (James 4:1–2) points us away from focusing on our spouses and makes us look toward God. Often, marital conflict arises because we want something and do not get it. The book of James specifically says that we are not getting it because we are looking in the wrong place. Looking in the right place reduces the demand we place on our spouses. When we look to God, He will provide unconditionally the love we crave. This will change us to become Christ-like, and we will approach our spouses with the spirit of humility and servanthood. A word of caution is that there are many exceptions to the above norm.

Since all wars and fighting come from the corruptions of our own hearts, it is right to mortify those lusts that war in the members. Worldly and fleshly lusts are distempers that will not allow content or satisfaction, and this will work against our peace with God. Sinful selfish desires and affections of the world are a hindrance to our prayer lives and work against our desires toward God. We should be careful that we do not misuse, by the disposition of our hearts, the mercies we receive when God grants our prayers.

Dr. Elizabeth Thambiraj

Mathew Henry tells us, "When men ask of God prosperity, they often ask with wrong aims and intentions. If we thus seek the things of this world, it is just in God to deny them."[5] - Mathew Henry commentary.

As we try to fathom the unconditional love of God, who gave His only Son, Jesus Christ, to humanity, we get a glimpse of what love really is: "For God so loved the world, that He gave His only begotten Son, that whosoever believeth in Him should not perish, but have everlasting life" (John 3:16).

During his earthly ministry, Jesus Christ moved with very sinful people and loved them unconditionally. He taught them to love others as they wished others to love and honor them. He loved Judas, the betrayer; the woman at the well, a sexual libertine; the conniving financial cheat, Zacchaeus; Peter, who denied Him; and many others steeped in sin. Jesus Christ was the only perfect human being who ever lived. He loved others unconditionally and taught us to love and honor our neighbors, especially in the highest priority of all the relationships—that is, in marriage. Our relationships, and especially our marriages, can become platforms where we can exercise unconditional love, at least to a certain extent, when we try to fathom God's everlasting love (Romans 8).

The message here is that no human being can love us the way we long to be loved, because no other human being will be able to alleviate the spiritual ache that God has placed in us. Why don't we search for that love in the right place?

Faithfulness

Faithfulness is a word that humanity does not know anymore. Betrayal by a trusted friend, by a spouse, by children, in working relationships, and even among Christian circles is becoming the normal way of life. Many people seem to love dogs, and when I asked them why, they invariably gave me a common answer. They said 'dogs are our best friends and is very faithful to us'. People have been betrayed so many times, even by their best friends, and we have almost lost the word *faithfulness* from the human dictionary. If there is any term that captures the essence of humanity's character at this time, it is *faithlessness*. Let us explore together the true meaning of faithfulness and why it is worth understanding biblically.

The dictionary then compares *faithful* with its synonyms: "*Faithful* implies steadfast adherence to a person or thing to which one is bound as by an oath or obligation; *loyal* implies undeviating allegiance to a person, cause, or institution that one feels morally bound to support or defend; *constant* suggests freedom from fickleness in affections or loyalties; *staunch* implies such a strong allegiance to one's principles or purposes as not to be turned aside by any cause; *resolute* stresses unwavering determination, often in adhering to one's personal ends or aims".[1]

[1]*The Fruit of the Spirit: Faithfulness*

www.org/index.cfm/ ... sr/CT/ ... /Fruit-of-Spirit-Faithfulness.htm

Other synonyms include *dedicated, steadfast, devoted, dependable, accurate, true, conscientious, dutiful, careful, scrupulous,* and *thorough.*

Faithless means "not keeping faith; dishonest; disloyal; unreliable; undependable; unbelieving." Its synonyms include *doubting, treacherous,* and *unscrupulous.*[2]

[2] *Collins Thesaurus of the English Language*

Dr. Elizabeth Thambiraj

In the Greek of the New Testament, the word used for *faithfulness* is the noun *pistis*, which has both an active and a passive sense or use. First, in its active use, it often refers to "faith, belief, and trust." But in the passive sense, it means "faithfulness, reliability, fidelity."[3]

[3] *Mark #14: Faithfulness | Bible.org - World's Largest Bible Study Site*

Faithfulness, in the final analysis, hinges upon what we value and how committed we are to it. We can be faithful to a friendship, an employer, a spouse, a family name, an athletic team, or even a small thing. "But know this, that in the last days perilous times will come: For men will be lovers of themselves, lovers of money, boasters, proud, blasphemers, disobedient to parents, unthankful, unholy, unloving, unforgiving, slanderers, without self-control, brutal, despisers of good, traitors, headstrong, haughty, lovers of pleasure rather than lovers of God, having a form of godliness but denying its power. And from such people turn away!" (2 Timothy 3:1–5). The above passage lists nineteen characteristics including "lovers of themselves" and points to faithfulness.

Instructions for Marriage

"Jesus said, 'Wherefore they are no more twain, but one flesh, What therefore God hath joined together, let not man put asunder'" (Matthew 19:6).

In this verse, Jesus puts forward the fundamental doctrine of the Christian faith concerning marriage and human sexuality. The leaders of the people were questioning about divorce and remarriage: "Is it lawful for a man to put away his wife for every cause?" (Matthew 19:3). The leaders wanted to know if divorce was acceptable, and Jesus pointed them to the first book of the Bible, Genesis 1:27, and said, "Have ye not read, that he which made them at the beginning made them male and female?" (Matthew 19:4). In the previous chapter, we discussed the topic of God's brilliance in creating male and female. God made the sexes, and He made marriage. By determining the nature of human sexuality in the beginning, He ordained that a man should desire and cleave unto his wife and a wife to her husband.

Mystery of Relationships through the Lens of Scriptures

We can assess the society we are living in and say confidently that faithfulness is not a norm.

Joseph was a character in the Bible whom God blessed for his faithfulness toward God in all circumstances. In his life, he was rejected, kidnapped, enslaved, and imprisoned. His family thought genuinely that he was dead and gone! Although his brothers were unfaithful to him, he graciously forgave them, helped them during the time of great famine, and shared his prosperity with them. When we read the book of Genesis chapter 45, we see that Joseph finally revealed himself to his brothers and helped them when they were in trouble. How many of us would share our prosperity with our brothers if they had hurt us very badly?

Joseph promised to take care of his father and the whole family during the years of famine, and he was in a position to do so as a lord of Egypt. Pharaoh was also respectful of Joseph, because Joseph had served Pharaoh very faithfully all his life and brought much good to Pharaoh. Likewise, Joseph was respectful to his father and brothers, and he gave them provisions and blessed them:

> Then Joseph came and told Pharaoh, and said, My father and my brethren, and their flocks, and their herds, and all that they have, are come out of the land of Canaan; and, behold, they are in the land of Goshen. And he took some of his brethren, even five men, and presented them unto Pharaoh. And Pharaoh said unto his brethren, What is your occupation? And they said unto Pharaoh, Thy servants are shepherds, both we, and also our fathers. They said moreover unto Pharaoh, For to sojourn in the land are we come; for thy servants have no pasture for their flocks; for the famine is sore in the land of Canaan: now therefore, we pray thee, let thy servants dwell in the land of Goshen. And Pharaoh spake unto Joseph, saying, Thy father and thy brethren are come unto thee: The land of Egypt is before thee; in the best of the land make thy father and brethren to dwell; in the land of Goshen let them dwell: and if thou knowest any men of activity among them, then make them rulers over my cattle. (Genesis 47:1–6)

Dr. Elizabeth Thambiraj

Here we see the faithfulness of Joseph in God's Word. His faithfulness affected his entire family. Joseph's brothers threw him in a pit, and eventually he ended up in prison. He must have wondered about his future many times when he was going through very rough life situations. Yet he had unwavering faith in God, and instead of despairing, he loved God, obeyed Him, and did what was right. God honored him and blessed the work of his hands for his faithfulness, and he became a lord of Egypt in a position of power and authority to bless people around him because of his hard work and faithfulness. God blessed the work of his hands, and he found favor in the sight of God and Pharaoh.

Joseph demonstrated how God forgives us and showers us with goodness even though we have sinned against Him. The same forgiveness and blessings will be ours if we ask for them. Here there is a comparison between Joseph and our Lord Jesus Christ. He was exalted above all powers, and His will is that all that are His should be with Him one day (John 17:24). Are we willing?

Religion or the Gospel

"At the very moment of that vain-glorious thought, a qualm came over me, a horrid nausea and the most dreadful shuddering ... I looked down ... I was once more Edward Hyde."[1]- Robert Louis Stevenson, *The Strange Case of Dr. Jekyll and Mr. Hyde.*

When circumstances go wrong, we are angry at God because we believe, like Job's friends, that anyone who is good deserves a comfortable life. When criticized, we are furious or devastated because we are self-righteous and feel we must destroy threats to that self-image at all costs. It could be our talents, moral records, personal discipline, social status, and so on, and we should have them so that they serve as our main hope, meaning, happiness, security, and significance, regardless of what we say our belief about God is!

Pharisaic religion not only destroys the soul but has a tremendous effect socially. Often people who would fall into the category of practising pharisaic religiosity have a sense of self-righteousness and despise and attack others who do not share their doctrinal beliefs and religious practices. They are people building their self-worth based on moral and spiritual performance, and it is a sort of a résumé they would like to present to God and the world. When self-righteous, angry, insecure, exclusive, moralistic people fill churches, the bride of Christ becomes very unattractive, and ordinary people become confused about the nature of Christianity. For an unbeliever who is exploring from outside, this is only another religion, and mostly no one would want to come near to explore what this religion is all about!

If we move in that religious pharisaical mode, we end up as anxious, insecure, irritable people. In that case, we are far worse off than an irreligious group, because Pharisees knew deep down inside that they cannot live up to that standard. This, in other words, is a do-it-yourself religion, and they inwardly believe that God accepts them only when they obey. Their full motivation is based on fear and insecurity. They obey in order to get things from God and do not care whom they hurt in order to gratify themselves! An enormous capacity for egotism and self-absorption hides in the hearts of most,

Dr. Elizabeth Thambiraj

which leads to violence, crime, warfare, and total disintegration of the society. "I knew myself, at the first breath of this new life, to be more wicked, tenfold more wicked, sold a slave to my original evil; and the thought in that moment, braced and delighted me like wine ... [Edward Hyde's] every act and thought centered on self."[2]

[2]Timothy Keller. 'The Reason for God" Belief in an age of Skepticism.

The Gospel, on the other hand, contains the resources to build a unique identity in Christ alone. The Word of God says, "For all have sinned, and come short of the glory of God" (Romans 3:23). The Gospel is good news for fallen humanity. It says that we are flawed human beings and that Jesus died for our sins because we are so loved, valued, and accepted. This indeed is a vast contrast to pharisaical religiosity. Understanding our fallenness will lead to humility and deeper confidence in Christ. One cannot feel superior to others while comprehending that Christ died for the whole world. Here the motivation is joy. We delight in obeying God because we want to resemble Christ and are in the process of being transformed into His image.

When circumstances go wrong, we begin to take comfort in the hope that Jesus Christ took all of our punishment and sin. During the training process for eternity, God continues to be faithful and shows His fatherly love during our trials. An unbeliever does not have this encouragement. When criticized, we can continue to cherish what Christ has done on the cross for us and rest on His pain because He has taken all of our shame. We have to remember that our identities are not built on our performance but on Christ's love for us. We are saved by sheer grace, so we cannot look down on those who believe or practice something different from us. It is only by grace that we are what we are, and this brings peace and elevates us spiritually to a position where we have no inner need to win arguments. When we base our identity and self-worth on the One who died for His enemies, we escape the spiral of bitterness, self-recrimination, and despair when something goes wrong in our lives.

There is a world of difference between the understanding that God accepts us because of our efforts and the understanding that God

Mystery of Relationships through the Lens of Scriptures

accepts us just as we are because of what Christ has done on the cross for humanity. This obviously results in two radically different motivations, two radically different spiritual identities, and two radically different kinds of lives. Most believers oscillate between these two, but we have to come to the knowledge and understanding of this unconditional grace of God, which requires a complete change in our thought process. Only grace frees us from the slavery of self that lurks in the midst of religion, morality, and all good things. The message here is that we are not saved by our records but by Christ's record on Calvary!

Whom Am I Living For?

Everyone has to live for something or somebody; otherwise, there is no meaning for life! That something or somebody invariably becomes the most important thing in our lives, and we focus our attention and energy on attaining affirmation, security, and significance from this. Knowingly or unknowingly, this becomes the lord of our lives, and we begin to live for it!

As we explore this together, we have to think for a minute about the personal consequences of sin. In several ways, sin has destroyed us personally, and we try to find our self-worth in something or somebody apart from God. In our contemporary individualistic culture, we try to get our self-worth from our achievements, or social status, or talents, or education, or love relationships, or power and position. In a traditional Asian culture, often self-worth is measured in terms of the identity that comes from fulfilling duties to family, or serving society, or owning an expensive car, or money in the bank. In Western culture, we also find our security and self-worth in education, the positions we hold in society, and the knowledge we attain! It is strange sometimes to think that we love ourselves too much and want affirmation and significance from something that is temporary and apart from God.

If anything threatens our identity, fear paralyzes us, and we go through tremendous internal pain without victory. Often, we crucify ourselves between the regrets of our past and the fears of our futures, and we begin to worship ourselves. We are very good at turning good things into ultimate things, and if we do not base our identity on God, this can eventually turn into a deep form of addiction. In other words, if we take our self-worth from achievements, social status, the family we come from, or work apart from God, these things enslave us. The good things become substitutes for God in our lives, because our love becomes inordinate. Then we fall into patterns of life that are like substance addiction. This situation can give rise to uncontrollable anguish if anything goes wrong in the life pattern.

Mystery of Relationships through the Lens of Scriptures

Let us look briefly at what Apostle Paul wrote to the believers at Philippi when he was imprisoned in Rome.

> Though I might also have confidence in the flesh. If any other man thinketh that he hath whereof he might trust in the flesh, I more: Circumcised the eighth day, of the stock of Israel, of the tribe of Benjamin, an Hebrew of the Hebrews; as touching the law, a Pharisee; Concerning zeal, persecuting the church; touching the righteousness which is in the law, blameless. But what things were gain to me, those I counted loss for Christ. Yea doubtless, and I count all things but loss for the excellency of the knowledge of Christ Jesus my Lord: for whom I have suffered the loss of all things, and do count them but dung, that I may win Christ. (Phil 3:4–8)

Apostle Paul is saying that he is counting all things loss for the excellence of the knowledge of Christ Jesus his Lord. He continues to say that he has suffered many things, and he counts them as rubbish so that he may gain Christ and be found in Him. He affirms that he is robed in the righteousness of Christ and does not have his own righteousness, which is from the law. The righteousness he has now is through faith in Christ, the righteousness that is from God by faith. His heart's desire is to know Him and the power of His resurrection and the fellowship of His sufferings. He wishes to be conformed to His death so that he may attain the resurrection from the dead. This is a very humbling statement on his part, because he has begun to understand the mysteries of the Kingdom of God and the power of the resurrection of Christ. He affirms that he has not obtained perfection yet but will continue to press forward to attain that perfection in Christ Jesus.

"Brethren, I count not myself to have apprehended: but this one thing I do, forgetting those things which are behind, and reaching forth unto those things which are before, I press toward the mark for the prize of the high calling of God in Christ Jesus. Let us therefore, as many as be perfect, be thus minded: and if in anything ye be otherwise minded, God shall reveal even this unto you. Nevertheless, whereto we have already attained, let us walk by the same rule, let us mind the same thing" (Phil 3:13–16).

Dr. Elizabeth Thambiraj

When one's life does not center on God, it is centered on something else, often on the self, and this eventually will lead to emptiness and hurt, however successful one may be. This in itself is sin, because anyone in this situation becomes a worshipper of self. This sin has serious social consequences and devastating effects on the world system. Dorothy Sayers, an English writer, saw many British intellectual elites in despair about the direction of human society in the wake of World War II. In her 1947 book *Creed or Chaos,* she mentions that their hopelessness was due to their loss of belief in the Christian doctrine of original sin and humanity's inherent pride and self-centeredness. Human society can become deeply fragmented when we substitute other gods for God, the author of the universe.

God who created us, and formed us in our mother's womb, who fashioned us individually is the only One who will be able to understand us in depth. It is common sense and wise to argue then the deepest chambers of our souls cannot be filled by anything less than God. If Jesus Christ is God incarnate, then by definition, nothing can satisfy the deepest parts of our souls the way He can. Then the author of glory becomes our significance, security, and affirmation, and He becomes that someone for whom we live!

How Great Is Our God!

Psalm 8 talks about the greatness of God. This Psalm begins and ends with the transcendence Excellency of God. This Psalm is a solemn meditation on the greatness and Excellency of God, and as created beings we are called to admire the beauty and greatness of God.

> O Lord our God, how excellent is Thy Name in all the earth! who hast set Thy glory above the heavens. Out of the mouth of babes and sucklings hast thou ordained strength because of Thine enemies, that Thou mightest still the enemy and the avenger. When I consider Thy heavens, the work of Thy fingers, the moon and the stars, which Thou hast ordained; What is man, that Thou art mindful of him? and the son of man, that Thou visitest him? For Thou hast made him a little lower than the angels, and hast crowned him with glory and honour. Thou madest him to have dominion over the works of Thy hands; Thou hast put all things under his feet: All sheep and Oxen, yea, and the beasts of the field; The fowl of the air, and the fish of the sea, and whatsoever passeth through the paths of the seas. O Lord our Lord, how excellent is Thy Name in all the earth! (Psalm 8)

If we really believe that God is the Lord of all of our affairs in this world, we should acknowledge Him. Creation proclaims that there is an infinite being who governs and rules. This Psalm reminds us that human beings are different from the other animals in creation; in a sense, the beasts of the field are so framed as to look downward, whereas man is made erect to look up toward heaven. The heavens are the handiwork of the Lord. He placed and ordained the moon and the stars. What our great God ordained cannot be altered but by Him alone. Compared to all His creation, He made human beings in His own image, and that means something; it demonstrates His love for humanity.

When we consider God's glory and His handiwork, we may well wonder why He would take notice of such a mean creature as human beings. God talked with Abraham and considered him His friend. It is very humbling to realize that it pleases God to talk with us as

Dr. Elizabeth Thambiraj

friends because of His care for humanity. Is it possible to fathom in our human minds His care for us, which led him to give His only Son so that we would not perish?

"For God so loved the world that He gave His only begotten Son, that whosoever believeth in Him should not perish, but have everlasting life" (John 3:16). The love of God the Father is the origin of our regeneration by the Spirit and our reconciliation by the lifting up of the only Son, Jesus Christ. He not only sent Him into the world to negotiate peace between heaven and earth but gave Him up to suffer and die for us as the great propitiation or expiatory sacrifice. Jesus Christ came and died for us so that we might not die by the sentence of the law. It is the unspeakable joy of all true believers, for which we are indebted to Jesus Christ that we are saved from the miseries of hell. This salvation is available to all who accept Jesus Christ. They will not die of their wounds in wilderness but will reach Canaan and enjoy the promised rest.

Romans 5:6 says, "For when we were yet without strength, in due time Christ died for the ungodly." Although we were in a sad condition, helpless and totally lost, with no visible way open for our recovery, vile and obnoxious, unworthy of any favor from a Holy God, the great God, as part of His great plan, gave His Son as a ransom for the whole world.

Here is the great Gospel duty—that is, to believe in Lord Jesus Christ, which is a great gift from a great God! The intention of the Great Giver is that humanity not perish. One must yield an unfeigned assent and consent to the record God has given in His Word concerning His Son. This is a very serious, sobering food for thought, and it is up to each one of us how seriously we take it to our minds and hearts. We must give ourselves to be ruled, taught, and saved by Him. This is good news to a convinced conscience, healing to broken bones and bleeding wounds: Christ indeed came not to condemn but to save.

Isaiah 30:15 says, "For thus saith the Lord God, the Holy One of Israel; In returning and rest shall ye be saved; in quietness and in confidence shall be your strength: and ye would not." We can all limit God by the way we think or act. We can also worry about a potential

Mystery of Relationships through the Lens of Scriptures

bad situation so much that we take things into our hands, forgetting that there is divine hope. We can use whatever descriptive words we want to describe our situations: *worse, difficult, hard, agonizing, frustrating, strenuous, debilitating, horrific, sorrowful, confusing, perturbing, penetrating,* or *painful.* According to God's Word, He is all-powerful, and no problem is too awful or too hard for God to handle. Our God is a great and limitless God who dwells in eternity and operates in infinity. He has all things within His understanding and under His control. This is a blessed hope for a believer in Christ Jesus.

Time and again, we see reminders that we are human and are limited in our ability. We are forced to look up to someone who can scale the unscalable. The One who is infinite and able in all circumstances and situations is God alone. Especially when we face difficult relationships, destructive and sinful habits, and other stresses in life, where do we run? The ability of human beings is limited, and the Word of God explicitly says that humanity is finite and so is our understanding. Like the grass in the field, we wither. Whether the problems we face are mountains or molehills, we cannot overcome them without the intervention of a loving heavenly Father who alone has the ability to scale the unscalable!

As the Deer Panteth for the Water ...

Mystery of Relationships through the Lens of Scriptures

Above are pictures of a deer in constant search of water. Eventually finding a brook, it quenches its thirst to its heart's content.

The writer of this Psalm probably was David, and we can conjecture that he wrote it when King Saul was persecuting him or at the time of his son Absalom's rebellion. Psalm 42 shows David's zeal in serving God in spite of his unfavorable situation. This was a very difficult time when he was driven away from entering the sanctuary and cut off from the privilege of serving and waiting upon God in public ordinances. This psalm is a great proof that he had a very earnest desire to have communion with God. It also shows that He trusted His plans for his life to God. This psalm in particular kindles and excites a gracious and fervent desire to have devout, pious affection for God, who alone can quench this desire and thirst.

Faith in God indeed brings holy desires for God and communion with Him. "As the hart panteth after the water brooks, so panteth my soul after thee, O God" (Psalm 42:1). Nothing is more grievous to the gracious soul than that which shakes its hope and confidence in God. "My tears have been my meat" (Psalm 42:3). This is holy love, mourning for God's withdrawn presence when David was forced to be away from God's house. His enemies would have teased him because God was absent from the ark, the token of God's presence. The enemies could have concluded that David had lost his God. This is a very hard position to be in, and the Psalmist compares this miserable feeling to that of a deer panting for water! This feeling also could be compared to the restlessness of a child in the process of being weaned by its mother.

David constantly communicated with God, and when his soul felt dejected, he told God about it and found peace in doing so. He had to escape to the borders of the land of Canaan to shelter himself from the rage of his persecutors: "O my God, my soul is cast down within me: therefore will I remember thee from the land of Jordan, and of the Hermonites, from the hill Mizar" (Psalm 42:6).

"Deep calleth unto deep at the noise of the waterspouts; all thy waves and thy billows are gone over me" (Psalm 42:7). Compare this to Jonah's prayer from the fish's belly: "For thou hast cast me into the

Dr. Elizabeth Thambiraj

deep, in the midst of the seas; and the floods compassed me about: all thy billows and thy waves passed over me" (Jonah 2:3). The mariners cast Jonah into the deep sea, but Jonah did not accuse the mariners, because he saw the hand of the Lord casting him there. The channels and the waters of the sea surrounded him on every side, and Jonah struggled for his life; and one can imagine how his feelings would have been. We can compare David's complaint to Jonah's cry.

Jonah's case was unique, and David faced a different situation but made a similar complaint. He complained of God's waves and billows going over him. Sometimes the condition of God's people may be such that they feel excluded from God's presence. Let us extrapolate this to our situation and see how we respond to God in adversity. The response from these people is only unbelief at that point of time, and God will never cast away His people, whom He has chosen. This reproach aims to discourage their hope in the Living God. God listened carefully to the complaints these men of God made in their depression, and He eventually came to rescue them. God commanded the waves and the billows, and they obeyed Him.

Our search for God should be like a deer's search for the water, a continuous search. Even when we do not know where to find His ark, there is a way heavenward if we genuinely search for God. God did not appear immediately to deliver David out of the hands of his enemies; the enemies concluded that God had abandoned him. The enemies were deceived into thinking that David had lost his God! David expected his deliverance to come from God's favor. He also knew that all his joy and peace had to come from God.

God indeed taught David and Jonah in their special circumstances to endure and stay firm in believing that He was in control and involved in their lives. Our comfort is that God is our rock, a rock to build our lives upon and to shelter in during times of adversity. May our souls continue to search for the living God, and may we find the fountain of living water. The only hope we have in times of misery is to take comfort in God through His inerrant word and to check all unbelieving doubts and fears.

Holding Loose ...

What does it mean to hold loose? It means not holding tight to anything we value—a career, wealth, relationships, an accomplishment, even a ministry or a bigger picture of life. The Word of God says that the life of a human being withers soon. Let us get a little perspective on *holding loose*.

A dear friend of mine wrote the following from her heart when in great pain after her husband passed away in a road accident. They were a loving, god-fearing couple who read the Bible daily and discussed what they read. He helped his wife in her weaknesses, always thankful for her; he thanked her for making his lunch on the day of the accident. The accident on the highway took his life, and the wife could hardly believe what had happened! Of course her heart and mind could not make a connection on that day, and she asked me, "Why us?" This is quite an example of a fiery trial!

Here are her own words: (*From the blog of Joslyn: A well-watered garden*). "Ministry was going great, our marriage was at the sweetest it had ever been, Julius was looking to retirement wanting to serve the Lord and asking for His direction, plans, dreams for our girls ... But God ..." Then my friend quoted Isaiah 55:8–9: "For my thoughts are not your thoughts, neither are your ways my ways, saith the Lord. For as the heavens are higher than the earth, so are my ways higher than your ways, and my thoughts than your thoughts."

When I heard what had happened, I was in agony for my friend's loss. Trials in life come in various forms. Sometimes they drive us to the deepest valleys where no one can help, and all we can do is cry, "God help me!" Often they are so difficult that they may even try to take away our faith in God if we do not immerse ourselves in His word. I do not mean to minimize the emotional pain or the reality of some of these fiery trials. But when the rubber hits the road, where is our sustenance and stability? Who is our real hope?

1 Peter 4:12–13 says, "Beloved, think it not strange concerning the fiery trial which is to try you, as though some strange thing

Dr. Elizabeth Thambiraj

happened to you: But rejoice, in as much as ye are partakers of Christ's sufferings; that when His glory shall be revealed, ye may be glad, ye may be glad also with exceeding joy." Below are some important terms to think about so that we can understand better our situation when we go through trials.

The *soul* expresses who one is and includes the mind, will, and emotions. It has thoughts.

The *spirit* is one's essential being and is in the Spirit. God breathed Spirit into human beings, and we came to life.

Satan's power is in the *lying tongue.* With it, he confuses the mind, affects the body, and gains power and control.

The Biblical word *heart* refers to the inner aspect of a person, which consists of all three of the above parts. The heart includes the following three things:

1. mental processes that direct actions and reactions and lead a person in his or her life;
2. emotions, which are reactions that act as icing to enrich our lives; and
3. the will, where we make decisions between the rational and the emotive.

Luke 6:45 tells us, "A good man out of the good treasure of his heart bringeth forth that which is good; and an evil man out of the evil treasure of his heart bringeth forth that which is evil: for of the abundance of the heart his mouth speaketh."

The heart is the center of a person's character—who he or she really is (Matthew 15:18). The heart is the seat of physical life (Acts 14:17 and James 5:5). It is the seat of moral nature and spiritual life and of grief (John 14:1, Romans 9:2, and 2 Corinthians 2:4). It also is the seat of joy (John 16:22 and Ephesians 5:19); desires (Matthew 5:28 and 2 Peter 2:14); affections (Luke 24:32 and Acts 21:13); perceptions (John 12:40 and Ephesians 4:18); thoughts (Matthew 9:4 and Hebrews 4:12); understanding (Matthew 13:15 and Romans 1:21); reasoning

Mystery of Relationships through the Lens of Scriptures

powers (Mark 2:6 and Luke 24:38); imagination (Luke 1:51); and conscience (Acts 2:37 and 1 John 3:20). Finally, the heart holds intentions (Hebrews 4:12 and 1 Peter 4:1); purpose (Acts 11:23 and 2 Corinthians 9:7); will (Romans 6:17 and Colossians 3:15); and faith (Mark 11:23, Romans 10:10, and Hebrews 3:12). The heart, in its moral significance in the Old Testament, includes the emotions, the reason, and the will.

"And they that use this world, as not abusing it: for the fashion of this world passeth away". 1 Cori: 7:31. "Not the matter and substance, but the fashion, form, and scheme of it, kingdoms, cities, towns, houses, families, estates, and possessions, are continually changing, and casting into different hands, and different forms; the men of the world, the inhabitants of it, are continually removing; one generation goes, and another comes, new faces are continually appearing; the riches and honours of the world are fading, perishing, and transitory things; everything is upon the flux, nothing is permanent; which is another argument why the world, and the things of it, are not to be loved": *Gills Exposition of the entire Bible.*

As our hearts remember previous life experiences and identities we have had, it is obvious that our experiences of ourselves become part of our hearts. When we lose something or somebody that we hold dear, Satan confuses our minds, affect our bodies and try to gain control and destroy us from inside out, robbing us of the glory that God has in a believer and trying to strip us away from His divine plan.

Our heavenly Father graciously showers blessings on us, and this confirms God's Word. Sometimes we allow His gifts to become more important to us than our commitment to Him. Anything we value—a career, wealth, relationships, an accomplishment, or even a ministry—can interfere with our devotion to Him. The Lord loves us unconditionally, and sometimes He does something to get our undivided attention in order to win us back to Himself. The Lord sometimes has to strip away the good things He has given, and this may be painful to us. Eventually, it brings spiritual blessings that we cannot see at the time. The life principle here is that anything we hold too tightly we will lose, and it is a painful truth. This is probably

Dr. Elizabeth Thambiraj

something none of us wants to hear because of the pain when we lose something or someone that is special to us.

An awful sense of the divine perfection is the best antidote against suffering in trials and persecutions. The faith and hope of a Christian are defensible against the entire world. This leads every believer to declare the hope that is in him or her even in difficult circumstances and in fiery trials.

Prayer

Lord, because You are God and we are mere human, it is impossible for us to understand the mystery of Your ways. "But we speak the wisdom of God in a mystery, even the hidden wisdom, which God ordained before the world unto our glory: Which none of the princes of this world knew: for had they known it, they would not have crucified the Lord of glory. But as it is written, Eye hath not seen, nor ear heard, neither have entered into the heart of man, the things which God hath prepared for them that love him" 1 Corinthians 2:7–9. Just like the many men and women of faith who died before receiving the fulfillment of Your promises, we want to seek Your intervention, cling to Your assurance of faithfulness, and look forward to a better place (Hebrews 11:13, 16).

Emotional Abuse in a Nutshell

Recently, quite a bit of study has been going on regarding the relationship between emotional abuse and mental health. No one wants to hear the word *abuse* in a relationship. Especially in relationships between couples, nobody wants to use the word *abuse* and no one wants to hear it.

Denying emotional care and affection, shunning a person's efforts to interact, and neglecting someone's mental and emotional health are forms of psychological abuse. Women often experience psychological abuse in dating relationships, and this happens not only in our culture but around the globe. Emotional abuse seems to be a worldwide problem and can affect people of any age and gender. Emotional abuse often starts as an occasional occurrence in a relationship but escalates if not checked. Verbal abuse seems to be normal in families and in spousal relationships and frequently plays a major role in violence and major crimes. Statistics on violent crime show that women are victimized around five to eight times more often than men by an intimate partner or spouse.

Emotional abuse can happen between spouses, friends, parents and children, or in working relationships. Berating, belittling, criticizing, name calling, screaming, threatening, excessive blaming, and sarcasm and humiliation are some forms of emotional abuse. Blowing a person's flaws out of proportion and making fun of that person in front of others is one form of abuse. In normal relationships, over time, this type of abuse erodes one's sense of self-confidence and self-worth, and the abused person begins to feel very small. No one has the right to do this to someone, because as believers, our self-worth and self-esteem come from the Lord. As children of God, we have to understand that the master artist formed us in our mothers' womb and called us by name. He is omniscient and very much involved in our lives.

Verbal assaults can happen in the following ways. People who verbally assault the others often are very insecure, and were assaulted verbally when young and probably they accept this as norm. Abusers often project their words and actions toward a victim because they were hurt

Dr. Elizabeth Thambiraj

during childhood and have not dealt with their wounds in a mature way. Victims of abuse often become abusers, because they do not know the love of Christ. Emotionally wounded victims wound others and victimize people around them, often close family members but sometimes more distant relations or even colleagues at work. If abuse happens in a marriage, we need extra vigilance and strength from God to be wise and enforce boundaries with clever choices.

Emotional and Verbal Abuse

Emotional abuse is hard to define.

"All forms of abuse follow a pattern that, left unchecked, will only increase over time."[1]

*[1]Focus Helps | **Emotional** and verbal **abuse** |*

*www.focushelps.ca/article/addictions-**abuse**/verbal-**and-emotional** ...*

If a person is jealous and possessive, he or she may become emotionally abusive. If this happens in a marriage, the emotionally abusive spouse could deny his or her partner other normal relationships, cut him or her off from the social support system, and bully him or her with manipulative mind games. Yelling, offering degrading remarks, minimizing someone's accomplishments, verbal abuse, and elder neglect are all common around the world. People often engage in this destructive behaviour toward others, because the underlying desire of their hearts is power and control.

Imagine, for a minute, Hitler's regime and the way he abused people! People who do not stay on the path of truth, people in positions of authority who are dishonest in their speech, have the capacity to abuse people emotionally. People who experience abuse as part of military training also may become abusive, and studies show that abused people often abuse others. Many cases are not reported, and it is extremely sad to note that this often happens even in Christian circles.

Definitions of Emotional Abuse

"No one is immune from encountering abusive people, but everyone can make healthy choices to end destructive relationship patterns".[2]
By: Beth J. Lueders

"An emotionally abusive person may dismiss your feelings and needs, expect you to perform humiliating or unpleasant tasks, manipulate you into feeling guilty for trivial things, belittle your outside support system or blame you for unfortunate circumstances in his or her life".[3]

By: Beth J. Lueders

The online KJV Dictionary defines abuse as follows:

"ABU'SED, pp. s as z. Ill-used; used to a bad purpose; treated with rude language; misemployed; perverted to bad or wrong ends; deceived; defiled; violated".[4]

[4]*ABUSE - Definition from the KJV Dictionary*

av1611.com/kjbp/kjv-dictionary/abuse.html

["**Psychological abuse**, also referred to as **emotional abuse** or **mental abuse**, is a form of abuse characterized by a person subjecting or exposing another to behavior that may result in psychological trauma, including anxiety, chronic depression, or post-traumatic stress disorder. [1] HYPERLINK "http://en.wikipedia.org/wiki/Emotional_abuse"[2] HYPERLINK "http://en.wikipedia.org/wiki/Emotional_abuse"[3] Such abuse is often associated with situations of power imbalance, such as abusive relationships, bullying, and abuse in the workplace.[2] HYPERLINK "http://en.wikipedia.org/wiki/Emotional_abuse"[3]"][5]

[5]*Psychological abuse - Wikipedia, the free encyclopedia*

en.wikipedia.org/wiki/Emotional_abuse

Emotional Abuse

Emotional abuse is an abnormal behavior specifically designed to subjugate another human being. The abuser may choose to subjugate

Dr. Elizabeth Thambiraj

another human being through fear, humiliation, intimidation, guilt, manipulation, coercion, and other similar tactics. Emotional abuse is psychological and causes severe mental anguish; it is not physical in nature. Emotional abuse includes everything from constant criticism to more subtle tactics to degrade the victim. Repeated disapproval and refusal to be pleased can intensify the target's mental anguish.

["Emotional abuse victims can become so convinced that they are worthless that they believe that no one else could want them".][6]

[6]Emotional Abuse - EQI

eqi.org/eabuse1.htm

Victims often stay in emotionally abusive situations because they falsely believe they have no other place to go. They fear being alone. This form of emotional abuse also is called psychological abuse and is a form of mental abuse. Even in different cultures and societies, emotional abuse happens. If it happens within a family setting, it is called psychological incest or emotional incest.

When a person experiences emotional abuse for a long time, there definitely will be scars, and the person will lose his or her self-confidence. Systematic brainwashing leads to a lack of self-confidence, a loss of self-worth, and a loss of self-concept, and it produces severe anxiety. The victim tends to trust his or her own perceptions. He or she loses personal value, because he or she cannot fight the abuser. These emotional scars cut to the core of the victim's heart and are much deeper than physical scars.

Continuous emotional abuse, insults, insinuations, criticism, and accusations, may slowly eat away at the victim's self-esteem until he or she is incapable of judging the situation realistically. People in this situation may become so beaten down emotionally that they blame themselves for the abuse and think they are the reason for their new reality. Their self-esteem may be so low that they cling to the abuser. That is the worst scenario, and it is not what God wants in a marriage.

Mystery of Relationships through the Lens of Scriptures

"Emotional abuse is underneath all other types of abuse - the most damaging aspect of physical, sexual, mental, etc. Abuse is the trauma to our hearts and souls from being betrayed by the people that we love and trust."[7]

[7]*Emotional abuse is Heart and Soul Mutilation*

www.joy2meu.com/emotional_abuse.html

I am going to explain below some important terms and signs of emotional abuse.

Emotional abuse can happen to anyone, and it can happen in a family, a work situation, or a school. Rejecting a person means not valuing him or her and communicating devaluing thoughts about that person to someone else. Degrading means thinking of a person as having little dignity and worth; it also involves humiliating that person with insulting, harsh remarks privately and publicly. Terrorizing a person is intimidating the person and trying to induce fear or even to cause physical harm to that person or to that person's loved ones.

Isolating a person is physically confining a person to restrict his or her freedom. The abuser in this situation generally has a dark secret that he or she does not want to be exposed. Exploitation is using a person for one's own personal advantage; good examples include selling drugs and prostitution. Detachment is denying emotional support, care, and affection and shunning a person's efforts to interact.

In general, we can say that all types of abuse involve some form of emotional abuse. Very often, emotional abuse happens to people who are less powerful or have fewer financial resources. The idea of emotional abuse is to brainwash a person into believing that what the abuser does is right.

According to the National Coalition against Domestic Violence, for many people, emotional abuse is even more devastating than physical abuse. Emotional abuse tears down the self-esteem and self-worth of a person and can cause great psychological damage. It even greatly affects the person's social interactions. Emotional abuse can reduce

Dr. Elizabeth Thambiraj

and hinder intelligence, attention, and the ability to feel and express emotions appropriately and can do lifelong damage to a person. It can cause severe anxiety, fear, self-blame, and self-abuse (such as substance abuse) in children and adults. Emotionally abused seniors may feel extreme guilt, inadequacy, depression, or powerlessness. Unfortunately, many psychologically abused elderly people are labeled senile or inept. *Inept* means "showing no skill" or "clumsy and lacking judgement." Seniors receive these labels because they are unskilled, amateurish, and incompetent.

Verbal Abuse

We all have heard the old saying, "Sticks and stones may break my bones, but words can never hurt me," and we know it is a lie. Words can either build or break, encourage or discourage, and our tongues are very powerful. People can be caring, careless, conniving, careful, comforting, or caustic with their words. We need to be careful in our speech so that we do not break people.

As Dr. Grace Kettering writes in her book *Verbal Abuse*, "Cruel names and labels can hurt us — dreadfully! Crippling comments may seem so trivial to the speaker as to be soon forgotten. But at a crucial moment or from an important person, certain words spoken to a vulnerable, receptive individual can make or break a life."

Hurling hurtful words, insulting, offering degrading remarks, name-calling, nagging, ridiculing, trivializing, screaming, ranting, yelling, using rude and foul language, withholding communication, and making disparaging comments disguised as jokes are all verbal abuse. God's Word has stern warnings about this form of verbal abuse, and we are called to severe accountability. Individuals who are teased at work, particularly if they grew up in a home where verbal abuse was the norm or experienced verbal abuse in school, may eventually take out their pent-up frustrations at home, especially to their spouses. In general, they verbally attack their spouses, loved ones, and even their close friends, and no one can be safe around them.

Hurtful words may sound like this: "You're a nag, just like your parents!" "You don't know how to do anything right." "It's your fault!" "You're too sensitive." "Come on, can't you take a joke?" "That

Mystery of Relationships through the Lens of Scriptures

outfit makes you look fat." "You're worthless in bed." "Who asked you?" "You don't need that second helping." "All you do anymore is go to church stuff." "Your ex sure screwed you up emotionally."

We should not ignore wounds caused by emotional and verbal abuse, because they have devastating effects. In general, women are on the receiving end of this very destructive behavior. The injuries can leave lasting scars, and it is extremely hard to be normal for these abused individuals. We must stop abuse as soon as it arises, because it only increases over time. We can reason and argue, saying there are no bruises or broken bones and hence the abuse is not serious, but it is not so!

In *Boundaries,* Henry Cloud and John Townsend write, "Our pain motivates us to act." These resources are available to guide individuals into safe, loving relationships. If pain motivates you to act against emotional and verbal abuse, listen to it. In doing so, you may save more than your own life; you may become a blessing to those who suffer silently.

In one Canadian study on abuse in university and college dating relationships, 81% of male respondents reported that they had psychologically abused a female partner.

The 1990 National Survey on Abuse of the Elderly in Canada estimated that: - 4% of seniors residing in private homes reported experiencing abuse and/or neglect.

http://www.thisisawar.com/AbuseEmotional.htm

Abuse is on the rise, and women undergo tremendous emotional abuse in general compared to men. Even in dating relationships, women were emotionally abused more often than men were, and some men have even admitted that they have psychologically traumatized their lovers or partners. Researchers have observed chronic verbal abuse in some senior homes not only in North America but also around the world. Abuse, once it starts, does not end in insults, swearing, and threats but may also extend to material abuse.

It is worth noting some signs of emotional abuse. Unlike physical abuse, emotional abuse is elusive, and both the abuser and the victim

Dr. Elizabeth Thambiraj

may be unaware of what is happening. We have to ask certain questions to see if we are abusers or abused in the following ways. The following are indications of abuse:

- humiliation, degradation, discounting, negating, judging, and criticizing;
- domination, control, and shame;
- accusing and blaming, trivial and unreasonable demands or expectations, denial of one's own shortcomings;
- emotional distancing and the silent treatment, isolation, and emotional abandonment or neglect; and
- Codependence and enmeshment.

Below are the definitions of *codependency* and *enmeshment*.

[8]Bing Dictionary

Co·de·pen·den·cy
[kò di péndənssee]

- mutual need: the dependence of two people, groups, or organisms on each other, especially when this reinforces mutually harmful behavior patterns
- relationship of mutual need: a situation in which a person such as the partner of an alcoholic or a parent of a drug-addicted child needs to feel needed by the other person][8]

Codependency is defined as a psychological condition or a relationship in which a person is controlled or <u>manipulated</u> by another who is affected with a pathological condition (typically <u>narcissism</u> or <u>drug addiction</u>); and in broader terms, it refers to the dependence on the needs of, or control of, another.[1][9]

[9]***Codependency*** - *Wikipedia, the free encyclopedia*

*en.wikipedia.org/wiki/**Codependency***

The leading proponents of behavioral and cognitive family systems therapy are Richard Stuart, Gerald Patterson, and Robert Liberman. Albert Ellis and Aaron Beck contributed to emotional cognitive

112

Mystery of Relationships through the Lens of Scriptures

therapy along with the work of the leading proponents. Ellis even said conflict between couples occurs when partners maintain unrealistic beliefs and expectations about their relationship. Ellis focused on emotional therapy part and Beck on cognitive therapy, and they complemented each other in developing behavioral cognitive therapy. Codependency occurs because some problematic responses within a family are mediated by distorted or dysfunctional beliefs (schemas), attitudes, and expectations.

The following are some of the symptoms associated with codependent people:

- They wish to please people and very much need of validation and approval when they care for people and rescue people from problems.
- They may have poor boundaries and fears of being alone without an intimate partner.
- They may deny their own desires and emotions.

"Enmeshment is a state of cross-generational bonding within a family, whereby a child (normally of the opposite sex) becomes a surrogate spouse for their mother or father.[1] The term is also applied more generally to engulfing codependent relationships [2] where an unhealthy symbiosis is in existence.[3]"[10]

[10]*Enmeshment - Wikipedia, the free encyclopedia*

en.wikipedia.org/wiki/Enmeshment

Enmeshment can occur in any close relationship. Enmeshment includes the idea of being caught in a situation and therefore not free. Salvador Minuchin, the family therapist who is the leading figure of structural therapy, introduced the concept of enmeshment to describe families with poorly defined personal boundaries. According to this therapist, enmeshment forms subsystems in which individuals are undifferentiated and have excessive concern for the others in the family, and this leads to a loss of autonomous development. A child brought up in this environment may lose his or her capacity for self-direction under the weight of psychic incest. If this situation

Dr. Elizabeth Thambiraj

continues, and if the family pressure increases, the child may end up as the identified patient or a family scapegoat.

Boundaries

When we live as a family unit, it is important to establish necessary boundaries. If not, one will have no idea where to begin and where to end, and it will become increasingly confusing when dealing with delicate situations. As a result, one who holds the power begins to rule, control, and compromise, and abuse becomes a normal way of life.

Breaking Away

In an enmeshed situation, guilt and fear make it hard to break away and put up boundaries. If people do not know what it is like to live with necessary boundaries, they experience fear when they begin to put their needs first. Guilt also shows its ugly head. The familiarity and safety of enmeshment make the ego mind question what will happen without it.

Some of the Effects of Abuses

1. Children who see their mothers being abused are themselves victims of emotional abuse.
2. Emotional abuse can have psychological and physical consequences for women, such as severe depression, anxiety attacks, migraine headaches, back and limb problems, and even stomach problems like ulcers. Women who have been psychologically traumatized and not physically abused are much more likely to misuse alcohol than women who have not experienced abuse.
3. Senior abuse can come from a partner, adult children, relatives, formal or informal caregivers, or even someone in a position of trust. Seniors who are emotionally traumatized may experience extreme feelings of inadequacy, guilt, low self-esteem, and symptoms of depression, fear of failure, powerlessness, hopelessness, and low self-worth. These signs are easy to confuse with loss of memory or mental capability, and it is possible for victims of this kind of abuse

Mystery of Relationships through the Lens of Scriptures

to be branded as senile. They may not actually be senile but only emotionally abused.

How to Deal with the Aggressors and Abusers in Our Lives

1. Aggression is any violation of your personal, emotional, spiritual, and mental space, and these are yours to protect. Find biblical ways to protect yourself from an aggressor.
2. You do not need anyone in your life who is aggressive and abuses you. It is not normal, healthy, or natural. Tell them to stop this behavior.
3. As an adult, you can take responsibility and put your own boundaries into place. Every day, we make choices about how we want to live.
4. You have the power within you to set boundaries to avoid emotional abuse. Do not allow an abuser to violate your sense of self-respect. This is not easy, but we can learn how, especially if we are living with an abuser.
5. Tell the abuser, "I am willing to be a part of your life only if you treat me with respect and dignity." (This does only refer to marriage but can extend to friendship, other family relationships, workplace relationships, and so forth.)

This may be a hard thing to do, but God gives the necessary grace and strength in all situations to fulfill His calling for us. When one sets boundaries with abusers, they are terrified. Remember that they are very insecure people. Surprisingly, they often shape up and get your point. In general, these abusers are very insecure people. Many of them probably experienced abuse early in life. Abused people generally become abusers because that is all they know, and they tend to think that if life has treated them badly, it is now their right to treat other people badly. We have to keep in mind that words can make or break people and that there is power in the tongue. The book of James talks about the tongue and points out that it has the capacity to produce a forest fire if not carefully guarded.

Emotions are good feelings or bad feelings that arise within us because of the varied situations and circumstances in our lives. People around us play a huge role in these feelings, and we have a wise way to deal

Dr. Elizabeth Thambiraj

with it. Negative emotions like fear, anxiety, depression, guilt, anger, hatred, stress, and resentment are God's warning sign that something is not right. They are like smoke detectors, and we would do well to pay attention to them if we wish to be emotionally stable. I have discussed these in detail on my book *Biblical Approach to Nonorganic Illnesses.*

In the last fifty years or so, well-meaning scholars have come up with many psychodynamic models to help people who have experienced verbal and emotional abuse. Behavioral therapy, cognitive therapy, cognitive behavioral therapy, the narrative model, the Milan model, systemic models, existential models, and Gestalt therapy are some of the psychodynamic models used to help alleviate the pain of abusive situations. Personal awareness of emotional abuse is important in order to prevent it from happening, because it is easy to be caught up in a spiral of potentially damaging emotions without realizing it.

Murray Bowen, a well-known family therapist, introduced eight interlocking concepts to help families to function to the best of their abilities and allow people to understand the emotional needs of other members of their families. They are triangles, differentiation of self, the nuclear family emotional system, the family projection process, the multigenerational transmission process, emotional cut off, sibling position, and the societal emotional process. The most important of these concepts is differentiation of self, and it has a huge impact on the family, community, and society.

In general, we can say that families, communities, and other social groups tremendously affect how people think, feel, and act. Individuals vary in their susceptibility to a particular group link. We can conclude that the differences between individuals and groups reflect differences in the level of differentiation of self. The less differentiation of self a person has, the more other people affect his or her functioning and the more he or she tries to control the functioning of others. Once established, a person's level of differentiation of self rarely changes unless he or she makes a structured and long-term effort to change.

Mystery of Relationships through the Lens of Scriptures

Differentiation of Self

"Differentiation of self is one's ability to separate one's own intellectual and emotional functioning from that of the family. Less differentiated people are thus more vulnerable to stress and find it challenging to adapt to life changes and contrary beliefs".[11]

[11]Murray Bowen - Wikipedia, the free encyclopedia

en.wikipedia.org/wiki/Murray Bowen

In general, people with very low differentiation of self want other people's approval and acceptance. They are more likely to be fused with predominant family emotions. They work hard to please others, trying to conform to others; or they may try to force others to conform to them. These individuals are more vulnerable to stress and anxiety, and it is important that they understand their own intellectual and emotional functioning. Now how do we apply this principle in our daily day today routines as believers in a family setting? Below are some Bible verses that talk about emotional abuse and how to overcome it with the strength of God.

There are some verses that talk about emotional abuse in the Bible. For example, 1 Corinthians 9:18 says, "What is my reward then? Verily that, when I preach the gospel, I may make the gospel of Christ without charge, that I abuse not my power in the gospel." In 1 Chronicles 10:4, we read, "Then said Saul to his armor bearer, 'Draw thy sword, and thrust me through therewith, lest these uncircumcised come and abuse me.' But his armor bearer would not, for he was sore afraid. So Saul took a sword and fell upon it." The same story appears in 1 Samuel 31:4: "Then said Saul unto his armour bearer, Draw thy sword, and thrust me through therewith; lest these uncircumcised come and thrust me through, and abuse me. But his armour bearer would not; for he was sore afraid. Therefore Saul took a sword, and fell upon it."

Dr. Elizabeth Thambiraj

Here are some verses to keep in mind when we encounter emotional abuse:

- "For ye have not received the spirit of bondage again to fear; but ye have received the Spirit of adoption, whereby we cry, Abba, Father. The Spirit itself beareth witness with our spirit, that we are the children of God" (Romans 8:15–16).
- "Who his own self bare our sins in his own body on the tree that we, being dead to sins, should live unto righteousness: by whose stripes ye were healed" (1 Peter 2:24).
- "When the even was come, they brought unto him many that were possessed with devils: and he cast out the spirits with his word, and healed all that were sick: That it might be fulfilled which was spoken by Esaias the prophet, saying, Himself took our infirmities, and bare our sicknesses" (Matthew 8:16–17).
- "And he said unto me, My grace is sufficient for thee: for my strength is made perfect in weakness. Most gladly therefore will I rather glory in my infirmities, that the power of Christ may rest upon me" (2 Corinthians 12:9).
- "If any of you lack wisdom, let him ask of God, that giveth to all men liberally, and upbraideth not; and it shall be given him" (James 1:5).
- "But my God shall supply all your need according to his riches in glory by Christ Jesus" (Philippians 4:19).
- "There hath no temptation taken you but such as is common to man: but God is faithful, who will not suffer you to be tempted above that ye are able; but will with the temptation also make a way to escape, that ye may be able to bear it" (1 Corinthians 10:13).
- "Peace I leave with you, my peace I give unto you: not as the world giveth, give I unto you. Let not your heart be troubled, neither let it be afraid" (John 14:27).
- "The righteous cry, and the Lord heareth, and delivereth them out of all their troubles. The Lord is nigh unto them that are of a broken heart; and saveth such as be of a contrite spirit. Many are the afflictions of the righteous: but the Lord delivereth him out of them all. He keepeth all his bones: not one of them is broken" (Psalm 34:17–20).

Mystery of Relationships through the Lens of Scriptures

- "But the God of all grace, who hath called us unto his eternal glory by Christ Jesus, after that ye have suffered a while, make you perfect, stablish, strengthen, settle you" (1 Peter 5:10).

It is impossible to be spiritually mature when one is emotionally immature, says Peter Scazzero in his book *Emotionally Healthy Spirituality*. He was a pastor of a growing church, and he says we have to stop trying to read minds and clarify expectations. As we continue to climb the ladder of integrity, it is important to develop a rule of life to implement emotionally healthy skills. A table below shows the works of the flesh or the deeds of the flesh. One may choose to study the works of the flesh instead of the fruit of the Spirit of God, which comes only from God.

Galatians 5:20 idolatry, sorcery, enmities, strife, jealousy, outbursts of anger, disputes, dissensions, factions, (NASB: Lockman)

Greek: eidololatria, pharmakeia, ecthrai, eris, zelos, thumoi, eritheiai, dichostasiai, haireseis,

Amplified: Idolatry, sorcery, enmity, strife, jealousy, anger (ill temper), selfishness, divisions (dissensions), party spirit (factions, sects with peculiar opinions, heresies), (Amplified Bible - Lockman)

Galatians HYPERLINK "http://www.preceptaustin.org/galatians_519-20.htm"
HYPERLINK "http://www.preceptaustin.org/galatians_519-20.htm"5 HYPERLINK
"http://www.preceptaustin.org/galatians_519-20.htm": HYPERLINK

www.preceptaustin.org/galatians 519-20.htm

Galatians 5 Commentary Galatians 5:16-23 ... Galatians 5:19-21 Commentary ...
KJV: Idolatry, witchcraft, hatred ...

Dr. Elizabeth Thambiraj

How Do We Know We Are Walking in the Spirit?

Often we think wrongly that walking in the Spirit is a mysterious act, that it is totally impossible, or that only a few know the secret. This indeed is a greatly mistaken view. Apostle Paul says that the flesh is continuously hostile to the spirit and that this will be evident in the works of the spirit. Plainly, if we are hostile to the working of the Spirit of God, it will manifest in the works of the flesh and in our behavior and will be evident to people around us. Even if we try to hide it beautifully, it will become evident. The Bible uses the analogy of a good tree and a bad tree. A tree is known by its fruit, and more literally, our actions and deeds reveal who we are. While the fleshly nature may not be visible every minute, its deeds become obvious. The King James Bible calls these deeds the desire of the flesh.

We can categorize sins in to the following four kinds: sexual sins (sensual sins), religious sins (idolatry and sorcery), social sins (interpersonal relationship), and drunkenness. When someone preaches on the lust of the flesh, we immediately think of sexual sins, but they are not the sole manifestation of the depraved flesh. Lust can manifest in any of the above categories. Unfortunately, the world clothes sin with such glamour that if we are not grounded in God's Word, anyone can be deceived. It is important that we check the glamor of sin with Scripture and check the issues of our heart, because the heart is a wellspring of life. Good and bad arise from the heart because of the connection between heart and mind, and God's Word substantiates this. What we sow in our minds eventually gives fruit.

It is important to realize that sin is often equated with smartness, and in our blissful ignorance, we fail to realize that sin can outsmart us and push us into a downward spiral that eventually becomes hard to escape. Sin can come in various forms and can look very attractive superficially. Changing the title of a book definitely does not change its content; in the same way, sin, in spite of its attractiveness, harms anyone who plunges into it. This sin can lead anyone to eternal ruin and doom. Unless we are washed by the precious blood of Jesus Christ, our souls can easily be tarnished.

Mystery of Relationships through the Lens of Scriptures

In a nutshell, when a Christian speaks of growing in the fruit of the Spirit that means how the Spirit of God works within us in this world and slowly conforms us to His image. The Spirit of God works to carry out His purposes for each believer on this earth and for each believer's future glory. The Spirit of God enables a believer to change his or her character from inside out, become a person of love, and begin to bear fruit. Such a person is like a tree planted in a garden; it has to be nurtured, pruned, watered, weeded, and cared for, and when the right time comes, it begins to yield its fruit. Similarly, the residing Spirit of God sometimes prunes us, and it may hurt us, but it is for our good so that we may yield fruit bountifully. Abundant spiritual fruit brings hope because of Jesus Christ in whom we believe.

Apostle Paul describes the fruits of the Spirit in Galatians 5:22 and deeds of the flesh in Galatians 5:19–20. "The nine fruits of the Spirit are love *(agape)*, joy (chara), peace *(eirene)*, patience *(makrothumia)*, kindness *(chrestotes)*, goodness *(agathosune)*, faithfulness *(pistis)*, gentleness *(prautes)*, and self-control *(egkrateia)*".[12] Another way to read this passage is that the latter eight fruits of the spirit all follow from the first, which is love. Exploring the meanings of the Greek words in the passage can give further understanding.

[12] ***Fruit Of The Spirit***

www.spirithome.com/fruits-of-the-spirit.html

Galatians 5:19–23 lists the deeds of the flesh: "Now the works of the flesh are manifest, which are these; Adultery, fornication, uncleanness, lasciviousness, Idolatry, witchcraft, hatred, variance, emulations, wrath, strife, seditions, heresies, envyings, murders, drunkenness, revellings, and such like: of the which I tell you before, as I have also told you in time past, that they which do such things shall not inherit the kingdom of God. But the fruit of the Spirit is love, joy, peace, longsuffering, gentleness, goodness, faith, Meekness, temperance: against such there is no law."

When Paul follows the list of the fruits of the Spirit by saying, "against such things there is no law," probably he has in mind that the religious authorities and the law recommend a life with these good

Dr. Elizabeth Thambiraj

traits. We know in our hearts that even our worst enemies on earth and the enemy of the Word will appreciate these traits in a person. No matter which part of the world we are living in, we generally tend to gravitate toward a person with these positive traits.

These fruits come from God, because they are the way God is, so wherever God is at work, these fruits are what it's like. As we continue to live in this fruitful way, we are being drawn closer to God and integrated more into God's purposes. And as we grow closer to God, we will think, act, and live more fruitfully.

The above discussion will be useless if I do not mention the love of Christ, the love so great that He was willing to die on the cross for us. Once we begin to fathom the love of God, our understanding deepens, and we generally become people of love. In 1 Corinthians 13:1–12, Paul talks about love; the King James Bible calls this love charity. Please read and meditate on the following verses.

> Though I speak with the tongues of men and of angels, and have not charity, I am become as sounding brass, or a tinkling cymbal. And though I have the gift of prophecy, and understand all mysteries, and all knowledge; and though I have all faith, so that I could remove mountains, and have not charity, I am nothing. And though I bestow all my goods to feed the poor, and though I give my body to be burned, and have not charity, it profiteth me nothing. Charity suffereth long, and is kind; charity envieth not; charity vaunteth not itself, is not puffed up, Doth not behave itself unseemly, seeketh not her own, is not easily provoked, thinketh no evil; Rejoiceth not in iniquity, but rejoiceth in the truth; Beareth all things, believeth all things, hopeth all things, endureth all things. Charity never faileth: but whether there be prophecies, they shall fail; whether there be tongues, they shall cease; whether there be knowledge, it shall vanish away. For we know in part, and we prophesy in part. But when that which is perfect is come, then that which is in part shall be done away. When I was a child, I spake as a child, I understood as a child, I thought as a child: but when I became a man, I put away childish things.

Mystery of Relationships through the Lens of Scriptures

For now we see through a glass, darkly; but then face to face: now I know in part; but then shall I know even as also I am known. And now abideth faith, hope, charity, these three; but the greatest of these is charity.

It is great if we can memorize these verses, and it does much good for those in emotionally abusive situations to become self-differentiated people of God.

Misplaced Priorities

We often mess up our lives because we make poor choices or make choices in the wrong order. We choose the most important activity as the first priority and place it at the top of our list on any particular day. Many of us do that unconsciously and do not think of its impact on our lives. We keep going, accomplishing whatever we wanted to do but in the wrong order. Where does the following verse of God's Word apply in our day-to-day lives? "But seek ye first the kingdom of God, and his righteousness; and all these things shall be added unto you" (Matthew 6:33).

Please note some other translations of Matthew 6:33 for our edification. The 1611 version of the King James Bible says, "But seeke ye first the kingdome of God, and his righteousnesse, and all these things shalbe added unto you." The New American Standard Version of 1995 reads, "But seek first His kingdom and His righteousness, and all these things will be added to you." The American Standard Version of 1901 says, "But seek ye first his kingdom, and his righteousness; and all these things shall be added unto you." The Basic English Bible translates the same verse, "But let your first care be for his kingdom and his righteousness; and all these other things will be given to you in addition." The Darby Bible says, "But seek ye first the kingdom of God and his righteousness, and all these things shall be added unto you." In Webster's Bible, the verse reads, "But seek ye first the kingdom of God, and his righteousness, and all these things shall be added to you." The Weymouth Bible says, "But make His Kingdom and righteousness your chief aim, and then these things shall all be given you in addition." The World English Bible says, "But seek first God's Kingdom, and his righteousness; and all these things will be given to you as well." The Wycliffe Bible reads, "Therfor seke ye first the kyngdom of God, and his riytfulnesse, and alle these thingis shulen be cast to you." Youngs Literal Bible says, "but seek ye first the reign of God and His righteousness, and all these shall be added to you."

The chart below is divided into eight sections, and at the center is the issue of the heart. The foremost priority should be our relationship

Mystery of Relationships through the Lens of Scriptures

with God, and we develop this priority by going to church, reading God's Word regularly, having prayer-filled lives filled with God's Spirit, and daily witnessing to others. This relationship with God affects us in all areas, especially in all other relationships. One of the foremost relationships in this world is the marital relationship. In general, if a person has a good relationship with God, it will flow to his or her marriage. This indeed affects our relationships with peers and in our professional lives. It also affects our self-esteem and self-worth, because these come from the Lord when we are at peace with God.

We need to understand that we have to keep our bodies fit, because our bodies are temples of the Holy Spirit. In other words, regular exercise, a healthful diet, and good sleep habits must become part of our focus if we are to get our priorities right. Relationship with God indirectly helps us to view our finances at home in a godly way, and we eventually will be good stewards of our wealth. We also will begin to understand that wealth is from God and learn to hold loosely what we have as we begin to understand what is written in God's Word. In family life, we will learn to be responsible and begin to discipline our children in godliness. We will want to move forward in our walks with the Lord. In general, all these are issues of our hearts. When there is turmoil within our hearts, it will affect all these different relationships to various degrees.

Dr. Elizabeth Thambiraj

Below is a chart for the total structuring and different priorities. Please note that this is just an example; readers must adjust the chart to match their own priorities.

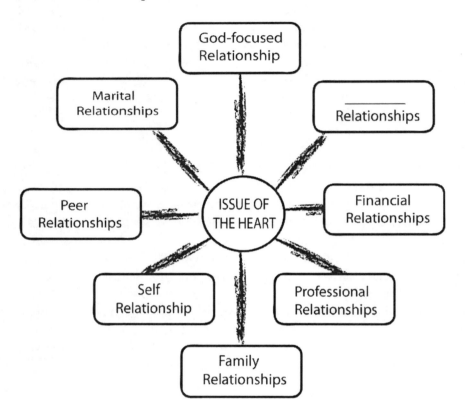

Reference: Jay E. Adams. *A Theology of Christian Counseling, More than Redemption.*

How Do We Seek God's Will in Our Lives?

A list of priorities will help us to assess our conflicts and make our priorities right with the help of God.

- As believers in Christ Jesus, we have the privilege of having God involved in every aspect of our lives. In fact, God wants to be part of every decision-making process, whether it is a move, a new job, or any other choice. We can prioritize based

Mystery of Relationships through the Lens of Scriptures

on the understanding that God is very much involved, and we can make a list.

- All of us are equipped differently, and it is our responsibility to do our jobs well so that we bring glory and honor to His name. We need to cultivate the habit of talking to God every day, and this communion is called prayer.
- God is concerned about the health of our souls, and He wants us to bear fruit bountifully. It is important for us to realize that we have to have a lifestyle that is pleasing to Him.
- When we put our focus on God and acknowledge His presence and guidance in all areas of our lives, we begin to have great confidence and security and the assurance that God is with us all the time. This is a great blessing for believers in Jesus Christ.
- If we are married, where do our spouses fit in? What priority do they have?

Let us meditate on 2 Peter 1:1-11 and try to apply on our day-to-day walk with God.

Simon Peter, a servant and an apostle of Jesus Christ, to them that have obtained like precious faith with us through the righteousness of God and our Saviour Jesus Christ: Grace and peace be multiplied unto you through the knowledge of God, and of Jesus our Lord, According as his divine power hath given unto us all things that pertain unto life and godliness, through the knowledge of him that hath called us to glory and virtue: Whereby are given unto us exceeding great and precious promises: that by these ye might be partakers of the divine nature, having escaped the corruption that is in the world through lust. And beside this, giving all diligence, add to your faith virtue; and to virtue knowledge; and to knowledge temperance; and to temperance patience; and to patience godliness; and to godliness brotherly kindness; and to brotherly kindness charity. For if these things be in you, and abound, they make you that ye shall neither be barren nor unfruitful in the knowledge of our Lord Jesus Christ. But he that lacketh these things is blind, and cannot see afar off, and hath forgotten that he was purged from his old sins. Wherefore the rather, brethren, give diligence to make your calling and election sure: for if ye do these things,

Dr. Elizabeth Thambiraj

ye shall never fall: for so an entrance shall be ministered unto you abundantly into the everlasting kingdom of our Lord and Saviour Jesus Christ.

How can the following diagram help us correctly prioritize in our walks with God?

Right Way vs. Wrong Way

- One way we can put the passage above into practice is to have open hearts and to ask God to explore all areas of our lives, hidden as well as exposed.
- When sensitive areas of our lives are touched, this may be painful; but trust God, because He wants the best for each

Mystery of Relationships through the Lens of Scriptures

of us. Slowly, the Spirit of God is changing us inside out and conforming us to His image and likeness.

Marriage was the first divine institution, and it should be our priority. In today's context, the Fall affects all of our marriages to a certain extent. What are the steps we can take to protect our marriages in a Fallen world? One question that will come up is whether we are to prioritize our spouses or our jobs. Believers and nonbelievers make many decisions every day. The decisions we make hugely affect our lives—and our families and marriages—for better or for worse. How do we prioritize our activities?

The main theme of the article below this: "What the Lord has joined together let no one put asunder." This Word of God is part of many marriage ceremonies, but in actual life, does it have any effect at all? This is the million-dollar question!

Please read the article at the URL below to enrich your knowledge.

Article Source: http://EzineArticles.com/ HYPERLINK "http://ezinearticles.com/837701"837701

"This declaration implies that no man, or ordinances proposed by man should interfere with the unity that exist in marriage. Once this unity is compromised by either party's misplaced priority, the union is on its path to demise. You do not need psychic to predict what the end would be. This also includes parents, siblings, friends, children, employers and even the priest that joined both parties in marriage."

- Article Source: http://EzineArticles.com/ HYPERLINK "http://ezinearticles.com/837701"837701

Not only in our Canadian culture and society but also throughout the world, the sanctity of marriage has been ranked lower and has been consigned to an inferior place. The world as a whole has less regard and importance to marriage than it used to be. There are not many people in today's culture around us think that marriage is the first divine institution and we see there is little commitment. Also we often notice that our priorities have been misplaced and sanctity

Dr. Elizabeth Thambiraj

of marriage takes a lower priority. These disordered priorities begin in our minds and then descends to our hearts, and our hearts carry them out. Throughout the world, human beings have so misplaced our priorities that it is not clear whether we value allegiance to our spouses. This doubt plays out even in the minds of church-going people.

It has also becoming normal to flirt with the boss to get a job or a promotion. Can we imagine the intensity of our culture's moral degradation? Of course, the depraved society that we live in sees flirting at work as normal; having illicit relationships and sex with office colleagues, fornication, adultery, and scandal are the order of the day. As a counselor, I think it is a sign of total depravity, and that means we are declining morally, spiritually, and emotionally. We are bankrupt in our views and have adopting a distorted form of truth. We think it is truth, but it is only a counterfeit truth. The spouse's first allegiance should be to God and then to his or her spouse, and this is vital for healthy thinking. A job, a boss, an employer, or money should not even matter when the unity of the couple is threatened. The unity, sanctity, and sanity of the couple should be protected at all costs; it should be an urgent priority.

"One do not need to attend under peer pressure or fear of not being promoted or accusations of being anti-social. One must have clear priorities, values and boundaries which you must abide to eliminate any thing that may breed doubt or suspicion in your home. One's job is temporal but marriage is a lifelong commitment. One will definitely retire one day, may change jobs several times before retirements but one's marriage is till death do us apart."

- Article Source: http://EzineArticles.com/HYPERLINK "http://ezinearticles. com/837701"837701

In our routine activities, how do we prioritize? What is our priority— our spouse or a promotion? A paycheck or our spouse's love? Acceptance by our colleagues at work or our spouse's trust? Our boss's affirmation or peace at our home? We live by the decisions we make daily. Every decision we make or do not make has an effect on our lives, marriages, and families. In situations like this, if we do not make a decision, someone else makes it for us, and this is a serious matter.

True Love

Christ showed the ultimate true love on the cross two thousand years ago, and today we remember that love and wonder sometimes whether there was any other way for God to show true love for humanity. J.C. Ryle expresses love the following way: "The highest proof of the spirit is love. Love the eternal thing which can already on earth possess as it really is." He adds, "The great thing in prayer is to feel that we are putting our supplications into the bosom of omnipotent love."

Forgiveness

Forgiveness means not to dwelling on the sin that we have forgiven, whether with the offender or others. Even thinking about the offence or brooding over the issue is a violation to the promise granted to the offender when we say, "I forgive." In a way, the word *forgive* means "to wipe clean." Forgiveness is a very hard topic. We all have forgiven others, and others have forgiven us in different situations, but our beloved Lord and Savior Jesus Christ showed the ultimate forgiveness on the cross.

The word *forgive* means "to wipe the slate clean, to pardon, to cancel a debt." When we wrong someone, we seek his or her forgiveness in order to restore the relationship. It is important to remember that we do not grant forgiveness because a person deserves to be forgiven. Instead, it is an act of love, mercy, and grace.[1]

[1]*Definition for Forgiveness - AllAboutGOD.com*

www.allaboutgod.com/definition-for-forgiveness-faq.htm

See more at http://www.allaboutgod.com/definition-for-forgiveness faq.htm#sthash.Zv8smiZj.dpuf

Luke 23:32–34 says, "And there were also two other, malefactors, led with him to be put to death. And when they were come to the place, which is called Calvary, there they crucified him, and the

Dr. Elizabeth Thambiraj

malefactors, one on the right hand, and the other on the left. Then said Jesus, Father, forgive them; for they know not what they do. And they parted his raiment, and cast lots."

We forgive because God has forgiven us (Ephesians 4:32). God forgave us because of His tremendous love for humanity, and when we call on His name, we are forgiven. Jesus performed this act of love on Calvary two thousand years ago.

Salvation

In the Old Testament, we see in the book of Exodus that God delivered Israel from the bondage of Egypt. This is the concept of salvation. In the New Testament, salvation came through Jesus Christ dying for our sins. Sin separates humanity from the holy God according to Isaiah 59:2 and Romans 3:23. Scripture teaches us that no amount of human goodness or religious activity can gain acceptance with God or get us to heaven. According to Romans 2:23, sin separates all humanity from God: "For all have sinned, and come short of the glory of God." Jesus Christ was God's salvation plan for humanity, and He alone bridges the gap between sinful humanity and God.

"Biblical salvation is God's way of providing his people deliverance from sin and spiritual death through repentance and faith in Jesus Christ. The New Testament reveals the source of salvation in our Lord and Savior Jesus Christ. By faith in Jesus Christ, believers are saved from God's judgment of sin and its consequence—eternal death".[2]

[2]Salvation - What is God's Plan of Salvation?

christianity.about.com/od/conversion/p/salvation.htm

It is important for the sinner to recognize his or sinfulness and to rely totally on God. One of the malefactors next to Jesus on the cross railed against him, but the other came to the humble recognition of his sinfulness and received salvation: "And one of the malefactors which were hanged railed on him, saying, if thou be Christ, save thyself and us. But the other answering rebuked him, saying, Dost

Mystery of Relationships through the Lens of Scriptures

not thou fear God, seeing thou art in the same condemnation? And we indeed justly; for we receive the due reward of our deeds: but this man hath done nothing amiss. And he said unto Jesus, Lord, remember me when thou comest into thy kingdom. And Jesus said unto him, Verily I say unto thee, today shalt thou be with me in paradise" (Luke 23:39–43).

Affection

noun

1. fond attachment, devotion, or <u>love</u>: *the affection of a parent for an only child.*

2. Often, **affections.**

a. emotion; feeling; sentiment: *over and above our <u>reason</u> and affections.*

b. the emotional realm of love: *a place in his affections.*

3. the state of being affected.[3]

[3] *Affection | Define Affection at Dictionary.com*

dictionary.reference.com/browse/Affection

Parents love their children. As Jesus died on the cross, His mother wept. It was not easy for Mary when she saw her son hanging on the cross and knew that her son was going to leave her permanently in a short time. Jesus was a responsible son, and Jesus does not want to leave her without the emotional support and love that she received from Him while He was with her. Jesus wanted and gave the responsibility of caring for her after He was gone to His beloved disciple John. This shows the affection He had for His mother. Mary was in a state of emotional pain, and the affection of John, Jesus's beloved disciple, comforted her. John 19:23–27 describes this interaction:

Dr. Elizabeth Thambiraj

Then the soldiers, when they had crucified Jesus, took his garments, and made four parts, to every soldier a part; and also his coat: now the coat was without seam, woven from the top throughout. They said therefore among themselves, Let us not rend it, but cast lots for it, whose it shall be: that the scripture might be fulfilled, which saith, they parted my raiment among them, and for my vesture they did cast lots. These things therefore the soldiers did. Now there stood by the cross of Jesus his mother, and his mother's sister, Mary the wife of Cleophas, and Mary Magdalene. When Jesus therefore saw his mother, and the disciple standing by, whom he loved, he saith unto his mother, Woman, behold thy son! Then saith he to the disciple, Behold thy mother! And from that hour that disciple took her unto his own home.

Anguish

"The noun *anguish* refers to severe physical or emotional pain or distress. In modern times, *anguish* has the parallel and related meanings of "physical torment" and "emotional suffering." Both kinds might be experienced at the hands of a dentist who likes to make his patients squirm in agony".[4]

[4]anguish - Dictionary Definition : Vocabulary.com

www.vocabulary.com/dictionary/anguish

The Latin word *angustus* means "distress" or "the feeling of being forced into a small space." One may face tremendous emotional and mental distress in life, especially when experiencing health issues, when a loved one is dying, or when going through a court case. Christians who are persecuted around the world for their faith also experience intense mental anguish! When I visited Rome the place where the Christians were thrown to the lions, I could well empathize their mental anguish, and for a brief moment I could hardly move from that place.

Mystery of Relationships through the Lens of Scriptures

I just came back from a mission trip to Nepal, where many are becoming Christians. Nepal though it is a secular state, many of the people are Hindus and Buddhists, and some new believers have to pay a huge price when they become Christians. Sometimes their families disown them, and every new believer has a story. We cannot fully fathom their situation or their mental and emotional anguish when they lose their close ties with their families for the sake of Christ. The anguish they feel, which cannot be expressed in words and hides behind their smiles, is beyond our understanding.

"Now from the sixth hour there was darkness over all the land unto the ninth hour. And about the ninth hour Jesus cried with a loud voice, saying, Eli, Eli, lama sabachthani? that is to say, My God, my God, why hast thou forsaken me? Some of them that stood there, when they heard that, said, This man calleth for Elias" (Matthew 27:45–47).

Suffering

Noun 1. Suffering- a state of acute pain

excruciation, agony

hurting, pain - a symptom of some physical hurt or disorder; "the patient developed severe pain and distension"

throe - severe spasm of pain; "the throes of dying"; "the throes of childbirth"

Passion of Christ, Passion - the suffering of Jesus at the Crucifixion[5]

[5]*suffering - definition of suffering by the Free Online ...*

www.thefreedictionary.com/suffering

Suffering is a part of Christian life, and the life of Jesus Christ during His earthly ministry demonstrated this. Gethsemane, Gabbatha, and Golgatha are three places where Jesus suffered.

Dr. Elizabeth Thambiraj

At Gethsemane, Satan tried his best to stop Jesus from dying on the cross, shedding blood, and this was a huge satanic attack. Gethsemane was Satan's hour, and this was the hour of travail:

"And he took with him Peter and the two sons of Zebedee, and began to be sorrowful and very heavy. Then saith he unto them, My soul is exceeding sorrowful, even unto death: tarry ye here, and watch with me. And he went a little farther, and fell on his face, and prayed, saying, O my Father, if it be possible, let this cup pass from me: nevertheless not as I will, but as thou wilt" (Matthew 26:37–39).

At Gabbatha, Jesus suffered at the hands of sinful men: "Then cometh he to his disciples, and saith unto them, Sleep on now, and take your rest: behold, the hour is at hand, and the Son of man is betrayed into the hands of sinners" (Matthew 26:45). This was the hour of trial.

At Glogatha, Jesus suffered at the hand of God's sovereignty: "And they crucified him, and parted his garments, casting lots: that it might be fulfilled which was spoken by the prophet, They parted my garments among them, and upon my vesture did they cast lots" (Matthew 27:35).

This became the hour of triumph when God raised Him up from the death on the third day. Our Lord Jesus Christ experienced agony, spasms, and severe pain on the cross, and He is indeed the suffering Messiah. "After this, Jesus knowing that all things were now accomplished, that the scripture might be fulfilled, saith, I thirst. Now there was set a vessel full of vinegar: and they filled a spunge with vinegar, and put it upon hyssop, and put it to his mouth" (John 19:28–29).

Victory

Here we are discussing Christ's victory on the cross.

"Victory (from <u>Latin</u> *Victoria*) is a term, originally applied to <u>warfare</u>, given to success achieved in personal <u>combat</u>, after military operations in general or, by extension, in any <u>competition</u>. Success in a <u>military campaign</u> is considered a <u>strategic victory</u>, while the success in a <u>military engagement</u> is a <u>tactical victory</u>".[6]

Mystery of Relationships through the Lens of Scriptures

[6]*Victory - Wikipedia, the free encyclopedia*

en.wikipedia.org/wiki/Victory

noun, plur al **vic·to·ries.**

1. a success or triumph over an enemy in battle or war.

2. an engagement ending in such triumph: *American victories in the Pacific were won at great cost.*

3. a success or superior position achieved against any opponent, opposition, difficulty, etc.: *a moral victory*[7].

[7]*Victory | Define Victory at Dictionary.com*

dictionary.reference.com/browse/victory

It is possible that Satan thought for a minute that he had defeated God on that day when Jesus was hanging on the cross. The apparent defeat on the cross was victory over Satan and his schemes. Jesus's ultimate victory on the cross came because of His total obedience to God the Father. At Calvary outside Jerusalem in AD 33, He hung on the cross. It was a public display with tremendous humiliation, and God raised Him up from the death, and that was the final victory over Satan. In the place of sin and suffering and separation from God, there was forgiveness of sin for humanity; there still is tremendous healing and resurrection of life. This was a huge victory over Satan's ploy to destroy humanity. "When Jesus therefore had received the vinegar, he said, It is finished: and he bowed his head, and gave up the ghost" (John 19:30).

Contentment

Contentment cannot come naturally to a fallen human being. It especially cannot come from material things, because they never satisfy the heart. Only God can satisfy the longing of the heart, and when we have God, we have all we need, because He is the only One who is going to be with us everlastingly. When Jesus was dying on the cross, His relationship with God the Father was deep, and He

Dr. Elizabeth Thambiraj

was content because He knew He had to put off this earthly tent and fulfill the plan His Father had for Him on this earth. Jesus knew He was fulfilling the plan to rescue humanity, and He was content.

"Contentment is the acknowledgment and satisfaction of reaching capacity. The level of capacity reached may be sought after, expected, desired, or simply predetermined as the level in which provides contentment".[8]

[8]*Contentment - Wikipedia, the free encyclopedia*

en.wikipedia.org/wiki/Contentment

Luke 23:44–46 says, "And it was about the sixth hour, and there was a darkness over all the earth until the ninth hour. And the sun was darkened, and the veil of the temple was rent in the midst. And when Jesus had cried with a loud voice, he said, Father, into thy hands I commend my spirit: and having said thus, he gave up the ghost."

Godliness and contentment are indeed rare gems, but since they can only be found inseparably combined, they are the rarest of gems to be found in humanity. "Hearken, my beloved brethren, Hath not God chosen the poor of this world rich in Faith, and heirs of the Kingdom which He hath promised to them that love Him?" (James 2:5).

J.C. Ryle writes, "Look at the Cross, think of the cross, meditate on the cross, and then go and set your affections on the world if you can. I believe that holiness is nowhere learned so well as on Calvary."

Thomas Brooks writes, "It was good counsel one gave, 'Never let go out of your minds the thoughts of a crucified Christ.' Let these be food and drink unto you; let them be your sweetness and consolation, your honey and your desire, your reading and your meditation, your life, death, and resurrection."

The Word of God asks us to compare ourselves with Jesus Christ, who owned nothing. His goal was to fulfill the plans of His Father, and this indeed was a Holy calling, and He was content. A good way to be content is to know whom we believe and to trust Him for today

Mystery of Relationships through the Lens of Scriptures

and tomorrow. He is God of the present, past, and future, and He is omniscient.

Apostle Paul spent his later days writing about Christ and the church. He used physical love as an analogy for Christ and His bride. One example is Ephesians 5:25–27: "Husbands, love your wives, even as Christ also loved the church, and gave himself for it; That he might sanctify and cleanse it with the washing of water by the word, That he might present it to himself a glorious church, not having spot, or wrinkle, or any such thing; but that it should be holy and without blemish."

Song of Solomon 4:1–16 talks about Christ and the church and genuine love. Let us meditate upon that. May our understanding if that true love deepen.

> Behold, thou art fair, my love; behold, thou art fair; thou hast doves' eyes within thy locks: thy hair is as a flock of goats that appear from mount Gilead. Thy teeth are like a flock of sheep that are even shorn, which came up from the washing; whereof every one bear twins, and none is barren among them. Thy lips are like a thread of scarlet, and thy speech is comely: thy temples are like a piece of a pomegranate within thy locks. Thy neck is like the tower of David builded for an armoury, whereon there hang a thousand bucklers, all shields of mighty men. Thy two breasts are like two young roes that are twins, which feed among the lilies. Until the day break, and the shadows flee away, I will get me to the mountain of myrrh, and to the hill of frankincense. Thou art all fair, my love; there is no spot in thee. Come with me from Lebanon, my spouse, with me from Lebanon: look from the top of Amana, from the top of Shenir and Hermon, from the lions' dens, from the mountains of the leopards. Thou hast ravished my heart, my sister, my spouse; thou hast ravished my heart with one of thine eyes, with one chain of thy neck. How fair is thy love, my sister, my spouse! how much better is thy love than wine! and the smell of thine ointments than all spices! Thy lips, O my spouse, drop as the honeycomb: honey and

Dr. Elizabeth Thambiraj

milk are under thy tongue; and the smell of thy garments is like the smell of Lebanon. A garden inclosed is my sister, my spouse; a spring shut up, a fountain sealed. Thy plants are an orchard of pomegranates, with pleasant fruits; camphire, with spikenard, Spikenard and saffron; calamus and cinnamon, with all trees of frankincense; myrrh and aloes, with all the chief spices: A fountain of gardens, a well of living waters, and streams from Lebanon. Awake, O north wind; and come, thou south; blow upon my garden that the spices thereof may flow out. Let my beloved come into his garden, and eat his pleasant fruits.

Charles Spurgeon wrote, "The Cross is the lighthouse which guides poor weather-beaten humanity into the harbour of peace."

J.C. Ryle tells us, "Humility and love are precisely the graces which the men of the world can understand, if they do not comprehend doctrines. They are the graces about which there is no mystery, and they are within reach of all classes. The poorest Christian can every day find occasion for practicing love and humility."

Isn't that true love?

A Scriptural View of Marriage

God's Word addresses many topics: attitudes, children, commitment, contentment, courage, the decisions we make, the differences between spouses, how we face difficult times, and the encouragement we need as couples are all parts of marriage. Faithfulness, finances, forgiveness, future goals, grace for day-to-day living, healing, hope, and joy in all circumstances are parts of the overall package in a marriage.

Patience, which is a fruit of the spirit, is essential for building a strong marriage. Peace, perseverance, and prayer are also parts of a healthy marriage. (Prayer, in particular, is the backbone of a strong marriage, and the Bible calls us to pray in all circumstances.) Dealing with pride and misplaced priorities; resolving conflicts; and finding rest and renewal for the body, mind, and spirit are essential in any marriage. Romance is part of marriage, and along with that, how we serve our spouses and how we both grow spiritually are constant challenges in marriage. We need strength, thankful hearts, and trust in one another. Genuine love becomes a continuous ache in many marriages. A strong marriage requires wisdom, strength, and unity as brothers and sisters in Christ. How we handle worry is a continuous tug-of-war in most marriages. With all of our differences, how do we worship the true triune God?

The third chapter of Nehemiah talks about the rebuilding of the walls of Jerusalem. The work was divided in such a way as to give everyone a part to play without causing contention or divided interests. In other words, the work was for the common good. Even some women had work to do, and nobles worked without contention for the common good of the people. Because each person did his or her part to mend the walls of Jerusalem, the walls were mended.

The present state of the walls of Jerusalem—they are rubble—reflects the state of marriage in this world. We must do something in order to remove chaos. Bringing order requires work and lots of organization and planning. Some people tried to hinder the rebuilding of Jerusalem, and similarly, we all encounter malicious people when we do the work of God. When we work together, we can defend the

Dr. Elizabeth Thambiraj

cause of truth and godliness against the assaults of enemies. The workers, without complaint, stood next to each other shoulder to shoulder, focusing on their own sections.

There is a principle here that applies to marriage. Different marriages are different, and their situations, circumstances, and goals are different, but in every good marriage, the spouses work for a common purpose. Some marriages have incredible parenting challenges, some have serious medical issues to cope with, and some have financial difficulties. These issues may affect the marriages, and some marriages suffer from trust issues because one spouse has deflated the trust in the marriage. Whatever the circumstances, all marriages suffer under the weight of the Fall. The Fall has profoundly affected the first divine institution, and we all need help and need God desperately. In other words, every marriage has crumbling walls that need to be rebuilt!

Often we begin to realize the omniscience of God when we look at our spouses. Spouses may seem totally different from one another and have different gifts, but God has united them as a couple for a special purpose. One spouse with tremendous gifts for overcoming difficult situations may be linked to one who has the patience to endure. An impatient person may be married to a patient one; God, in His omniscience, knows it is a perfect match that will fulfill His purpose and allow the spouses to learn from each other. Marriage becomes a school where we learn from each other as one flesh. Very often, one spouse's strength is another spouse's weakness.

Patience is a fruit of the Spirit, and the Word of God says that patience is better than pride. To build a marriage, we all have to work on this particular fruit of the Spirit. "Better is the end of a thing than the beginning thereof: and the patient in spirit is better than the proud in spirit. Be not hasty in thy spirit to be angry: for anger resteth in the bosom of fools" (Ecclesiastes 7:8–9). Scriptures that support patience in marriage are 1 Corinthians 13:4–7; Proverbs 14:29; Romans 8:25; Galatians 5:22–23; Psalm 37:3–7; Psalm 40:1–3; and 2 Corinthians 1:6–7.

Above all other relationships, marriage relationship requires heavy doses of forgiveness. As a basic principle, God wants us to forgive

Mystery of Relationships through the Lens of Scriptures

our offenders whether they ask for forgiveness or not: "And forgive us our debts, as we forgive our debtors" (Matthew 6:12). Forgiveness is a means of getting over the valleys of anger, depression, and bitterness. It is important to forgive so that the offended party does not fall into a downward spiral. When the offended forgives the offender, this releases the offended person so that he or she becomes free. This may be humanly impossible, but the offended person does not have to operate with his or her own strength alone; our omniscient God is there to provide His strength.

If we read Genesis chapters 42 through 45, we see that Joseph had a chance to take vengeance on his brothers who had sold him into slavery, but he decided to forgive them. The brothers of Joseph did not ask his forgiveness, but God gave Joseph grace and he forgave his brothers voluntarily. Each one of us has the freedom and responsibility to choose to forgive our offenders. The intimacy of marriage brings not only joy but also many moments of hurt, which may be small or large. Love means not only saying we are sorry when we are wrong but, more importantly, choosing to forgive even before we are asked. This is God's way of training us in love and changing us into His image and likeness. I understand this is a very hard school of training, but can we trust that God is training us for something glorious!

One of the ways of solving conflicts in marriage is to keep short accounts with God and with our spouses. Agreeing on a direction for a couple's relationship can be a huge hurdle, and praying can become harder as a couple. Bringing family matters to the throne room of God every day in prayer not only helps a family draw closer to God but also continually rebuilds the ruined walls! When handled with a prayerful heart, conflicts often become an area of growth where God brings issues of our hearts to our attention.

Where Is True Love?

Ephesians 5:21–32 talks about Christ and the church as the model for our marriages in this part of eternity:

> Submitting yourselves one to another in the fear of God.
> Wives, submit yourselves unto your own husbands, as unto

Dr. Elizabeth Thambiraj

the Lord. For the husband is the head of the wife, even as Christ is the head of the church: and he is the saviour of the body. Therefore as the church is subject unto Christ, so let the wives be to their own husbands in everything. Husbands, love your wives, even as Christ also loved the church, and gave himself for it; That he might sanctify and cleanse it with the washing of water by the word, That he might present it to himself a glorious church, not having spot, or wrinkle, or any such thing; but that it should be holy and without blemish. So ought men to love their wives as their own bodies. He that loveth his wife loveth himself. For no man ever yet hated his own flesh; but nourisheth and cherisheth it, even as the Lord the church: For we are members of his body, of his flesh, and of his bones. For this cause shall a man leave his father and mother, and shall be joined unto his wife, and they two shall be one flesh. This is a great mystery: but I speak concerning Christ and the church.

While the above is the model for true love, attaining it seems to be a huge struggle in this fallen world. While our earthly relationships let us down again and again, our relationship with God can genuinely and fully meet our deepest needs for significance and self-worth. Psalm 23 is a poetic reminder to us when we face difficult challenges in our marriages or in other relationships. Our Good Shepherd is always there to restore our souls, which were made in the image and likeness of God. He is able to comfort us and to meet the deepest needs and desires of our souls. This is a huge comfort a child of God has in Christ Jesus.

Genesis talks about Joseph's life and how his earthly father met his needs until one day, to his shock, he lost it all. When Joseph's jealous brothers sold him into slavery, in a moment, Joseph lost everything including his family. In the long journey to Egypt, where was Joseph's trust? Probably Joseph never would have learned to depend on God completely but for his difficult circumstances in a foreign land. "But as for you, ye thought evil against me; but God meant it unto good, to bring to pass, as it is this day, to save much people alive" (Genesis 50:20).

Mystery of Relationships through the Lens of Scriptures

Whom do we put our trust in during good times and bad? Some may trust in people in authority, some may trust in family members, and some may even trust in their possessions. Our things, just like Joseph's, could be gone in a minute; and if we put our trust in people, invariably they will disappoint us. If our happiness and trust come from people and things, this will inevitably lead us to misery and loss of hope. "Blessed is the man that trusteth in the Lord, and whose hope the Lord is. For he shall be as a tree planted by the waters, and that spreadeth out her roots by the river, and shall not see when heat cometh, but her leaf shall be green; and shall not be careful in the year of drought, neither shall cease from yielding fruit" (Jeremiah 17:7–8).

We cannot look for happiness and security in marriage, because this puts too much pressure on marriage. Happiness, security, self-worth, and confidence should come from the One who formed us in our mothers' wombs. He wired us and fashioned us individually and no one can know us better than God, and this includes the emotional part of us. He will never leave or forsake us, because His love is true and unconditional.

Isaiah 30:15 says, "For thus saith the Lord God, the Holy One of Israel; In returning and rest shall ye be saved; in quietness and in confidence shall be your strength: and ye would not." Sometimes we limit God through the way we think, especially in very bad circumstances. Hard, difficult, agonizing, frustrating, strenuous, debilitating, horrific, sorrowful, confusing, perturbing, penetrating, or painful situations come to humanity, and this may force some to think there is no hope. This is the normal reaction of humanity when we do not have hope in Christ.

I want to bring assurance and hope for the hopeless here. There is always hope in the blood and resurrection of Christ, and because He lives today, we have hope for tomorrow. Problems in life force us to look at the face of God with hope, and then we begin to wonder if God can help us out. Our God is a great and limitless God. He dwells in eternity, operates in infinity, and has all things within His understanding and all things under His control. God is able to lift us out of our valleys if we can give Him control and look up.

145

Dr. Elizabeth Thambiraj

In a corporation, when someone owns 51 percent of the stock, that person has all the say. We often try to get the 51 percent of the shares so that we can have the final word. Is God really in our marriages? If He is, what percentage of the stock does He own? How much do we really want to involve God in our marriages?

Gender Roles: A Glimpse.

Genesis 1:26–28 tells us,

> Then God said "Let us make human kind in our image
> according to our likeness and let them have dominion over
> the fish of the sea and over the birds of the air and over
> the cattle and over all the wild animals of the earth." So
> God created humankind in His image. In the image of
> God He created them; male and female He created them.
> God blessed them and God said to them, "Be fruitful and
> multiply, and fill the earth and subdue it and have dominion
> over the fish of the sea and over the birds of the air and over
> every living thing that moves upon the earth."

In the second chapter of Genesis, we find a more detailed description
of the creation of woman:

> And the Lord God said, it is not good that the man should
> be alone; I will make him an help meet for him. And out of
> the ground the Lord God formed every beast of the field,
> and every fowl of the air; and brought them unto Adam to
> see what he would call them: and whatsoever Adam called
> every living creature that was the name thereof. And Adam
> gave names to all cattle, and to the fowl of the air, and to
> every beast of the field; but for Adam there was not found
> a help meet for him.

> And the Lord God caused a deep sleep to fall upon Adam,
> and he slept: and he took one of his ribs, and closed up the
> flesh instead thereof; And the rib, which the Lord God had
> taken from man, made he a woman, and brought her unto
> the man. And Adam said, this is now bone of my bones,
> and flesh of my flesh: she shall be called Woman, because
> she was taken out of Man. Therefore shall a man leave his
> father and his mother, and shall cleave unto his wife: and
> they shall be one flesh. And they were both naked, the man
> and his wife, and were not ashamed. (Genesis 2:18–25)

Dr. Elizabeth Thambiraj

The Outline of Creation

1. God created man first from dust of the earth (Genesis 2:7).
2. God created woman from Adam, and unlike the rest of creation, the woman was taken from another creature, not from nature (Genesis 2:22).
3. Adam named the woman Eve (2:23).
4. The relationship between the man and the woman is the reason for a man to leave his family to be with his wife (Genesis 2:24).

In Genesis 3, we find that sin enters in and gender roles become confused when man and woman began to sin together. In the cool of the day, when God comes to them, He calls for Adam, and for the first time, Adam begins to feel ashamed before the holy God. Adam also shifts the blame to the woman for his disobedience. We see that pattern repeated often following disobedience, and we are called to get help. Help from where? The curse of the Fall applies to all of humanity, but the emphasis of the curse is different for men and women. To summarize the curses, God talks about the difficulty of the man's work and the difficulty of the woman's relationships, especially with her husband and children.

5. Satan tempts Eve to disobey (Genesis 3:1).
6. Eve brings Adam into the matter (Genesis 3:6).
7. Women are cursed because of Eve's actions (Genesis 3:16).
8. Men are cursed because of Adam's actions (Genesis 3:17-19).

It is important to understand the physical and emotional differences between men and women if we want to understand relationships. We have to keep in mind that men and women are wired differently. It would be a huge mistake to clone the emotional nature of the other person, because God made us to be different. The main goal should be to communicate with each other attentively and to expose from each perspective the issues that come along. This is especially important in a marriage relationship, and the merging perspective is often a better one than just the man or the woman's initial opinion.

Mystery of Relationships through the Lens of Scriptures

In general, people can say that men are stronger physically; are more realistic, logical, objective, literal, aggregate thinkers. When it comes to judgment they need an input; and are very task oriented. Also we can say that women are physically weaker, more idealistic, more intuitive, more subject to their feelings, more tangential thinkers, quick to grasp details, quick to judgment, and very family oriented. One may choose to disagree with the above statements because in some cases the opposite views could be true and here I am making a general point that male and female are wired differently, they think and act very often differently to the same event or situations around them.

In general, one can say that two worlds in our thought lives affect decisions. One is the world of objective reality, and the other is the subjective world of imagination. The world of imagination includes speculation about the intent and motives of others. When unguarded, imagination can inflict havoc.

In the realm of objective reality, the wife has an indispensable role. Research has shown that men find their wives often have better judgment in matters of detail. This is a gift of God, and we should not despise it, because that would be like despising the Giver of all gifts. There are many examples in the Bible showing that men and women are different in the way they deal with things, but God empowers them differently to accomplish God's purposes on this earth. For example, if Moses's father was as insensitive to details as many men are and had woven the basket that carried baby Moses, the child could have drowned!

In Greek mythology, Eros is the god of love, son of Aphrodite. Male and female though wired differently being in love while married will not destroy the marriage between two sensible decent people or couples. Some couples idolize Eros, and their marriages are in danger. Such couples expect the feeling of being in love stay with them permanently. Married couples will agree with me that this expectation does not match reality. When disappointed, such people often blame Eros or their spouses. Eros is like a godparent who has made vows, and it is up to the couple to keep the vows. The couple must work hard to continue to be in love even when Eros is not

149

Dr. Elizabeth Thambiraj

present. There are valleys and mountains in normal life. Lovers with a little common sense will understand that and take the good and the bad in a marriage. The scriptures affirm that humility, charity, and divine grace are necessary in Christian married life. C.S Lewis makes a similar point when he writes, "And all good Christian lovers know that this programme, modest as it sounds, will not be carried out except by humility, charity and divine grace; that it is indeed the whole Christian life seen from one particular angle." C.S Lewis.-The Four Loves, p. 114-115

Wise men respect the views of their wives and respect their wives' talents. When they listen to their wives, they gain better perspectives and superior understanding. It is also important that husbands speak to their wives in soft tones. Even when spoken in kindness, loud words can be misconstrued, and they seem heavier to a women's heart than to a man's heart. This is how women are wired, and the Bible says they are weaker vessels. In the subjective realm of imagination and speculation, their roles are reversed. Men in general have the God-given capacity and responsibility to be a sponge that diffuses the speculation of their wives. Sometimes when the husband says to his wife, "We will wait on the Lord," it will be wiser and safer for her to listen to him respectfully. Below are some quotes from C.S Lewis to think through for God's glory and for the blessing of humanity.

Many writers and even preachers and well-meaning theologians understand the headship of a husband differently from what God's Word says. We have to go back to the Bible and fall on our knees before God to get the right understanding. C.S Lewis says the following: "The husband is the head of the wife just in so far as he is to her what Christ is to the Church. He is to love her as Christ loved the Church—read on—and give his life for her." C.S Lewis. -The Four Loves, p. 105

Lewis goes on to write, "The sternest feminist need not grudge my sex the crown offered to it either in the Pagan or in the Christian mystery. For the one is of paper and the other of thorns." - C.S Lewis. -The Four Loves, p. 106

Mystery of Relationships through the Lens of Scriptures

The things happening in the world are enough to make us tremble. Both believers and nonbelievers are shocked and divided over gender roles, and everyone craves a safety net. When the Word of God talks about gender roles, it focuses on the church and the family, and that is my focus here. In business, politics, health care, law enforcement, science, research and development, and art and education, there is no safety net, no plan for repentance and forgiveness when we hurt one another. There is no covenantal commitment outside the church and the family, and indeed, the church and the family offer the safety net that will free us. Because of the relationship between Christ and the church described in Ephesians 5:21–33, we have a safety net; we are free to swing from this trapeze with confidence. If one member falls, the body of believers will be there to catch him or her. We will help those who are weak to climb up and move forward once again.

Men and women form a team. If they would dance together for the common good, it would be amazing. This is almost like two wings of an airplane, which are alike and yet not the same but correspond beautifully and take people to different destinations. The question for our hearts to ponder is which wing is more important. I would say we need them both to play their separate roles for the common cause. If we look at our society, we notice people with different gifts, talents, and jobs. Some of us are housewives, some women work outside home, some are soldiers, and all may be citizens in their countries. Yet we all march in step together wearing the uniforms of our social and political statuses for the good of our country. Does that not happen in a marriage between spouses? What one spouse does will be different from what the other spouse does, but they both work for the family, marching in lockstep.

"What a gift it is, then, to come into the home or the church and done our ball gowns and tuxedos. Some of us dance forward, some of us dance backward. This is a gift from God not to be despised or to be taken lightly." - C.S. Lewis.

Part III

Diagrams on Relationships

I have included some diagrams to help readers to get a better biblical understanding of relationships, especially marriages.

Diagram 1

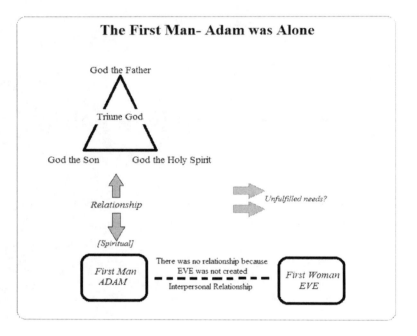

Mystery of Relationships through the Lens of Scriptures

The above diagram shows that Adam was alone before the creation of Eve. Adam had a good relationship with God, and obviously, there was no interpersonal relationship, because there was no Eve. In general, we can say that personality develops in the interpersonal relationships that an individual enjoys, and very often that is with the person we interact more in our routine life. We can explain personality, to certain extent, as the characteristic way a person deals with other people in interpersonal relationships.

From the above, we can conclude that even though Adam had a fantastic relationship with God, there were unfulfilled needs in his life, because he had no other human being to relate to. The unfulfilled needs were both internal and external, and we can classify them as social needs. Internal needs include the needs to be loved and to love and also to find sexual fulfillment and companionship. External needs include the desires to work together, to walk together, to be together, and to be one flesh together. God pronounced that it was not good for a man to be alone. The book of Genesis shows the importance God places on relationships. God knew that without intimacy with an equal, Adam would be lonely even with creation and the Creator.

Diagram 2

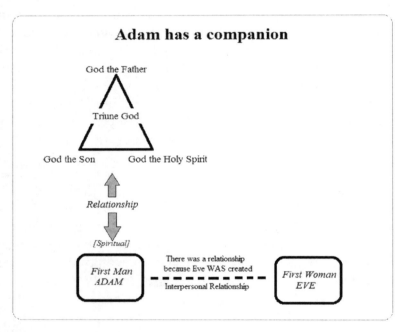

Mystery of Relationships through the Lens of Scriptures

Adam's relationship to God was vertical, and when God created Eve, the horizontal relationship became complete. Adam needed human relationships and companionship for inner happiness and satisfaction, and God said that it was not good for man to be alone. Only that complete relationship could meet the internal and external social needs of human beings. God pronounced that the creation of Eve was good. God created Adam for relationship, and He made a woman from the rib He had taken out of the man and brought her to the man (Genesis 2:18, 21–22).

Diagram 3

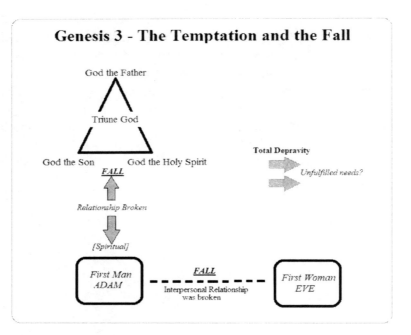

Mystery of Relationships through the Lens of Scriptures

Here comes the tempter and the Fall in Genesis 3, and our rebellion, and the consequences of our sin. "The wrath of God is being revealed from heaven against all godlessness and wickedness of men who supress the truth by their wickedness" (Romans 1:18). The Fall affects relationships very badly. The relationship between God and humanity broke, and so did the relationship between the man and the woman. This broken relationship affects humanity both internally and externally. Internally, human beings lost our true identities, and as a result, we became anxious; fearful; and full of guilt, rage, and anger. We lost the joy we had and became depressed. Because of this huge distortion, externally, human beings became evildoers filled with jealousy, rage, and murderous intent. Human beings begin stealing, coveting, lying, and trying hard to fulfill needs by searching out adulterous relationships. Here total depravity sets in, and humanity's needs are unfulfilled. The point to remember is that after sin entered the world, the loneliness that Adam felt before the Fall returned, this time with a huge sigh and is a heartrending cry!

Diagram 4

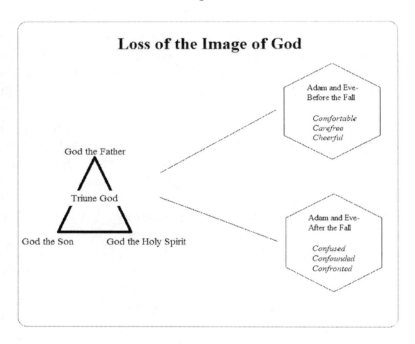

Mystery of Relationships through the Lens of Scriptures

At the Fall, human beings (Adam and Eve) lost the image of God. The lies of Satan continue to take the place of absolute truth and it began in the Garden of Eden. Satan flattered the human ego, telling Adam and Eve, "Ye shall be gods." After the Fall, the need for close relationships grew, and in general, relationships suffered greatly because of the severe distortion. Before the Fall, Adam and Eve were comfortable, carefree, and cheerful, communing with God in the cool of the day regularly. After the Fall, our first parents were confused, conflicted, and confounded, because their relationship with God was broken completely. We need God desperately to correct that distortion, and we must go to the cross with that humble petition. Correcting this huge distortion is humanly impossible, and only God is able to do this.

Diagram 5

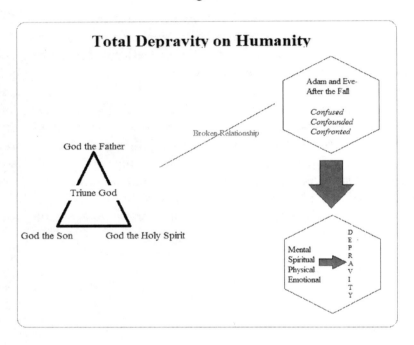

Mystery of Relationships through the Lens of Scriptures

At the Fall, both Adam and Eve were confused, confronted, conflicted, and confounded, and total depravity set in. Total depravity affects all human beings mentally, physically, spiritually, and emotionally, and this results in broken relationships.

The nervous system is a complex network of nerves and cells that carry messages to and from the brain and spinal cord to various parts of the body. The human nervous system consists of the peripheral nervous system (autonomic and somatic) and the central nervous system (the brain and spinal cord). The brain cannot function beyond how it is programmed.

Our central nervous system affects our thinking, will, mind, and emotions. We need brokenness and humility before God to understand the Scriptures, and we have to keep in mind that God resists the proud but gives grace to the humble.

Diagram 6

The Effect of Total Depravity on Humanity

MAN in the image of God

Man's Deepest Needs Met through God

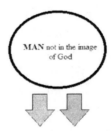

MAN not in the image of God

Rejection and Alienation from God

To whom we serve affects every aspect of our thoughts, emotions, will, desires, conceptions, and ultimately our hearts. When we are alienated from God, we lose everything and eternal death is the ultimate end. In our total depravity, if we continue to be alienated from God we lose it all.

Here is another way of looking at the whole picture. Before the Fall, God met humanity's deepest needs, and human beings had access to the absolute truth and existed in God's image. After the Fall, humanity experienced rejection and alienation from God and began to live a lie of Satan. As a result, human beings have divided selves. At the Fall, the unified self divided, and there emerged a needing self and a rejected self. The needing self needs to belong or be affiliated with someone. It needs self-esteem and affection as well as strength and affirmation, because we have lost the absolute truth. The rejected self is self-pitying: it feels rejected and ashamed, does not feel a sense of belonging, has low self-esteem, and feels weak and hopeless because of the absence of absolute truth. In general, people are caught up between these two selves, and there is tension and alienation because we are trying to live on assumptive truth and not the real truth.

Diagram 7

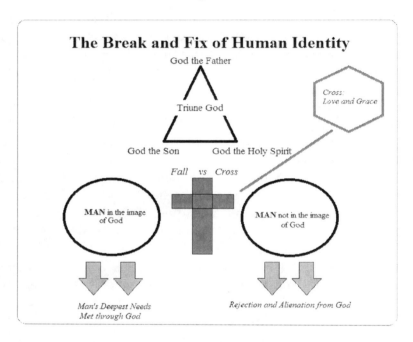

Mystery of Relationships through the Lens of Scriptures

Now that our relationship with God is broken, only God can fix it. We need to understand this, and this understanding also has to come from God, because in our total depravity, it is hard to understand this absolute truth. In a marriage, if one of the spouses does not understand this, it can cause tremendous upheaval in the relationship. God overcame rejection and alienation on the cross through the blood of Christ, and we have hope for the restoration of human identity at the foot of the cross. The proper perspective on this side of the cross is total dependence on our Father's grace: "I am loved and accepted by my Father in heaven." This brings us to the place of acceptance and the restoration of human identity.

Diagram 8

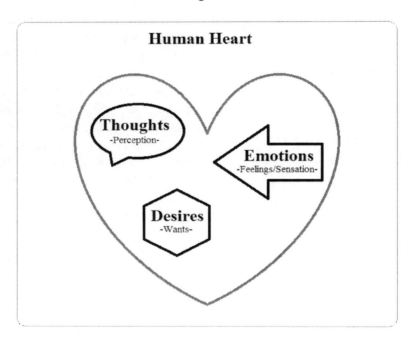

Mystery of Relationships through the Lens of Scriptures

Refer to the chapter on holding loose for further explanation.

Emotions are complex in nature, and so is the soul, which includes the heart. Emotions are signals from God, and we need to pay attention to them, because they are outward expressions of inward reality. The Bible repeatedly instructs us to guard our hearts, because out of them comes the living water. What we sow in our minds has a tremendous effect in our hearts, so we must be careful what we sow in our minds. For example, if we sow seeds of discord in the minds of others, this can turn into bitterness and can spiral down.

Consider the different aspects of the human heart:

Cognition is made up of our thoughts and conceptions.

Volition includes the will and the desires of the heart.

Affect consists of the feelings and emotions that arise because of cognition and volition.

The proper way of viewing the heart is as follows: The heart, which includes cognition, volition, and affect, is psychological, spiritual, and physical.

Now, where is the work of the Spirit? We have only God's Spirit or the spirit of the world or of Satan. To whom do we yield? Whom we serve affects every aspect of our thoughts, emotions, will, desires, conceptions, and ultimately our hearts.

Reference: William T. Kirwan. *Biblical Concepts for Christian Counseling; A case for Integrating Psychology and Theology.* Grand Rapids, Michigan: Bake Book House, 1984.

Part IV

Prayers for Relationships

Preface

Struggles in our relationships often point to deeper issues that God alone knows. God works in our lives continuously in those struggles to change us into His image. The mountains we face in our relationships are often molehills to God, and with God, we are able to scale the unscalable.

We all can agree wholeheartedly that we need someone to lean on in our lives. God created Adam, and He realized that it was not good for the man to be alone and wanted to provide a suitable helper. "And the Lord God said, It is not good that the man should be alone; I will make him an help meet for him" (Genesis 2:18). God gave Eve to Adam, and she was wired differently from Adam. Men and women have to learn to live their lives in their context of human relationships.

All men and women were created with a God-shaped hole, which we could call a *relationship hole*. This hole is both vertical and horizontal. God has to fill the vertical void, and friendship fills the horizontal void. When these two intersect, we can come to many conclusions as Paul mentions in the book of Philippians: "Wherefore, my beloved, as ye have always obeyed, not as in my presence only, but now much more in my absence, work out your own salvation with fear and trembling. For it is God which worketh in you both to will and to do of his good pleasure. Do all things without murmurings and disputings: That ye may be blameless and harmless, the sons of God, without rebuke, in the midst of a crooked and perverse nation, among whom ye shine as lights in the world" (Philippians 2:12–15).

God, in His omniscience, did not create individuals but people whom He expects to live in harmony. Naturally, men and women yearn to share their lives with a person of the opposite sex. It is obvious that when people enjoy good relationships with their spouses, they are very happy; when they do not, they are very lonely. This shows that God has wired us for relationships.

The Scripture below talks about unity and diversity in one body and shows beautifully that each part has to function properly for

Dr. Elizabeth Thambiraj

the health of the body. The community that emerges out of the local body of believers, the loving relationships in their own families, and their friendships with each other in the context of our life-giving relationship with Jesus Christ form the missing piece in the jig-jaw puzzle. This is the relationship the world longs for.

> For as the body is one, and hath many members, and all the members of that one body, being many, are one body: so also is Christ. For by one Spirit are we all baptized into one body, whether we be Jews or Gentiles, whether we be bond or free; and have been all made to drink into one Spirit. For the body is not one member, but many. If the foot shall say, Because I am not the hand, I am not of the body; is it therefore not of the body? And if the ear shall say, because I am not the eye, I am not of the body; is it therefore not of the body? If the whole body were an eye, where were the hearing? If the whole were hearing, where were the smelling? But now hath God set the members every one of them in the body, as it hath pleased him. And if they were all one member, where were the body? But now are they many members, yet but one body. And the eye cannot say unto the hand, I have no need of thee: nor again the head to the feet, I have no need of you. Nay, much more those members of the body, which seem to be feebler, are necessary: And those members of the body, which we think to be less honourable, upon these we bestow more abundant honour; and our uncomely parts have more abundant comeliness. For our comely parts have no need: but God hath tempered the body together, having given more abundant honour to that part which lacked. That there should be no schism in the body; but that the members should have the same care one for another. And whether one member suffer, all the members suffer with it; or one member be honoured, all the members rejoice with it. Now ye are the body of Christ, and members in particular. (1 Corinthians 12:12–27)

Many of us do not want to agree that our relationships serve as an important gauge of our walks with God. In other words, if our

Mystery of Relationships through the Lens of Scriptures

relationships with God are mature and sincere, this will affect our relationships with our spouses and with godly men and women in the body of Christ. A pattern of strained relationships points to an area in our lives that needs attention and further work and maturation. Relationship with God directly correlates to relationship with our spouses and with godly friendships in general.

I have heard the saying, "The family that prays together stays together." Family is important, because throughout the Scriptures, God uses the family unit as the principal means of dealing with His people. I have included some prayers in this section for deeper issues and behaviors in relationships. God can use these issues to bring us closer to Him and to conform us to His image. In other words, God is pruning certain areas in our lives, and this is a painful process, but He is good and wants us to be fruitful and multiply. This may sound very complex and crude, but God is able to help us grow and mature and be fruitful. I have included some prayers for strained relationships, and these prayers are fully based on the Word of God. As we pray, may we meditate on His word. I pray that the Spirit of God will minister His words to our hearts and bring healing and comfort in our areas of strain.

Please take note that we can personalize these prayers as we pray.

A Prayer for Healing Strained Relationships with Parents

Omniscient, omnipotent, and omnipresent God, Thou art worthy, and your Name is worthy to be praised at all times. Father in heaven, it is a true blessing, as believers, to call You Abba, Father. It is again a great blessing to know that Jesus Christ, our mediator and intercessor, is always praying for us in our weaknesses and the Holy Spirit, the comforter, is always with us when we face trials and temptations, especially when we face strained relationships with our earthly parents. Your Word says, "Honour thy father and mother; which is the first commandment with promise; That it may be well with thee, and thou mayest live long on the earth" (Ephesians 6:2–3).

According to Your Word, we children are called to honor our fathers and mothers, and You have promised long life for children. The hurt they have inspired in our lives is big, and this makes obedience to Your Word very hard. Very often, it is extremely hard, and our hearts are resilient to make things right.

We pray, O God, that You would pick us out of the miry clay of this strained relationship so that, by the power of the Holy Spirit, we can communicate on the solid ground of truth and grace. Give me the grace to forgive them, and remind me of this verse: "And be ye kind one to another, tender hearted, forgiving one another, even as God for Christ's sake hath forgiven you" (Ephesians 4:32). Father, even though it is extremely hard, I trust that You are able to give me grace in abundance in times of need so that I can forgive my parents for the hurts they have caused intentionally or unintentionally, whether they are severe, slight, or even inexcusable. I want to release every offense to Your precious throne room of grace, because Your Word says, "For my yoke is easy, and my burden is light" (Matthew 11:30).

Lord, I pray, "breathe on me, breath of God," so that my wounds will be healed. Heal me so that I can leave the past behind me. Remove the blinders from my eyes so that I can see the truth in the light of Your grace, which will help me to understand if there is any pride, or

Mystery of Relationships through the Lens of Scriptures

rebellion, selfishness, or hypersensitivity on my part that has allowed my wounds to fester.

In a similar fashion, open the eyes of the hearts of my parents to see their wrongdoing, because in Your Word it is written, "And, ye fathers, provoke not your children to wrath: but bring them up in the nurture and admonition of the Lord" (Ephesians 6:4). Remove the veil from their eyes so they can see clearly their fault and the reason for this strained relationship and conflict.

May You restore us to humility and peace. Even if they refuse to be restored, give me a heart to forgive their offences. By doing so, I am honoring You. Grant me, O Lord, the courage to take the necessary steps to seek forgiveness so that I will be restored. Give me the boldness to approach them in sincerity, meekness, love, and wisdom.

Dear Father in heaven, Your Word constantly reminds me that all things work together for the good of those who love You: "And we know that all things work together for good to them that love God, to them who are the called according to his purpose" (Romans 8:28). I want to give all the stress, strain, and anxiety caused by this strained relationship to You so that I will have peace. I want to rest in You so that You will be honored and glorified through this. Only You can ease the strain in our strained relationships, because You are the prince of peace.

Lord, I pray that you may give me grace upon grace in my life so that I may understand as it is written in Your Word: "and to know the love of Christ, which passeth knowledge, that ye might be filled with all the fullness of God. Now unto him that is able to do exceeding abundantly above all that we ask or think, according to the power that worketh in us, unto him be glory in the church by Christ Jesus throughout all ages, world without end. Amen" (Ephesians 3:19–21).

Mending Broken Relationships

Our Father in heaven, we want to praise You and honor You for making human beings in Your image and likeness and for building a relationship between human beings and God. Father, You alone are the architect of all relationships, and You formed the first relationships in the Garden of Eden between God and man and between man and woman, and there was perfect communication between You and human beings. The Fall came as described in Genesis chapter 3 and brought devastation to this relationship. As a result of this, conflict, quarrels, and divisions became the norm on this planet earth.

Thank you for giving us Jesus Christ, who broke the wall of separation between God and humanity. Because of Him, the curse from the Garden of Eden is completely broken, and we have hope in Christ Jesus. Who can mend a broken spirit? Who can bring healing and restoration apart from God, who formed relationships in the Garden of Eden?

Father, it is very disheartening, painful, and difficult when family members or church members have chosen to inflict severe wounds with words, actions, or occult practices. Lord, it is to our glory to forgive the offender, but the painful memories of those events could haunt and destroy the wounded person except for Christ and Christ alone. Embrace us with Your grace and love so that those wounds become less painful and we can walk victoriously in Christ Jesus.

Lord, I am reminded of Your Word in Colossians 3:12–17:

> Put on therefore, as the elect of God, holy and beloved, bowels of mercies, kindness, humbleness of mind, meekness, longsuffering; forbearing one another, and forgiving one another, if any man have a quarrel against any: even as Christ forgave you, so also do ye. And above all these things put on charity, which is the bond of perfectness. And let the peace of God rule in your hearts, to which also ye are called in one body; and be ye thankful. Let the word of Christ dwell in you richly in all

Mystery of Relationships through the Lens of Scriptures

wisdom; teaching and admonishing one another in psalms and hymns and spiritual songs, singing with grace in your hearts to the Lord. And whatsoever ye do in word or deed, do all in the name of the Lord Jesus, giving thanks to God and the Father by him.

We pray that the Spirit of God, who is the perfect Counselor, will continue to minister to our aching hearts, weed out areas that need attention and correction, and bring us to perfection and Your peace. Lord, time and again, we remember that we are human and that we are limited in our ability, and we are forced to look up! Grant us the capacity to assess ourselves with sober judgment so that we can take responsibility for any wrongdoing and repent. Lord, You have promised in Your Word that You will give grace abundantly to judge ourselves rightly in the Lord. "For I say, through the grace given unto me, to every man that is among you, not to think of himself more highly than he ought to think; but to think soberly, according as God hath dealt to every man the measure of faith" (Romans 12:3).

Loving Father, as You continue to soften our hearts, we pray that You would soften the hearts of our offenders and speak to them by the power of the Holy Spirit in the areas they may have caused the division and conflict. If they committed these acts out of jealousy, we pray that You would continue to minister to their hearts and give them a change of heart. We refuse to usurp the power and work of the Holy Spirit, and we release them into Your hands. For our part, give us grace abundantly so we may forgive them completely, and help us to grow in the fruit of the Spirit. "But the fruit of the Spirit is love, joy, peace, longsuffering, gentleness, goodness, faith, meekness, temperance: against such there is no law" (Galatians 5:22–23). Replace all of our selfishness with the fruit of the Spirit.

Time and again, we are reminded that the One who is infinite and able is God alone in Christ Jesus, who helps us and gives us grace continuously in need, especially when we face difficult relationships, destructive and sinful habits, and other stresses in life. We want to acknowledge that no matter what we face, mountains or molehills, we can overcome them only with the intervention of a loving heavenly

Dr. Elizabeth Thambiraj

Father who alone has the ability to scale the unscalable! By praying this, we acknowledge that You are sovereign and omniscient.

We pray, O God, that You would help us scale the unscalable through the precious blood that Jesus Christ shed for the remission of sins on Calvary. Through Him alone are redemption and sanctification and restoration to God, the Father, who is wise and all-powerful. Lord, we pray that if it is in Your will, you will bring the restoration of our relationship with the offender to bring glory and honor to Yourself. Thank You for the indwelling power of the Holy Spirit, who is able to help every believer who calls upon God in Christ Jesus.

As we pray, please remind us of this Word of God: "Now unto Him that is able to keep you from falling, and to present you faultless before the presence of His glory with exceeding joy, To the only wise God our savior, be glory and majesty, dominion and power, both now and forever; Amen" (Jude: 24–25).

A Prayer for Conflict between Husband and Wife

"For where envying and strife is, there is confusion and every evil work. But the wisdom that is from above is first pure, then peaceable, gentle, and easy to be intreated, full of mercy and good fruits, without partiality, and without hypocrisy. And the fruit of righteousness is sown in peace of them that make peace" (James: 3:16–18).

Omniscient, omnipresent, omnipotent God, the architect of all relationships, who cares for us deeply, we want to praise You and honor You, because You alone are worthy of all our praises. Thank you for the gift of Your Son, Jesus Christ, and for placing a blessed hope in our hearts. Thank you, because You know everything about us even before we speak to you.

Just like a child talking to an earthly father, we want to approach Your throne room of grace, fully acknowledging that You alone have the ability to scale the unscalable. Lord, my relationship with my spouse is muddled up, and I do not even know where to begin. More than changing my spouse, my humble petition is that You would change me. Show me areas of weakness in my life that need divine attention and speak to me through Your Word. Overwhelm me with Your love and compassion, and I pray that I do not allow a wedge to grow between the two of us. Lord, I am constantly reminded that what You have joined together, my spouse and I must not take for granted. "Wherefore they are no more twain, but one flesh. What therefore God hath joined together, let not man put asunder" (Mathew 19:6).

Almighty God, the Father, Your Word proclaims that all things work together for the good of those who love You in Romans 8:28: "And we know that all things work together for good to them that love God, to them who are the called according to his purpose." Even though it is beyond my comprehension in the midst of my marital strife, I trust that You are doing something good.

Dr. Elizabeth Thambiraj

Search my heart, O God, and show me areas of pride. Weed out any areas that are not pleasing to You, and if I am the reason for my problem, convict and confront me through the wonder-working power of the Holy Spirit. Convict me of my sin and cultivate Your humility so that I learn openly to confess my wrongdoing so I can be restored in my relationship with my spouse.

Father, I come to the conclusion that no matter how hard I try or how well I argue or reason, I am incapable of changing my spouse. This is the work of the Holy Spirit, and I refuse to usurp Your role in my spouse's life. To whatever extent my spouse is responsible for our conflict, change her or him for Your glory and honor.

I want to lay aside all anger, wrath, dissension, and bitterness and any offenses of the past. According to Your Word, love never keeps any record of wrongs; instead, it always protects, always trusts, always hopes, and always perseveres. Love "Doth not behave itself unseemly, seeketh not her own, is not easily provoked, thinketh no evil; Rejoiceth not in iniquity, but rejoiceth in the truth; Beareth all things, believeth all things, hopeth all things, endureth all things" (1 Corinthians 13:5–7). Please remind me of Proverbs 19:11—"the discretion of a man deferreth his anger; and it is to his glory to pass over a transgression"—so that I will understand it is to my glory to overlook an offence. I want to forgive my spouse for all the hurts he or she has inflicted, whether intentional or accidental. I do not want to be ensnared by foolish discussions and arrogant disputes and waste time on this earth. "But foolish and unlearned questions avoid, knowing that they do gender strifes. And the servant of the Lord must not strive; but be gentle unto all men, apt to teach, patient" (2 Tim: 2:23–24).

Please remind me that each time I feel resentful and prolong a dispute, I am giving the evil one a place in my heart, and this decreases my communion, fellowship, and joy with You. Lord, place a hedge of protection around our household so that the enemy will find no place in the covenant my spouse and I have established with You. Give us deep discernment to understand that as a couple we are fighting the common enemy of all believers. This enemy is Your enemy if we genuinely want to follow You.

Mystery of Relationships through the Lens of Scriptures

Lord, grant me wisdom from above so that I can distinguish my fleshly desires from the truth. Give me a sense of which battles are worth fighting and which are not. Restore me and revive me, O Lord, so that my spouse and I can live together again in agreement. Strengthen us as a result of this conflict and draw us closer to You and to each other. Let the seeds we sow in our relationship produce and yield a harvest of righteousness. "And the fruit of righteousness is sown in peace of them that make peace" (James 3:18).

Now to You, O Lord, wisdom, dominion, power, and majesty reign. Grant us grace upon grace to understand the depth of Your knowledge and wisdom according to Your Word in Ephesians 3:18–21, that we "May be able to comprehend with all saints what is the breadth, and length, and depth, and height; And to know the love of Christ, which passeth knowledge, that ye might be filled with all the fullness of God. Now unto him that is able to do exceeding abundantly above all that we ask or think, according to the power that worketh in us, Unto him be glory in the church by Christ Jesus throughout all ages, world without end; Amen."

Physical and Emotional Abuse

It is impossible to be spiritually mature when one is emotionally immature, says Peter Scazzero in his book *Emotionally Healthy Spirituality*. As the prophet Isaiah says, "For thus saith the Lord GOD, the Holy One of Israel; In returning and rest shall ye be saved; in quietness and in confidence shall be your strength: and ye would not" (Isaiah 30:15). Are we limiting God by the way we think? Imagine a circumstance that we consider bad. We can use whatever descriptive words we want to use—*difficult, hard, agonizing, frustrating, strenuous, debilitating, horrific, sorrowful, confusing, perturbing, penetrating,* or *painful.* Is there a problem too awful or too hard for God to handle? If our answer to this question is anything other than no, our understanding of God is too small. Our God is a great and limitless God. He dwells in eternity and operates in infinity. He has all things within His understanding and all things under His control, because He is omniscient, omnipotent, and omnipresent.

"Emotional abuse is difficult to define, and many cases are never reported; nevertheless, it's clear that this form of destructive behavior is based on power and control. An emotionally abusive person may dismiss your feelings and needs, expect you to perform humiliating or unpleasant tasks, manipulate you into feeling guilty for trivial things, belittle your outside support system, or blame you for unfortunate circumstances in his or her life. Jealousy, possessiveness, and mistrust characterize an emotionally abusive person".[1]

"Widely recognized types of emotional abuse include rejecting, degrading, terrorizing, isolating, exploiting, and detaching. Some examples include denying someone access to other relationships, taunting on the playground, yelling degrading remarks, downplaying accomplishments, and threatening to take the children away. From bullying and manipulative mind games to sexual harassment and elder neglect, emotional and verbal abuse are rampant in our society. No one is immune from encountering abusive people, but everyone can make healthy choices to end destructive relationship patterns".[2]

Mystery of Relationships through the Lens of Scriptures

[1,2]*Focus Helps* | **Emotional** *and verbal* **abuse** |

*www.focushelps.ca/article/addictions-**abuse**/verbal-**and-emotional*** ...

Apart from making healthy choices, we have a great God who empathizes and sympathizes with our situation, and we can go to Him in prayer for wisdom and discernment to make right choices in varied situations. The prayer below can be personalized and used for God's glory and honor.

Prayer

Dear Father in heaven, we come to Your throne room of grace knowing that Jesus, when He was on this earth, was abused, degraded, bullied, and even called Beelzebub. The finale came when Jesus was hanging on the cross. Those around him yelled, "Thou that destroyest the temple, and buildest it in three days, save thyself. If thou be the Son of God, come down from the cross" (Matthew 27:40). It is not surprising that we, as believers, experience similar abuse while on this earth, but at the same time, it is overwhelming, disheartening, and painful when we go through it.

We come to You as broken people, because an abusive spouse has battered us physically and emotionally to the point of despondency, and we pray for Your divine protection and intervention. We are in need of You, and we are desperate for You. Lord, You have said in Your Word that no one is to separate what you have joined together, and we pray that You would place a hedge of protection around our families according to Your Word. "Hast not thou made an hedge about him, and about his house, and about all that he hath on every side? thou hast blessed the work of his hands, and his substance is increased in the land" (Job 1:10). Shield us from further harm and allow us to find favor before You so that our families will not be dysfunctional but will be encouraged by Your love and by Your Word.

Lord, it is written in Your Word, that You will bless the righteous and will protect them: "For You, O Lord, will bless the righteous; With favor You will surround him as with a shield" (Psalm 5:12). We pray for a spouse entangled in the spirit of iniquity and the bondage of

Dr. Elizabeth Thambiraj

sin, corruption, anger, violence, and bitterness. Satan was a liar and a thief from the very beginning, and he wants to destroy family unity as he did in the Garden of Eden. Lord, we pray according to Your Word for abundant life for our spouses and our families. You said, "The thief cometh not, but for to steal, and to kill, and to destroy: I am come that they might have life, and that they might have it more abundantly" (John 10:10).

In 1 Corinthians 7:3–5, Apostle Paul writes, "Let the husband render unto the wife due benevolence: and likewise also the wife unto the husband. The wife hath not power of her own body, but the husband: and likewise also the husband hath not power of his own body, but the wife. Defraud ye not one the other, except it be with consent for a time, that ye may give yourselves to fasting and prayer; and come together again, that Satan tempt you not for your incontinency."

In accordance with Your Word, we pray for peace in our families and in our marriages so that our relationships may honor You. We pray for peace, harmony, calmness, and self-control in the abuser so that he or she may learn to love not only in word but also in deed and in truth. We want to remember Your Word, which says, "My little children, let us not love in word, neither in tongue; but indeed and in truth" (1 John 3:18). Change the heart of the abuser, O Lord, so that his or her eyes are opened to the truth. Transplant within the abuser a heart of flesh instead of a heart of stone. As You said in Your Word, "A new heart also will I give you, and a new spirit will I put within you: and I will take away the stony heart out of your flesh, and I will give you an heart of flesh" (Ezekiel 36:26).

We pray that the enemy will not condemn us forever and give us continuous guilt, because it is written, "There is therefore now no condemnation to them which are in Christ Jesus, who walk not after the flesh, but after the Spirit" (Romans 8:1). Lord, You have said in Your Word, that You are a God of generations, and You blessed Abraham's descendants through generations because of the covenant You made with him. We pray today that we may honor You in all of our ways, and if there is any generational pattern of sin in our families, we ask that You would uproot it completely so that we may be a genuine household of God.

Mystery of Relationships through the Lens of Scriptures

Dear God, as marriage is a covenant between two parties, and the heavenly Father is the genuine bride giver, we pray earnestly for Your divine intervention. We pray for repentance and restoration on both sides. Thank You for affirming Your love even for the evildoer in Your Word: "Say unto them, As I live, saith the Lord God, I have no pleasure in the death of the wicked; but that the wicked turn from his way and live: turn ye, turn ye from your evil ways; for why will ye die, O house of Israel?" (Ezekiel 33:11).

We pray for any venomous arrows that have pierced the heart of the abused person in the relationship and that could destroy the soul if not for the atoning blood of Jesus Christ. We ask for healing and atonement. "But he was wounded for our transgressions, he was bruised for our iniquities: the chastisement of our peace was upon him; and with his stripes we are healed" (Isaiah 53:5). Your promises assure us that You are our hiding place, that You preserve us from trouble, and that You will surround us with songs of deliverance whenever we call upon You. As the psalmist writes, "Thou art my hiding place; thou shalt preserve me from trouble; thou shalt compass me about with songs of deliverance" (Psalm 32:7).

When we are conflicted, confronted, confused, and confounded, You are our only refuge and shelter and the only One who is able to bring us out of confusion and instill within us the strength necessary for those situations. Thank you for warning in Your Word, "Wherefore take unto you the whole armour of God, that ye may be able to withstand in the evil day, and having done all, to stand" (Ephesians 6:13). We pray for courage so we can confide in someone who bears a burden. According to Your Word, "without counsel purposes are disappointed: but in the multitude of counsellors they are established" (Proverbs 15:22). Give us grace so that we can move with wisdom and discernment from here.

We want to sing the wondrous story of Jesus and His life, giving hope to others who walk through overwhelming, perilous situations. We ask You to bestow on us beauty for ashes, oil of joy for mourning, a garment of praise for heaviness, and may we be called a tree of righteousness and a planting of the Lord. Thank You for Your assurance of hope in Your Word.

Dr. Elizabeth Thambiraj

> The Spirit of the Lord God is upon me; because the Lord hath anointed me to preach good tidings unto the meek; he hath sent me to bind up the broken-hearted, to proclaim liberty to the captives, and the opening of the prison to them that are bound; To proclaim the acceptable year of the Lord, and the day of vengeance of our God; to comfort all that mourn; To appoint unto them that mourn in Zion, to give unto them beauty for ashes, the oil of joy for mourning, the garment of praise for the spirit of heaviness; that they might be called trees of righteousness, the planting of the Lord, that he might be glorified. (Isaiah 61:1–3).

Give us grace upon grace in our lives so that we may learn "And to know the love of Christ, which passeth knowledge, that ye might be filled with all the fulness of God. Now unto him that is able to do exceeding abundantly above all that we ask or think, according to the power that worketh in us, Unto him be glory in the church by Christ Jesus throughout all ages, world without end. Amen" (Ephesians 3:19–21).

A Prayer for an Unsaved Spouse

Dear heavenly Father, I come to You because You said in Your Word that it was not in Your will that anyone should perish. It is written that "The Lord is not slack concerning his promise, as some men count slackness; but is longsuffering to us-ward, not willing that any should perish, but that all should come to repentance" (2 Peter 3:9). I come to you in boldness, standing firmly on Your Word. "And this is the confidence that we have in him, that, if we ask any thing according to his will, he heareth us: And if we know that he hear us, whatsoever we ask, we know that we have the petitions that we desired of him" (1 John 5:14–15).

Lord Jesus, when You hung on the cross, it was not only for me but also for my spouse. When you rose up from the dead, You broke the powers of darkness in order to free humanity from the bondage of sin and death. This truth applies for my spouse too, and I stand in agreement with Your will and ask that You will free my spouse from bondage and darkness. I pray that You will shut his or her eyes to the enticing scenes of the enemy and remove any influences that would draw him or her away from You.

Father, You are worthy of all of our praises. "For ye have not received the spirit of bondage again to fear; but ye have received the Spirit of adoption, whereby we cry, Abba, Father" (Romans 8:15). I ask, according to Your Word, that You would send the spirit of adoption and adopt my spouse, and I release him or her to You so that he or she may be brought to the place of complete submission to Your sovereignty.

There is nothing I can do apart from asking You to do the divine work in my spouse's life to open his or her heart to Your truth. Place godly people around my spouse who will speak the truth in love in his or her life, and use them to change his or her heart of stone to a heart of flesh. Show me my part in Your redemptive work, and guide me so I may follow what You want me to do. Bring my spouse under the convicting power of the Holy Spirit. Replace our unequal yoke with an equal one. It is written, "Be ye not unequally yoked together

189

Dr. Elizabeth Thambiraj

with unbelievers: for what fellowship hath righteousness with unrighteousness? And what communion hath light with darkness?" (2 Corinthians 6:14). I want to serve You with all my family and with my spouse, and I pray that You will answer my prayer for Your glory and Your honor. Amen.

Professional Comment from the Author

This book is on a biblical view of marriage, and it is useful in general to get a biblical perspective on marriage. In my personal life and in my practice, I have witnessed that marriage is indeed work, and sometimes when the work is hard, we may need some help along the way. The God of the universe, who created marriage as the first divine institution, wants to be a part of our marriages. It is much easier to ignore this than to make it a reality in our marriages.

God is a God of generations, and if we don't deal with generational dysfunction biblically, it can pass on to future generations. We can use genograms to spot generational dysfunction and to work on various destructive issues. Above all, the Word of God stands inerrant in all situations.

If God is not the first priority in a marriage, something else becomes our god; it is very easy to make that thing an idol. This could be one of the three *A*'s: abuse, alcoholism, or addiction. Without even realizing, we can be lovers of ourselves rather than lovers of God. We can also be so selfish that there is no place for God and His leading in our marriages. It is possible we can worship ourselves because of our selfish nature rather than worshipping God of the universe.

God works through parents when we raise children. If the parents do not take authority or if the spouse with the stronger will does not intentionally share authority, the children inevitably begin to take advantage and rule. It is not God's way of parenting but rather worldly to side with a child rather than sharing parenting role with a spouse. This will lead to confusion and conflicts in a marriage. It is important that spouses respect each other's views in running the affairs of family life.

God is a God of truth, and if there is a third person in a marriage, there will be betrayal and loss of trust. This third person could be

Dr. Elizabeth Thambiraj

a parent, a work colleague, or an in-law. My question here is this: biblically, what does it means to leave and cleave?

God hates idolatry, and it is a religious sin. God gave the nation of Israel specific instructions not to follow the practices of the nations around them. If a member of the family or one of the spouses is involved in occult practices, it could cause havoc for the couple. In a way, their marriage is unequally yoked, and this could lead to devastation and huge trials. In other words, no matter how rich someone's education may be, if he or she is not rich toward God, he or she does not know the God of the Bible.

When women are more educated than their husbands are, how does biblical submission apply? What do we understand by biblical submission and biblical authority? How does the abuse of authority affect marriage? What is the difference between godly authority and ungodly authority?

My book on a biblical approach to nonorganic illnesses addressed many issues including fear, anxiety, bitterness, anger, resentment, jealousy, and depression, and it mentions tips to help relationships. An organic illness could bring devastation to a relationship if not handled in a godly way. Organic illnesses require medication, and we have to remind ourselves of the words of Jesus Christ: "The sick need the physician."

The above are areas where a marriage can suffer without careful attention. It is much easier for resentment to settle in if spouses take love for granted, and love could become bankrupt.

It is important to understand and realize the meaning of the following verses. Song of Solomon 2:16a says, "My beloved is mine, and I am his," and Song of Solomon 6:3a says, "I am my beloved's, and my beloved is mine." The only way we can own the Lord is to be owned by Him. "We love Him because He first loved us" (1 John 4:19). This is the common order of love between a husband and wife. The fair lady is easy to love, but the rough and rugged gentleman is less lovely. But the love of a man for his chosen bride will win the lady if it is sincere, genuine, and unrelenting. We cannot love that which

Mystery of Relationships through the Lens of Scriptures

we have not known. We cannot know the Lord until He has loved us. He loved and knew His elect before they were yet conceived in their mother's womb. - Dr. Jerry L. Ogles DD

It is vital to remind ourselves what the book of Deuteronomy says about the commandments and judgments of God.

> Now these are the commandments, the statutes, and the judgments, which the Lord your God commanded to teach you, that ye might do them in the land whither ye go to possess it: That thou mightest fear the Lord thy God, to keep all his statutes and his commandments, which I command thee, thou, and thy son, and thy son's son, all the days of thy life; and that thy days may be prolonged. Hear therefore, O Israel, and observe to do it; that it may be well with thee, and that ye may increase mightily, as the Lord God of thy fathers hath promised thee, in the land that floweth with milk and honey. (Deuteronomy 6:1–3)

It is exciting to explore God's design for marriage. I pray for all those who want to explore God's design that applying God's Word will change our marriages, strengthening and enriching them.

- Let us be willing to struggle rather than demanding a quick fix. Growth in marriage involves far more than demanding something right. It involves lot of involvement as a couple to pray and to search the Bible for truth about ourselves and our marriages.
- Let us be willing and open to talking with our spouses about the issues in our marriages. These issues could bring up deep emotions, and discussing them will be a difficult experience, but if the God of the Bible is in our relationships, we have hope.
- Commit to pray for each other daily in struggles as well as in joy.
- Be willing to dream rather than living with expectations that are far below God's design.

Dr. Elizabeth Thambiraj

The Route to Intimacy

Apostle Paul describes in his letters to Corinthians and Ephesians, "lives to glorify other." Marriage is hard work, and it is ministry, and God calls us to care less about ourselves than we do about our spouses. If we enter a relationship to find someone who will labor for our glory, then we will violate and drain that person's capacity to offer life.

We have to believe that even in deceit and betrayal, God's Spirit is at work, convicting, confronting, and conforming both spouses to a maturity that cannot be achieved without brokenness and suffering. Where is God in our marriages? What is His role, and how much do we believe His word?

It is written in the Scriptures that "Two are better than one; because they have a good reward for their labour. For if they fall, the one will lift up his fellow: but woe to him that is alone when he falleth; for he hath not another to help him up. Again, if two lie together, then they have heat: but how can one be warm alone? And if one prevail against him, two shall withstand him; and a threefold cord is not quickly broken" (Ecclesiastes 4:9–12).

From the above verses, it is clear that a monastic life was never intended for a state of perfection. When two are joined together in holy love and fellowship, Christ, by His Spirit, will come to them and make the third. Christ joined Himself with the two disciples going to Emmaus, and a cord of three strands can never be broken. This principle applies to Christian marriages, and this is good food for thought. By saying this I do not intend to say that by living alone one cannot attain a state of perfection in holy love and fellowship in Christ.

Truth, when we take it to heart and apply it in our lives, sets us free from any dysfunction. This may be difficult, but it will result in a victorious life. Through the tremendous mercy of God, I have seen addictions healed, divorced couples dating again their former spouses again, and many spouses in troubled relationships wanted to have victorious lives. There is power in God's truth that is able to break

Mystery of Relationships through the Lens of Scriptures

strongholds and defeat anything that rises against the knowledge of God.

We have to remember that our weapons of warfare are not carnal but spiritual. "For though we walk in the flesh, we do not war after the flesh: (For the weapons of our warfare are not carnal, but mighty through God to the pulling down of strong holds ;) Casting down imaginations, and every high thing that exalteth itself against the knowledge of God, and bringing into captivity every thought to the obedience of Christ; And having in a readiness to revenge all disobedience, when your obedience is fulfilled" (2 Corinthians 10:3–6).

My deepest desire is for the dreams of couples to be fulfilled in Christ Jesus and for marriages to enjoy intimacy mirroring the intimacy of the Father and His Son, Jesus Christ. John 17:21–23 says, "That they all may be one; as thou, Father, art in me, and I in thee, that they also may be one in us: that the world may believe that thou hast sent me. And the glory which thou gavest me I have given them; that they may be one, even as we are one: I in them, and thou in me, that they may be made perfect in one; and that the world may know that thou hast sent me, and hast loved them, as thou hast loved me."

The Word of God says, "For my people have committed two evils; they have forsaken me the fountain of living waters, and hewed them out cisterns, broken cisterns, that can hold no water" (Jeremiah 2:13). Jesus Christ is the fountain of living water, the true cistern that can hold water, and it is heart breaking to know that we run after broken cisterns that cannot hold water! May we humble ourselves and hunger and seek after what God has intended in our marriages.

Notes

Part I

End Notes

1. Genesis 4 - Matthew Henry's Commentary - Bible Commentary

   www.christnotes.org › ... › Matthew Henry's Commentary › Genesis

   Bible commentary about Genesis 4 (Matthew Henry's Commentary). Bible Commentary. Christ Notes. Bible Search | Commentaries | Dictionaries | Email | Daily Verse ...

2. Ibid.

3. Ibid.

4. "Full Armor of God," www.christianarsenal.com/Christian_Arsenal/Full_Armor_of_God.html.

   Using the Roman Soldier's armor as a visual example, the Apostle Paul describes the Armor of God in the Book of Ephesians as both ... 32 caliber 6 shot revolver

5. Mathew Henry, *The Matthew Henry's Commentary on Revelations 19:1-10.*

6. Ibid.

Website References

1. Ephesians 5 - Matthew Henry's Commentary - Bible Commentary

   www.christnotes.org › ... › Matthew Henry's Commentary › Ephesians

   Bible commentary about Ephesians 5 (Matthew Henry's Commentary). ...

   << Ephesians 4 | Ephesians 5 | Ephesians 6 >> (Read all of Ephesians 5) Related Commentaries.

Dr. Elizabeth Thambiraj

2. Ephesians 5:1 - Matthew Henry's Complete Commentary on the ...

    www.studylight.org/com/mhm/view.cgi?book=eph&chapter=5

    "Let no man deceive you with vain words, &c., Ephesians 5:6. ...

    "Complete Commentary on Ephesians 5:1". "Matthew Henry Complete Commentary.

3. Ephesians - Matthew Henry's Commentary - Bible Gateway

    www.biblegateway.com › Resources › Matthew Henry's Commentary

    Resources » Matthew Henry's Commentary » Ephesians. ... Chapter 5; Verses 1–2; Verses 3 ...

    Verses 10–18; Verses 19–24; Some think that this epistle to the ...

4. Matthew Henry's Complete Commentary on the Bible - Ephesians 6

    www.ewordtoday.com/comments/ephesians/mh/ephesians6.htm

    Complete commentary on the Bible by Matthew Henry. ... Introduction 1 2 3 4 5 6 ...

    which makes Paul's love to these Christian Ephesians the ...

5. Revelation 19 - Matthew Henry's Commentary - Bible ...

    www.christnotes.org › ... › Matthew Henry's Commentary › Revelation

    Bible commentary about Revelation 19 (Matthew Henry's Commentary).

    Bible Commentary. Christ Notes. Bible Search ...

6. Ephesians 6 - Matthew Henry's Commentary - Bible Commentary

    www.christnotes.org › ... › Matthew Henry's Commentary › Ephesians

    Bible commentary about Ephesians 6 (Matthew Henry's Commentary)

7. Ephesians 6:10-18 - Effective Spiritual Warfare

    www.xenos.org/teachings/?teaching=1366

    Effective Spiritual Warfare Ephesians 6:10-18.

Mystery of Relationships through the Lens of Scriptures

Teaching ... 6:10-20 tells us to "stand"—to trust God ... believe—that our acceptance by God is based on our.

8.   Sermon on Ephesians 6:10-18 | The spiritual warfare

www.virtualpreacher.org/sermon-outlines/spiritual-warfare

Text: Ephesians 6:10-18. 1. Tapping the source of strength. Read Ephesians 6:10-11. ...

Read Ephesians 6:12-13. A. In warfare gathering intelligence is key.

9.   The Invisible War Spiritual Warfare 101: What is (Part 1 ...

livingontheedge.org/ ... war-satan-demons-and-spritual-warfare.pdf · PDF file

Ephesians 6:11-18 Spiritual Warfare – Ray C. Stedman ... Ephesians 6:18-20 ... Ephesians 6:10-12 (NAS)

10. Revelation 21 Commentary - Matthew Henry Commentary on the ...

www.biblestudytools.com › Revelation

Read Revelation 21 commentary using Matthew Henry Commentary on the Whole Bible (Concise).

Study the bible online using commentary on Revelation 21 and more!

11. Chapter 21 - Matthew Henry's Commentary - Bible Gateway

www.biblegateway.com › ... › Matthew Henry's Commentary › Revelation

Resources » Matthew Henry's Commentary » Revelation » Chapter 21. ... II.

The vision itself, Rev. 21:10-27 ^ Go to the top of the page. Home; Passage Lookup

12. Ephesians 6 Pictures, Images & Photos - Photobucket

photobucket.com/images/Ephesians+6

Ephesians 6 Images, Ephesians 6 Pictures. Download photos or share to Facebook, ...

The Sword of The Spirit is the Word of God Resist the devil and He must flee ...

Dr. Elizabeth Thambiraj

Other References

1. Dan Allender and Tremper Longman III, *Intimate Allies* (Carol Stream, IL: Tyndale House, 1995).

2. I. Goldenberg and H. Goldenberg, *Family Therapy: An Overview* (Pacific Grove, CA: Brookes/Cole Publishing, 2007).

3. R. W. Richardson, *Family Ties That Bind* (Vancouver, BC: International Self-Counsel Press, 1995).

4. Gary Thomas, *Sacred Marriage: What If God Designed Marriage More to Make Us Holy Than to Make Us Happy* (Toronto: Harper Collins Canada, 2002).

5. Mary E. DeMuth, *Authentic Parenting in a Postmodern Culture: Practical Help for Shaping Your Children's Hearts, Minds, and Souls* (Eugene, OR: Harvest House Publishers, 2007).

6. William T. Kirwan, *Biblical Concepts for Christian Counseling: A Case for Integrating Psychology and Theology* (Grand Rapids, MI: Baker Book House, 1984).

Recommended Reading & Resources

7. Larry Crabb, *Effective Biblical Counseling: How caring Christians Can Become Capable Counselors* (Grand Rapids, MI: Zondervan, 1977).

8. Everett L. Worthington Jr. Author of Forgiving and Reconciling, *Hope-Focused Marriage Counseling* (IL: IVP Academic, 2005), ISBN-10: 0-8308-2764-1

9. Russell Barkley and Arthur Robin, *Your Defiant Teen: 10 Steps to Resolve Conflict and Rebuild Your Relationship* (New York: A division of Guilford Publications, 2008).

10. David Furlong, *Healing Your Family Patterns: How to Access the Past to Heal the Present* (London: Judy Piatkus, 1997).

Book References

1. Millard J. Erickson, *Christian Theology* (Grand Rapids, MI: Baker Book House, 19885), 947–1002.

2. R. T. Kendall, *Understanding Theology: Developing a Healthy Church in the 21st Century.* Christian Focus Publications; 1st Edition Thus edition (1998), 357-364.

Mystery of Relationships through the Lens of Scriptures

3. Jay E. Adams, *A Theology of Christian Counseling: More than Redemption* (Grand Rapids, MI: Zondervan, 1979), 249–275.

4. Louis Berkhof, *Systematic Theology* (Grand Rapids, MI: Eerdmans, 1996), 423–450.

5. Robert P. Lightner, *Handbook of Evangelical Theology: Historical, Biblical, and Contemporary Survey and Review* (Grand Rapids, MI: Baker Book House, 1986), 527–544.

6. Charles Ryrie, *Basic Theology* (Chicago: Moody Press, 1999), 374–377.

7. A. H. Strong, *Systematic Theology* (NJ: Fleming H. Revell, 1907), 869–881.

8. Wayne Grudem, *Systematic Theology: An Introduction to Biblical Doctrine* (Grand Rapids, MI: Zondervan, 1994), 736–761; 840–850.

9. Steven W. Waterhouse, *Not By Bread Alone: An Outlined Guide to Bible Doctrine* (Amarillo, TX: Westcliffe Press, 2007), 188–191.

10. John Theodore Muller, *Christian Dogmatics: A handbook of Doctrinal Theology for Pastors, Teachers, and Laymen* (St. Louis, MO: Concordia Publishing House, 1934) 384–386.

11. "Prayer to Move Your Mountains," *Powerful Prayers for The Spirit-Filled Life* (Nashville, Tennessee: Thomas Nelson, Inc, 2000).

12. John White, *Parables: The Greatest Stories Ever Told* (IL: Intervarsity Press, 1999).

13. *The ESV Study Bible* (Wheaton, IL: Crossway Bibles, 2008).

14. *The Matthew Henry Study Bible* (Iowa Falls, IA: World Bible Publishing, 1990).

Part II

A Litmus Test for Relationship with God

End Notes

1. "Prayer," *Wikipedia,* last modified May 17, 2015, http://en.wikipedia.org/wiki/Prayer.

    Prayer is an invocation or act that seeks to activate a rapport with a deity, an object of worship, or a spiritual entity through deliberate communication. Prayer can …

Dr. Elizabeth Thambiraj

2. "Prayers and Blessings," *Judaism 101,* www.jewfaq.org/prayer.htm.

    Tefilah: Prayer. The Hebrew word for prayer is tefilah. It is derived from the root Pe-Lamed-Lamed and the word l'hitpalel, meaning to judge oneself.

Website References

1. Prayer and relationship with God | daily meditation

    dailymedit.wordpress.com/2013/06/11/prayer-and-relationship-with ...

    2013-06-11 · Genesis 18:33: And the LORD went his way, when he had finished speaking to Abraham, and Abraham returned to his place. Communication is the mark of ...

2. Prayer and the God who listens - Resources for the seeking spirit

    www.spirithome.com/prayersp.html

    Prayer as communication within a living relationship with God. Praying for enemies. Praying amiss. What God is listening for, and what you might discover.

3. "How Do You Have A Relationship With God?" *Clarifying Christianity,* www. clarifyingchristianity.com/relationship.shtml.

    Although not part of the model prayer, when God does ... these examples show a belief system that does not allow a personal relationship with God. From Part ...

4. Prayer Secret #1 - Your Personal Relationship With God

    www.bible-knowledge.com/prayer-secret-1

5. Prayer Secret #1 Your Personal Relationship With God.

    This, in my opinion, is the #1 secret for being able to get more of your personal prayers answered by God the ...

Book References

1. Peter Scazzero, *Emotionally Healthy Spirituality* (Thomas Nelson, 2011).

2. I. Goldenberg and H. Goldenberg, *Family Therapy: An Overview* (Pacific Grove, CA: Brookes/Cole Publishing, 2007).

Mystery of Relationships through the Lens of Scriptures

3. Devotions excerpted from the NIV Marriage Devotional Bible, *God's Words of Life on Marriage* (Zondervan, 2000). ISBN 0-310-98358-5

Other References

1. Dan Allender and Tremper Longman III, *Intimate Allies* (Carol Stream, IL: Tyndale House, 1995).

2. I. Goldenberg and H. Goldenberg, *Family Therapy: An Overview* (Pacific Grove, CA: Brookes/Cole Publishing, 2007).

3. R. W. Richardson, *Family Ties That Bind* (Vancouver, BC: International Self-Counsel Press, 1995).

4. Gary Thomas, *Sacred Marriage: What If God Designed Marriage More to Make Us Holy than to Make Us Happy* (Toronto: Harper Collins Canada, 2002).

5. Mary E. DeMuth, *Authentic Parenting in a Postmodern Culture: Practical Help for Shaping Your Children's Hearts, Minds, and Souls* (Eugene, OR: Harvest House Publishers, 2007).

6. William T. Kirwan, *Biblical Concepts for Christian Counseling: A Case for Integrating Psychology and Theology* (Grand Rapids, MI: Baker Book House, 1984).

Recommended Reading & Resources

7. Larry Crabb, *Effective Biblical Counseling: How Caring Christians Can Become Capable Counselors* (Grand Rapids, MI: Zondervan, 1977).

8. Everett L. Worthington Jr., *Hope-Focused Marriage Counseling* (IL: IVP Academic, 2005).

9. Russell Barkley and Arthur Robin, *Your Defiant Teen: 10 Steps to Resolve Conflict and Rebuild Your Relationship* (New York: A division of Guilford Publications, 2008).

10. David Furlong, *Healing Your Family Patterns: How to Access the Past to Heal the Present* (London: Judy Piatkus, 1997).

Dr. Elizabeth Thambiraj

For Further Reading

1. Millard J. Erickson, *Christian Theology* (Grand Rapids, MI: Baker Book House, 1985), 947–1002.

2. R. T. Kendall, *Understanding Theology: Developing a Healthy Church in the 21ˢᵗ Century* (1996), 357–364.

3. Jay E. Adams, *A Theology of Christian Counseling: More than Redemption* (Grand Rapids, MI: Zondervan, 1979), 249–275.

4. Louis Berkhof, *Systematic Theology* (Grand Rapids, MI: Eerdmans, 1996), 423–450.

5. Robert P. Lightner, *Handbook of Evangelical Theology: Historical, Biblical, and Contemporary Survey and Review* (Grand Rapids, MI: Baker Book House, 1986), 527–544.

6. Charles Ryrie, *Basic Theology* (Chicago: Moody Press, 1999), 374–377.

7. A. H. Strong, *Systematic Theology* (NJ: Fleming H. Revell, 1907), 869–881.

8. Wayne Grudem, *Systematic Theology: An Introduction to Biblical Doctrine* (Grand Rapids, MI: Zondervan, 1994), 736–761; 840–850.

9. Steven W. Waterhouse, *Not by Bread Alone: An Outlined Guide to Bible Doctrine* (Amarillo, TX: Westcliffe Press, 2007), 188–191.

10. John Theodore Muller, *Christian Dogmatics: A Handbook of Doctrinal Theology for Pastors, Teachers, and Laymen* (St. Louis, MO: Concordia Publishing House, 1934), 384–386.

11. "Prayer to Move Your Mountains," *Powerful Prayers for The Spirit-Filled Life* (Nashville, TN: Thomas Nelson, 2000).

12. John White, *Parables: The Greatest Stories Ever Told* (IL: Inter varsity Press, 1999).

13. *The ESV Study Bible* (Wheaton, IL: Crossway Bibles, 2008).

14. *The Matthew Henry Study Bible* (Iowa Falls, IA: World Bible Publishing, 1990).

Mystery of Relationships through the Lens of Scriptures

How Can I Be a Loving Neighbor?

End Notes

1. *Dictionary.com,* s.v. "neighbor," dictionary.reference.com/browse/neighbor.

2. What is the Greek word for 'neighbor'? | ChaCha

   www.chacha.com/question/what-is-the-greek-word-for-%27neighbor%27

   What is the Greek word for 'neighbor'? ChaCha Answer: The English language word "neighbor" translates to "geitonas" in the Greek lang ...

3. Vern Sheridan Poythress, *Westminster Theological Journal* 50, no. 1 (1988): 27–64, used with permission.

4. *Babylon 9 Translation Software and Dictionary Tool,* www.babylon.com/definition/neighbor/Greek.

   English - Greek Technical Dictionary: Download this dictionary: neighbor (Lex**) γείτονας ... neighbour. γείτονας English Greek Technical Dictionary

Book References

1. Peter Scazzero, *Emotionally Healthy Spirituality* (Thomas Nelson, 2011).

2. I. Goldenberg and H. Goldenberg, *Family Therapy: An Overview* (Pacific Grove, CA: Brookes/Cole Publishing, 2007).

3. *God's Words of Life on Marriage* (Zondervan, 2000).

Other References

1. Dan Allender and Tremper Longman III, *Intimate Allies* (Carol Stream, IL: Tyndale House, 1995).

2. I. Goldenberg and H. Goldenberg, *Family Therapy: An Overview* (Pacific Grove, CA: Brookes/Cole Publishing, 2007).

3. R. W. Richardson, *Family Ties That Bind* (Vancouver, BC: International Self-Counsel Press. 1995).

Dr. Elizabeth Thambiraj

4. Gary Thomas, *Sacred Marriage: What If God Designed Marriage More to Make Us Holy than to Make Us Happy* (Toronto: Harper Collins Canada, 2002).

5. Mary E. DeMuth, *Authentic Parenting in a Postmodern Culture: Practical Help for Shaping Your Children's Hearts, Minds, and Souls* (Eugene, OR: Harvest House Publishers, 2007).

6. William T. Kirwan, *Biblical Concepts for Christian Counseling: A Case for Integrating Psychology and Theology* (Grand Rapids, MI: Baker Book House, 1984).

Recommended Reading & Resources

7. Larry Crabb, *Effective Biblical Counseling: How Caring Christians Can Become Capable Counselors* (Grand Rapids, MI: Zondervan, 1977).

8. Everett L. Worthington Jr., *Hope-Focused Marriage Counseling* (IL: IVP Academic, 2005).

9. Russell Barkley and Arthur Robin, *Your Defiant Teen: 10 Steps to Resolve Conflict and Rebuild Your Relationship* (New York: A division of Guilford Publications, 2008).

10. David Furlong, *Healing Your Family Patterns: How toAaccess the Past to Heal the Present* (London: Judy Piatkus, 1997).

For Further Reading

1. Millard J. Erickson, *Christian Theology* (Grand Rapids: Baker Book House, 1985), 947–1002.

2. R. T. Kendall, *Understanding Theology: Developing a Healthy Church in the 21st Century* (1996), 357–364.

3. Jay E. Adams, *A Theology of Christian Counseling: More than Redemption* (Grand Rapids, MI: Zondervan, 1979), 249–275.

4. Louis Berkhof, *Systematic Theology* (Grand Rapids, MI: Eerdmans, 1996), 423–450.

5. Robert P. Lightner, *Handbook of Evangelical Theology: Historical, Biblical, and Contemporary Survey and Review* (Grand Rapids, MI: Baker Book House, 1986), 527–544.

6. Charles Ryrie, *Basic Theology* (Chicago: Moody Press, 1999), 374–377.

Mystery of Relationships through the Lens of Scriptures

7.   A. H. Strong, *Systematic Theology* (NJ: Fleming H. Revell, 1907), 869–881.

8.   Wayne Grudem, *Systematic Theology: An Introduction to Biblical Doctrine* (Grand Rapids, MI: Zondervan, 1994), 736–761; 840–850.

9.   Steven W. Waterhouse, *Not by Bread Alone: An Outlined Guide to Bible Doctrine* (Amarillo, TX: Westcliffe Press, 2007), 188–191.

10. John Theodore Muller, *Christian Dogmatics: A Handbook of Doctrinal Theology for Pastors, Teachers, and Laymen* (St. Louis, MO: Concordia Publishing House, 1934), 384–386.

11. "Prayer to Move Your Mountains," *Powerful Prayers for The Spirit-Filled Life* (Nashville, TN: Thomas Nelson, 2000).

12. John White, *Parables: The Greatest Stories Ever Told* (IL: Intervarsity Press, 1999).

13. *The ESV Study Bible* (Wheaton, IL: Crossway Bibles, 2008).

14. *The Matthew Henry Study Bible* (Iowa Falls, IA: World Bible Publishing, 1990).

Male and Female: Divine Comedy or Brilliance?

For Further Reading

"The Hardwired Difference between Male and Female Brains Could Explain Why Men Are 'Better at Map Reading,'" *The Independent*, http://www.independent.co.uk/life-style/the-hardwired-difference-between-male-and-female-brains-could-explain-why-men-are-better-at-map-reading-8978248.html.

Intuition is thinking without thinking. It's what people call gut feelings.

End Notes

1.   A. Schaffer, "The Male/Female Brain," *Brain Health & Brain Fitness Blog*, www.fitbrains.com/blog/2008/10/ ... /the-malefemale-brai ...

21 Oct 2008 – He and his colleagues sampled speech from male and female college students, who ... translator of Dante's Divine Comedy from Italian into English verse. ... background with Lewis in terms of class and intellectual brilliance, ...

Dr. Elizabeth Thambiraj

2.	Hebrew, letters, love, maleness, femaleness, ahab, ahabah, agape

	spiritualsprings.org/ss-16.htm

	Strong's Number or Single Word Search. Spiritual Springs: File z = 16. Hebrew, letters, love, maleness, femaleness, ahab, ahabah, agape … This is the Hebrew word for femaleness love. The "strong … May God bless our relearning of His love.

3.	Dan Allender and Tremper Longman III, *Intimate Allies* (Carol Stream, IL: Tyndale House, 1995), 144, 158, 159.

4.	Ibid.

Website References

1.	A. Schaffer, "The Male/Female Brain," *Brain Health & Brain Fitness Blog,*

	www.fitbrains.com/blog/2008/10/ … /the-malefemale-brai …

	21 Oct 2008 – He and his colleagues sampled speech from male and female college students, who … … translator of Dante's Divine Comedy from Italian into English verse. … background with Lewis in terms of class and intellectual brilliance, …

2.	Hebrew, letters, love, maleness, femaleness, ahab, ahabah, agape

	spiritualsprings.org/ss-16.htm

	Strong's Number or Single Word Search. Spiritual Springs: File z = 16. Hebrew, letters, love, maleness, femaleness, ahab, ahabah, agape … This is the Hebrew word for femaleness love. The "strong … May God bless our relearning of His love.

Book References

1.	Gary Thomas, *Sacred Marriage: What If God Designed Marriage More to Make Us Holy than to Make Us Happy* (Toronto: Harper Collins Canada, 2002).

2.	Claire Smith, *God's Good Design: What the Bible Really Says about Men and Women* (Kingsford, Australia: Matthiasmedia, 2012), 105–155.

3.	Dan Allender and Tremper Longman III, *Intimate Allies* (Carol Stream, IL: Tyndale House, 1995).

Mystery of Relationships through the Lens of Scriptures

Further References

1. Peter Scazzero, *Emotionally Healthy Spirituality* (Thomas Nelson, 2011).

2. I. Goldenberg and H. Goldenberg, *Family Therapy: An Overview* (Pacific Grove, CA: Brookes/Cole Publishing, 2007).

3. *God's Words of Life on Marriage* (Zondervan, 2000).

Other References

1. Dan Allender and Tremper Longman III, *Intimate Allies* (Carol Stream, IL: Tyndale House, 1995).

2. I. Goldenberg and H. Goldenberg, *Family Therapy: An Overview* (Pacific Grove, CA: Brookes/Cole Publishing, 2007).

3. R. W. Richardson, *Family Ties That Bind* (Vancouver, BC: International Self-Counsel Press. 1995).

4. Gary Thomas, *Sacred Marriage: What If God Designed Marriage More to Make Us Holy than to Make Us Happy* (Toronto: Harper Collins Canada, 2002).

5. Mary E. DeMuth, *Authentic Parenting in a Postmodern Culture: Practical Help for Shaping Your Children's Hearts, Minds, and Souls* (Eugene, OR: Harvest House Publishers, 2007).

6. William T. Kirwan, *Biblical Concepts for Christian Counseling: A Case for Integrating Psychology and Theology* (Grand Rapids, MI: Baker Book House, 1984).

Recommended Reading & Resources

7. Larry Crabb, *Effective Biblical Counseling: How Caring Christians Can Become Capable Counselors* (Grand Rapids, MI: Zondervan, 1977).

8. Everett L. Worthington Jr., *Hope-Focused Marriage Counseling* (IL: IVP Academic, 2005).

9. Russell Barkley and Arthur Robin, *Your Defiant Teen: 10 Steps to Resolve Conflict and Rebuild Your Relationship* (New York: A division of Guilford Publications, 2008).

Dr. Elizabeth Thambiraj

10. David Furlong, *Healing Your Family Patterns: How to Access the Past to Heal the Present* (London: Judy Piatkus, 1997).

Marriage

End Notes

1. Dan Allender and Tremper Longman III, *Intimate Allies* (Carol Stream, IL: Tyndale House, 1995), 346–347.

2. Ibid.

3. Ibid., 211.

Book Reference

Dan Allender and Tremper Longman III, *Intimate Allies* (Carol Stream, IL: Tyndale House, 1995).

Other Book References

1. Peter Scazzero, *Emotionally Healthy Spirituality* (Thomas Nelson, 2011).

2. I. Goldenberg and H. Goldenberg, *Family Therapy: An Overview* (Pacific Grove, CA: Brookes/Cole Publishing, 2007)

3. *God's Words of Life on Marriage* (Zondervan, 2000).

Other References

1. Dan Allender and Tremper Longman III, *Intimate Allies* (Carol Stream, IL: Tyndale House, 1995).

2. I. Goldenberg and H. Goldenberg, *Family Therapy: An Overview* (Pacific Grove, CA: Brookes/Cole Publishing, 2007)

3. R. W. Richardson, *Family Ties That Bind* (Vancouver, BC: International Self-Counsel Press, 1995).

Mystery of Relationships through the Lens of Scriptures

4. Gary Thomas, *Sacred Marriage: What If God Designed Marriage More to Make Us Holy than to Make Us Happy* (Toronto: Harper Collins Canada, 2002).

5. Mary E. DeMuth, *Authentic Parenting in a Postmodern Culture: Practical Help for Shaping Your Children's Hearts, Minds, and Souls* (Eugene, OR: Harvest House Publishers, 2007).

6. William T. Kirwan, *Biblical Concepts for Christian Counseling: A Case for Integrating Psychology and Theology* (Grand Rapids, MI: Baker Book House, 1984).

Recommended Reading & Resources

7. Larry Crabb, *Effective Biblical Counseling: How Caring Christians Can Become Capable Counselors* (Grand Rapids, MI: Zondervan, 1977).

8. Everett L. Worthington Jr., *Hope-Focused Marriage Counseling* (IL: IVP Academic, 2005).

9. Russell Barkley and Arthur Robin, *Your Defiant Teen: 10 Steps to Resolve Conflict and Rebuild Your Relationship* (New York: A division of Guilford Publications, 2008).

10. David Furlong, *Healing Your Family Patterns: How to Access the Past to Heal the Present* (London: Judy Piatkus, 1997).

Other Book References

1. "Prayer to Move Your Mountains," *Powerful Prayers for The Spirit-Filled Life* (Nashville, TN: Thomas Nelson, 2000).

2. William R. Miller and Kathleen A. Jackson, *Practical Psychology for Pastors* (Upper Saddle River, NJ: Prentice-Hall, 1995).

3. Jay E. Adams, *The Christian Counselor's Manual: The Practice of Nouthetic Counseling* (Grand Rapids, MI: Zondervan, 1973).

4. John G. Kruis, *Quick Scripture Reference for Counseling* (Grand Rapids, MI: Baker Book House 1988, 1994, 2000), 169–170.

5. David G. Benner and Peter C. Hill, *Baker Encyclopaedia of Psychology and Counseling* (Grand Rapids: Baker Books, 1999).

Dr. Elizabeth Thambiraj

6. Larry Crabb, *Effective Biblical Counseling: How Caring Christians Can Become Capable Counselors* (Grand Rapids, MI: Zondervan, 1977), 100–104.

7. *The Matthew Henry Study Bible* (Iowa Falls, IA: World Bible Publishing, 1986.

8. Beth Moore, *David: Seeking a Heart Like His* (Nashville, TN: Life Way Christian Resources, 2010), 206–210.

9. Jay E. Adams, *Critical Stages of Biblical Counseling: Finishing Well, Breaking Through, Getting Started* (NJ: Zondervan, 2002).

10. Jay E. Adams, *How to Help People Change: The Four-Step Biblical Process* (Grand Rapids, MI: Zondervan, 1986).

11. John F. MacArthur Jr., Wayne A. Mack, and the Master's College Faculty, *Introduction to Biblical Counseling: A Basic Guide to the Principles and Practice of Counseling* (Nashville: Thomas Nelson, 1994).

12. Jay E. Adams, *Lectures on Counseling* (Grand Rapids, MI: Baker Book House, 1978), 192–203.

13. *Women of Destiny Bible: Women Mentoring Women through the Scriptures,* (Nashville, TN: Thomas Nelson, 1982)..

14. Stephen D. Eyre, *Deuteronomy: Becoming Holy People* (Downers Grove, IL: IVP Connect, 2004), 32–26.

15. Bruce M. Metzeger and Michael D. Coogan, eds., *The Oxford Companion to the Bible* (Oxford, UK: Oxford University Press).

16. Stephen Mitchell, *The Book of Job* (San Francisco: North Point Press, 1987), cited in R. T. Pennock, *Tower of Babel* (Cambridge, MA: MIT Press, 1999).

17. Stormie Omartin, *The Power of a Praying Wife* (Eugene, OR: Harvest House, 1997), 81–85.

18. Dan Allender and Tremper Longman III, *Intimate Allies* (Carol Stream, IL: Tyndale House, 1995).

19. Claire Smith, *God's Good Design: What the Bible Really Says about Men and Women* (Kingsford, Australia: Matthiasmedia, 2012), 157–180.

20. Everett L. Worthington Jr., *Hope-Focused Marriage Counseling* (IL: IVP Academic, 2005), 146–167.

Mystery of Relationships through the Lens of Scriptures

Triggers of Conflict in Marriages

Website References

1. Amazing Audio Bible Deutronomy 22 - YouTube

    www.youtube.com/watch?v=67Hn9HFUKBY11 Dec 2010 - 5 min - Uploaded by Jegarsahadutha

2. More videos for Deutronomy22:22"

3. GOD'S WORD AGAINST THE OCCULT

    www.exposeoccult.com/index.php?option=com_content ...

    With this assurance—and the knowledge that all angels, powers, and authorities have been subjected to Christ (1 Peter 3:22)—we can examine the occult ...

4. Angels - Supernatural ... Scary Just Got Sexy!

    supernatural.wikia.com/wiki/Angels

4.1 Powers possessed by all angels; 4.2 Powers accessed through the Heavenly ... Although not physically seen, an angel's true form has been seen as a ... being imbued with unimaginable and unmeasurable power and authority. ... Cosmic Awareness—All archangels have a superhuman knowledge of the universe.

5. Angelology: The Doctrine of Angels | Bible.org - Worlds Largest ...

    bible.org/article/angelology-doctrine-angels

    Though theologians have been cautious in their study of angels, in recent years we ... However, we have no assurance that what is true of cherubim and seraphim is true ... But as creatures they are limited in their powers, knowledge, and activities (1 ... Like all of creation, angels are under God's authority and subject to His ...

6. 1 Peter 3:18-22 Commentary

    preceptaustin.org/1_peter_318-22.htm

    As a result of His death in our place, believers have been "brought to God" and ... ... a "knowing with", a co-knowledge with oneself or a being of one's own witness in ... 22 let us draw near with a sincere heart in full assurance of faith, having our ... at God's right hand, with all angels, authorities and powers subservient to him.

213

Dr. Elizabeth Thambiraj

7. <u>Colossians 2 – Answering the Colossian Heresy</u>

   www.enduringword.com/commentaries/5102.htm

   For Paul, real riches were found in the believer's full assurance. ... Christ, in whom are hidden all the treasures of wisdom and knowledge: This is an important idea in ... We always have to be reminded of the things we have been taught. ... "Christ, in this picture, is the conquering general; the powers and authorities are the ...

8. 2 Samuel 11:1–5 (KJV 1900) - "And it came to pass ...

   biblia.com/bible/kjv1900/2Sa11.1-5

   Invest in a library of Bible study resources and use it on your computer, mobile device, and at Biblia.com!

Book References

1. Dan Allender and Tremper Longman III, *Intimate Allies* (Carol Stream, IL: Tyndale House, 1995).

2. Gary Thomas, *Sacred Marriage: What If God Designed Marriage More to Make Us Holy than to Make Us Happy* (Toronto: Harper Collins Canada, 2002).

Other Book References

1. Peter Scazzero, *Emotionally Healthy Spirituality* (Thomas Nelson, 2011).

2. I. Goldenberg and H. Goldenberg, *Family Therapy: An Overview* (Pacific Grove, CA: Brookes/Cole Publishing, 2007).

3. *God's Words of Life on Marriage* (Zondervan, 2000).

Other References

1. Dan Allender and Tremper Longman III, *Intimate Allies* (Carol Stream, IL: Tyndale House, 1995).

2. I. Goldenberg and H. Goldenberg, *Family Therapy: An Overview* (Pacific Grove, CA: Brookes/Cole Publishing, 2007).

Mystery of Relationships through the Lens of Scriptures

3. R. W. Richardson, *Family Ties That Bind* (Vancouver, BC: International Self-Counsel Press, 1995).

4. Gary Thomas, *Sacred Marriage: What If God Designed Marriage More to Make Us Holy than to Make Us Happy* (Toronto: Harper Collins Canada, 2002).

5. Mary E. DeMuth, *Authentic Parenting in a Postmodern Culture: Practical Help for Shaping Your Children's Hearts, Minds, and Souls* (Eugene, OR: Harvest House Publishers, 2007).

6. William T. Kirwan, *Biblical Concepts for Christian Counseling: A Case for Integrating Psychology and Theology* (Grand Rapids, MI: Baker Book House, 1984).

Recommended Reading & Resources

7. Larry Crabb, *Effective Biblical Counseling: How Caring Christians Can Become Capable Counselors* (Grand Rapids, MI: Zondervan, 1977).

8. Everett L. Worthington Jr., *Hope-Focused Marriage Counseling* (IL: IVP Academic, 2005).

9. Russell Barkley and Arthur Robin, *Your Defiant Teen: 10 Steps to Resolve Conflict and Rebuild Your Relationship* (New York: A division of Guilford Publications, 2008).

10. David Furlong, *Healing Your Family Patterns: How to Access the Past to Heal the Present* (London: Judy Piatkus, 1997).

Other Book References

1. "Prayer to Move Your Mountains," *Powerful Prayers for The Spirit-Filled Life* (Nashville, TN: Thomas Nelson, 2000).

2. William R. Miller and Kathleen A. Jackson, *Practical Psychology for Pastors* (Upper Saddle River, NJ: Prentice-Hall, 1995).

3. Jay E. Adams, *The Christian Counselor's Manual: The Practice of Nouthetic Counseling* (Grand Rapids, MI: Zondervan, 1973).

4. John G. Kruis, *Quick Scripture Reference for Counseling* (Grand Rapids, MI: Baker Books), 169–170.

Dr. Elizabeth Thambiraj

5. David G. Benner and Peter C. Hill, *Baker Encyclopaedia of Psychology and Counseling* (Grand Rapids, MI: Baker Books, 1999).

6. Larry Crabb, *Effective Biblical Counseling: How Caring Christians Can Become Capable Counselors* (Grand Rapids, MI: Zondervan, 1977), 100–104.

7. *The Matthew Henry Study Bible* (Iowa Falls, IA: World Bible Publishing, 1990).

8. Beth Moore, *David: Seeking a Heart Like His* (Nashville, TN: Life Way Christian Resources, 2010), 206–210.

9. Jay E. Adams, *Critical Stages of Biblical Counseling: Finishing Well, Breaking Through, Getting Started* (NJ: Zondervan, 2002).

10. Jay E. Adams, *How to Help People Change: The Four-Step Biblical Process* (Grand Rapids, MI: Zondervan, 1986).

11. John F. MacArthur Jr., Wayne A. Mack, and the Master's College Faculty, *Introduction to Biblical Counseling: A Basic Guide to the Principles and Practice of Counseling* (Nashville: Thomas Nelson, 1994).

12. Jay E. Adams, *Lectures on Counseling* (Grand Rapids, MI: Baker Book House, 1978), 192–203.

13. *Women of Destiny Bible: Women Mentoring Women through the Scriptures* (Nashville, TN: Thomas Nelson, 1982).

14. Stephen D. Eyre, *Deuteronomy: Becoming Holy People* (Downers Grove, IL: IVP Connect, 2004), 26-32.

15 Bruce M. Metzeger and Michael D. Coogan, eds., *The Oxford Companion to the Bible* (Oxford, UK: Oxford University Press).

16. Stephen Mitchell, *The Book of Job* (San Francisco: North Point Press, 1987), cited in R. T. Pennock, *Tower of Babel* (Cambridge, MA: MIT Press, 1999).

17. Stormie Omartin, *The Power of a Praying Wife* (Eugene, OR: Harvest House, 1997), 81–85.

18. Dan Allender and Tremper Longman III, *Intimate Allies* (Carol Stream, IL: Tyndale House, 1995).

19. Claire Smith, *God's Good Design: What the Bible Really Says about Men and Women* (Kingsford, Australia: Matthias Media, 2012), 157–180.

Mystery of Relationships through the Lens of Scriptures

20.　Everett L. Worthington Jr., *Hope-Focused Marriage Counseling* (IL: IVP Academic, 2005), 146–167.

A Little Glimpse into Marriages beyond the Fall

End Notes

1.　Dan Allender and Tremper Longman III, *Intimate Allies* (Carol Stream, IL: Tyndale House, 1995), 301.

2.　Ibid., 346.

3.　Ibid., 331.

Book References

1.　Dan Allender and Tremper Longman III, *Intimate Allies* (Carol Stream, IL: Tyndale House, 1995).

2.　Jay E. Adams, *Critical Stages of Biblical Counseling: Finishing Well, Breaking Through, Getting Started* (NJ: Zondervan, 2002).

3.　Jay E. Adams, *How to Help People Change: The Four-Step Biblical Process* (Grand Rapids, MI: Zondervan, 1986).

4.　John F. MacArthur Jr., Wayne A. Mack, and the Master's College Faculty, *Introduction to Biblical Counseling: A Basic Guide to the Principles and Practice of Counseling* (Nashville: Thomas Nelson, 1994).

5.　Jay E. Adams, *Lectures on Counseling* (Grand Rapids, MI: Baker Book House, 1978), 192–203.

6.　*Women of Destiny Bible: Women Mentoring Women through the Scriptures* (Nashville, TN: Thomas Nelson, 1982).

Tongues

End Notes

1.　Thesaurus.com, s.v. "taming," thesaurus.com/browse/taming.

Dr. Elizabeth Thambiraj

2. Synonyms of tame | Infoplease.com - Thesaurus Search Page ...

    thesaurus.infoplease.com/tame

    tame: synonyms, definitions, and usage ... Synonyms for tame Verb 1. tame, chasten, subdue, change, alter, modify usage: correct by punishment or discipline

3. James 3:1-12 Study Guide - BCBSR

    www.bcbsr.com/books/jam3a.html

    JAMES 3:1-12 Control of the ... (Compare Matt 12:36,37 also) vs 3-5 In what ways is you life ... into the role of teacher without having taken the time to study the ...

4. James 3:5-12 KJV - Even so the tongue is a little member ...

    www.biblegateway.com/passage/?search=James+3%3A5-12&version=KJV

    James 3:5-12. King James Version (KJV) 5 ... Amplified, KJV, NASB, & NIV Comparative Study Bible

Website References

1. **"Speaking in Tongues,"** bible.org/article/speaking-tongues

    Lehman Strauss writes on the subject of speaking in tongues ... Introduction. This is not the final chapter to be written on the subject of speaking in tongues.

2. What the Bible Says About Speaking in Tongues | Grace Communion ...

    www.gci.org/bible/tongues1

    Chapter 1: JESUS' PROMISE "What you are seeing is real," a church member told the visitor. "These people are filled with the Holy Spirit." The visitor was seeing a ...

3. Bible passages about speaking in tongues: Glossia and Xenoglossia

    www.religioustolerance.org/tongues3.htm

    Bible passages which deal with speaking in tongues (glossia & zenoglossia)

4. Bible Tongue Speaking and Modern Impostors!

    www.bible.ca/su-tongues-today.htm

First century: Today: Spoke a known language. Acts 2:8: Today don't even claim to use known languages. Were understood. Acts 2:6; I Cor. 14:19: Don't claim to …

5. James 3:2 NKJV - For we all stumble in many things. If - Bible Gateway

    www.biblegateway.com/passage/?search=James+3%3A2&version=NKJV

    For we all stumble in many things. If anyone does not stumble in word, he is a perfect man, able also to bridle the whole body.

6. James 3:2-6 NKJV - For we all stumble in many things. If - Bible …

    www.biblegateway.com/passage/?search=James+3%3A2-6&version=NKJV

    For we all stumble in many things. If anyone does not stumble in word, he is a perfect man, able also to bridle the whole body. Indeed, we put bits in horses …

7. James 3:1-9 - Scion of Zion

    www.scionofzion.com/james3_1-9.htm

    James 3:2 (KJV) For in many things we offend all. If any man offend not in word, the same is a perfect man, and able also to bridle the whole body.

Book References

1. Ed Murphy, *The Handbook for Spiritual Warfare* (Nashville: Thomas Nelson, 1996), 432–436.

2. Jay E. Adams, *Critical Stages of Biblical Counseling: Finishing Well, Breaking Through, Getting Started* (NJ: Zondervan, 2002).

3. Jay E. Adams, *How to Help People Change: The Four-Step Biblical Process* (Grand Rapids, MI: Zondervan, 1986).

4. John F. MacArthur Jr., Wayne A. Mack, and the Master's College Faculty, *Introduction to Biblical Counseling: A Basic Guide to the Principles and Practice of Counseling* (Nashville: Thomas Nelson, 1994).

5. Jay E. Adams, *Lectures on Counseling* (Grand Rapids, MI: Baker Book House, 1978), 192–203.

6. *Women of Destiny Bible: Women Mentoring Women through the Scriptures* (Nashville, TN: Thomas Nelson, 1982).

Dr. Elizabeth Thambiraj

7. Warren W. Wiersbe, *Devotions for Confidence & Integrity: Hebrews & John* (Colorado, Springs, Colorado: Honor Books, 2006).

8. Dan Allender and Tremper Longman III, *Intimate Allies* (Carol Stream, IL: Tyndale House, 1995).

Love … in All the Wrong Places?

End Notes

1. What is the Hebrew word for love

   wiki.answers.com › … › Translations › English to HebrewCached

   What is the Hebrew word for love? In: English to Hebrew [Edit categories]. Answer: noun = ahava (הבהא) verb = ahav (בהא). Contributor: Adamlance. First answer …

2. "Greek Words for Love," *Wikipeda*, en.wikipedia.org/wiki/Greek_words_for_love.

   Ancient Greek has four distinct words for love: agápe, éros, philía, and storgē. … other languages, it has been historically difficult to separate the meanings of …

3. Dan Allender and Tremper Longman III, *Intimate Allies* (Carol Stream, IL: Tyndale House, 1995).

4. Gary Thomas, *Sacred Marriage: What If God Designed Marriage More to Make Us Holy than to Make Us Happy* (Toronto: Harper Collins Canada, 2002), 73.

5. James 4 Commentary - Matthew Henry Commentary on the Whole …

   www.biblestudytools.com › James

   Read James 4 commentary using Matthew Henry Commentary on the Whole Bible (Concise). Study the bible online using commentary on James 4 and more!

Website References

1. The Love of God

   www.cyberhymnal.org/htm/l/o/loveofgo.htm

Mystery of Relationships through the Lens of Scriptures

The love of God is greater far. Than tongue or pen can ever tell; It goes beyond the highest star, And reaches to the lowest hell; The guilty pair, bowed down with ...

2. **"Love of God,"** *Wikipedia*, **en.wikipedia.org/wiki/Love_of_God**

Love of God (philotheia and philanthropia) are central notions in monotheistic and polytheistic religions, and are important in one's personal relationship with.

3. The Love Of GodHome Page -

www.theloveofgod.org

4. For the Love of God

thegospelcoalition.org/blogs/loveofgod

2 days ago – For the Love of God is a daily devotional designed to walk a person through the Bible in a year while assisting the reader in discovering the ...

5. The Attributes of God by A.W. Pink-The Love of God

www.pbministries.org/books/pink/Attributes/attrib_15.htm

There are many today who talk about the love of God, who are total strangers to the God of love. The Divine love is commonly regarded as a species of amiable ...

6. The Love of God - general-conference

www.lds.org/general-conference/2009/10/the-love-of-god?lang ...

Love is the measure of our faith, the inspiration for our obedience, and the true altitude of our discipleship.

7. Resources on The Love of God - Desiring God

www.desiringgod.org/resource-library/topic-index/the-love-of-god

Spirit-given assurance and enjoyment of the love of God is the secret to growing in hope through ... The Love of God Has Been Poured Out Within Our Hearts ...

8. Love of God

www.allaboutgod.com/love-of-god.htm

Dr. Elizabeth Thambiraj

Love Of God - Is the Creator a God of Love? God's Love revealed. God's Love foretold. God's Love manifested through His only Begotten Son.

9. What is the true meaning of love?

theguide2.com/true-meaning-love

4 Jan 2011 – Most people who claim to love someone don't really love them, because they don't know what love actually is. Sponsored Links: What is love ...

10. "Greek Words for Love," *Wikipeda*, en.wikipedia.org/wiki/Greek_words_for_love.

Ancient Greek has four distinct words for love: agápe, éros, philía, and storgē. ... other languages, it has been historically difficult to separate the meanings of ...

Book References

1. "Prayer to Move Your Mountains," *Powerful Prayers for The Spirit-Filled Life* (Nashville, TN: Thomas Nelson, 2000).

2. Timothy Keller, *Counterfeit Gods: The Empty Promises of Money, Sex, and Power, and the Only Hope That Matters* (New York: Penguin, 2009).

3. Jay E. Adams, *The Christian Counselor's Manual: The Practice of Nouthetic Counseling* (Grand Rapids, MI: Zondervan, 1973).

4. Timothy Keller, *The Prodigal God: Recovering the Heart of the Christian Faith* (New York: Penguin, 2008).

5. David G. Benner and Peter C. Hill, *Baker Encyclopaedia of Psychology and Counseling* (Grand Rapids, MI: Baker Books, 1999).

6. Larry Crabb, *Effective Biblical Counseling: How Caring Christians Can Become Capable Counselors* (Grand Rapids, MI: Zondervan, 1977).

7. *The Matthew Henry Study Bible* (Iowa Falls, IA: World Bible Publishing, 1990).

8   Beth Moore, *David: Seeking a Heart Like His* (Nashville, TN: Life Way Christian Resources, 2010), 206–210.

9. Jay E. Adams, *Critical Stages of Biblical Counseling: Finishing Well, Breaking Through, Getting Started* (NJ: Zondervan, 2002).

Mystery of Relationships through the Lens of Scriptures

10. Jay E. Adams, *How to Help People Change: The Four-Step Biblical Process* (Grand Rapids, MI: Zondervan, 1986).

11. John F. MacArthur Jr., Wayne A. Mack, and the Master's College Faculty, *Introduction to Biblical Counseling: A Basic Guide to the Principles and Practice of Counseling* (Nashville: Thomas Nelson, 1994).

12. Jay E. Adams, *Lectures on Counseling* (Grand Rapids, MI: Baker Book House, 1978).

13. *Women of Destiny Bible: Women Mentoring Women through the Scriptures* (Nashville, TN: Thomas Nelson, 1982).

14. Stephen D. Eyre, *Deuteronomy: Becoming Holy People* (Downers Grove, IL: IVP Connect, 2004), 32–26.

15. Bruce M. Metzeger and Michael D. Coogan, eds., *The Oxford Companion to the Bible* (Oxford, UK: Oxford University Press).

16. Stephen Mitchell, *The Book of Job* (San Francisco: North Point Press, 1987), cited in R. T. Pennock, *Tower of Babel* (Cambridge, MA: MIT Press, 1999).

17. Stormie Omartin, *The Power of a Praying Wife* (Eugene, OR: Harvest House, 1997), 69–75.

18. Timothy Keller, *The Reason for God: Belief in an Age of Skepticism* (New York: Penguin, 2008), 191–208.

19. William R. Miller and Kathleen A. Jackson, *Practical Psychology for Pastors* (Upper Saddle River, NJ: Prentice-Hall, 1995).

20. Gary Thomas, *Sacred Marriage: What If God Designed Marriage More to Make Us Holy than to Make Us Happy* (Toronto: Harper Collins Canada, 2002).

21. Dan Allender and Tremper Longman III, *Intimate Allies* (Carol Stream, IL: Tyndale House, 1995).

Faithfulness

End Notes

1. The Fruit of the Spirit: Faithfulness

   www.org/index.cfm/ … sr/CT/ … /Fruit-of-Spirit-Faithfulness.htm

Dr. Elizabeth Thambiraj

Faithlessness is the essence of mankind's general character at the end of the age. However, faithfulness is to be a hallmark of a true Christian. How.

2. *Collins Thesaurus of the English Language,* 2nd ed.

3. Mark #14: Faithfulness | Bible.org - Worlds Largest Bible Study Site

bible.org/seriespage/mark-14-faithfulness Faithfulness, then, is a quality that God wants to reproduce in us through the salvation that comes in Christ. It is another of the qualities of maturity to be sought in ...

Website References

1. The Fruit of the Spirit: Faithfulness

www.cgg.org/index.cfm/ ... sr/CT/ ... /Fruit-of-Spirit-Faithfulness.htm

Faithlessness is the essence of mankind's general character at the end of the age. However, faithfulness is to be a hallmark of a true Christian. How.

2. *The Free Dictionary,* s.v. "faithfulness," www.thefreedictionary.com/faithfulness.

3. *Dictionary.com,* s.v. "faithful," dictionary.reference.com/browse/faithful.

4. Mark #14: Faithfulness | Bible.org - Worlds Largest Bible Study Site

bible.org/seriespage/mark-14-faithfulness

Faithfulness, then, is a quality that God wants to reproduce in us through the salvation that comes in Christ. It is another of the qualities of maturity to be sought in ...

5. Faithfulness Quotes - BrainyQuote

www.brainyquote.com/quotes/keywords/faithfulness.html

Faithfulness Quotes from BrainyQuote, an extensive collection of quotations by famous authors, celebrities, and newsmakers.

6. Thesaurus.com, s.v. "faithfulness," thesaurus.com/browse/faithfulness.

7. "Great Is Thy Faithfulness"

www.hymntime.com/tch/htm/g/r/e/greatitf.htm

Mystery of Relationships through the Lens of Scriptures

Words: Thomas Chisholm, 1923. Music: William Runyan.

8. Scriptures On Faithfulness

    www.heavensinspirations.com/word-faithfulness.html

    These are scriptures from God's word on faithfulness. All the scriptures I've taken from the Amplified Bible unless otherwise stated. If you click on the scripture ...

9. Faithfulness

    www.spirithome.com/faithfulness.html

    Faithfulness is a quality the Holy Spirit grows within you. It holds life together. How you can make it a way of life for yourself, and toward others.

Book References

1. "Prayer to Move Your Mountains," *Powerful Prayers for The Spirit-Filled Life* (Nashville, TN: Thomas Nelson, 2000).

2. William R. Miller and Kathleen A. Jackson, *Practical Psychology for Pastors* (Upper Saddle River, NJ: Prentice-Hall, 1995).

3. Jay E. Adams, *The Christian Counselor's Manual: The Practice of Nouthetic Counseling* (Grand Rapids, MI: Zondervan, 1973).

4. John G. Kruis, *Quick Scripture Reference for Counseling* (Grand Rapids, MI: Baker Books), 169–170.

5. David G. Benner and Peter C. Hill, *Baker Encyclopaedia of Psychology and Counseling* (Grand Rapids, MI: Baker Books, 1999).

6. Larry Crabb, *Effective Biblical Counseling: How Caring Christians Can Become Capable Counselors* (Grand Rapids, MI: Zondervan, 1977), 100–104.

7. *The Matthew Henry Study Bible* (Iowa Falls, IA: World Bible Publishing, 1990).

8. Beth Moore, *David: Seeking a Heart Like His* (Nashville, TN: Life Way Christian Resources, 2010), 206–210.

9. Jay E. Adams, *Critical Stages of Biblical Counseling: Finishing Well, Breaking Through, Getting Started* (NJ: Zondervan, 2002).

Dr. Elizabeth Thambiraj

10. Jay E. Adams, *How to Help People Change: The Four-Step Biblical Process* (Grand Rapids, MI: Zondervan, 1986).

11. John F. MacArthur Jr., Wayne A. Mack, and the Master's College Faculty, *Introduction to Biblical Counseling: A Basic Guide to the Principles and Practice of Counseling* (Nashville: Thomas Nelson, 1994).

12. Jay E. Adams, *Lectures on Counseling* (Grand Rapids, MI: Baker Book House, 1978), 192–203.

13. *Women of Destiny Bible: Women Mentoring Women through the Scriptures* (Nashville, TN: Thomas Nelson, 1982).

14. Stephen D. Eyre, *Deuteronomy: Becoming Holy People* (Downers Grove, IL: IVP Connect, 2004), 32–26.

15. Bruce M. Metzeger and Michael D. Coogan, eds., *The Oxford Companion to the Bible* (Oxford, UK: Oxford University Press).

16. Stephen Mitchell, *The Book of Job* (San Francisco: North Point Press, 1987), cited in R. T. Pennock, *Tower of Babel* (Cambridge, MA: MIT Press, 1999).

17. Stormie Omartin, *The Power of a Praying Wife* (Eugene, OR: Harvest House, 1997), 81–85.

18. Timothy Keller, *The Reason for God: Belief in an Age of Skepticism* (New York: Penguin, 2008).

Religion or the Gospel?

End Notes

1. Timothy Keller, *The Reason for God: Belief in an Age of Skepticism* (New York: Penguin, 2008), 174.

2. Ibid., 175.

Website References

1. Religion vs. Gospel | Ordinary Pastor

   www.ordinarypastor.com › Gospel

Mystery of Relationships through the Lens of Scriptures

10 Jun 2007 – Here is a helpful list of distinctives articulated by Mark Driscoll between Religion and the Gospel. I have found these to be helpful in personal ...

2.   The Five Gospels Parallels

www.utoronto.ca/religion/synopsis/

HTML Gospel Parallels for Matthew, Mark, Luke, John, and Thomas A Teaching tool for the study of the New Testament and the literature of early Christianity.

3.   The Difference between Religion and the Gospel | The Resurgence

theresurgence.com/ ... /the-difference-between-religion-and-the-gospel

18 Jan 2012 – Tim Keller's Gospel in Life Study Guide is incredibly helpful and expounds upon the difference of religion and the gospel. We like it so much, we ...

4.   THE PENTECOSTAL GOSPEL

artsweb.bham.ac.uk/aanderson/publications/pentecostal_gospel.htm

by A Anderson

THE PENTECOSTAL GOSPEL, RELIGION AND CULTURE IN AFRICAN PERSPECTIVE. Allan Anderson. Graduate Institute for Theology and Religion ...

5.   Religion And The Gospel – Tullian Tchividjian

thegospelcoalition.org/blogs/tullian/2012/ ... /religion-and-the-gospel

14 Jan 2012 – But, the distinction between religion and the gospel that Jefferson makes does raise some important questions. For example, in the Bible, is the ...

6.   A Bible Online Religion Guide: Gospel of Jesus, Free Studies

www.gospelway.com/

2 Mar 2012 – Free online Bible study guides and Bible lesson studies. Study religion, gospel of Jesus Christ, holy Scripture, worship of God, salvation from ...

7.   Gospel vs. Religion - Acts 29 Network: Seattle, WA >

www.acts29network.org/acts-29-blog/gospel-vs-religion

Dr. Elizabeth Thambiraj

13 May 2010 – Gospel vs. Religion. Blog: Gospel VS Religion. By Scott Thomas, President of Acts 29 Network. If anyone is preaching to you a gospel contrary ...

8. Climate Change As Religion: The Gospel According To Gore - Forbes

www.forbes.com/ ... /climate-change-as-religion-the-gospel-according ...

26 Apr 2011 – Climate changes and shorter-term weather events are the way that nature balances itself.

9. "Gospel Music," *Wikipedia,* en.wikipedia.org/wiki/Gospel_music.

Gospel music is composed and performed for many purposes, including aesthetic pleasure, religious or ceremonial purposes, and as an entertainment product ...

10. The Differences Between Religion and The Gospel

www.christianpost.com/ ... /the-differences-between-religion-and-the- ...

8 Apr 2011 – Read the comparison list with humility and care. RELIGION: I obey-therefore I'm accepted. THE GOSPEL: I'm accepted-therefore I obey.

Book References

1. "Prayer to Move Your Mountains," *Powerful Prayers for The Spirit-Filled Life* (Nashville, TN: Thomas Nelson, 2000).

2. Timothy Keller, *Counterfeit Gods: The Empty Promises of Money, Sex, and Power, and the Only Hope That Matters* (New York: Penguin, 2009).

3. Jay E. Adams, *The Christian Counselor's Manual: The Practice of Nouthetic Counseling* (Grand Rapids, MI: Zondervan, 1973).

4. Timothy Keller, *The Prodigal God: Recovering the Heart of the Christian Faith* (New York: Penguin, 2008).

5. David G. Benner and Peter C. Hill, *Baker Encyclopaedia of Psychology and Counseling* (Grand Rapids, MI: Baker Books, 1999).

6. Larry Crabb, *Effective Biblical Counseling: How Caring Christians Can Become Capable Counselors* (Grand Rapids, MI: Zondervan, 1977), 100–104.

7. *The Matthew Henry Study Bible* (Iowa Falls, IA: World Bible Publishing, 1990).

Mystery of Relationships through the Lens of Scriptures

8. Beth Moore, *David: Seeking a Heart Like His* (Nashville, TN: Life Way Christian Resources, 2010), 206–210.

9. Jay E. Adams, *Critical Stages of Biblical Counseling: Finishing Well, Breaking Through, Getting Started* (NJ: Zondervan, 2002).

10. Jay E. Adams, *How to Help People Change: The Four-Step Biblical Process* (Grand Rapids, MI: Zondervan, 1986).

11. John F. MacArthur Jr., Wayne A. Mack, and the Master's College Faculty, *Introduction to Biblical Counseling: A Basic Guide to the Principles and Practice of Counseling* (Nashville: Thomas Nelson, 1994).

12. Jay E. Adams, *Lectures on Counseling* (Grand Rapids, MI: Baker Book House, 1978),192–203.

13. *Women of Destiny Bible: Women Mentoring Women through the Scriptures* (Nashville, TN: Thomas Nelson, 1982).

14. Stephen D. Eyre, *Deuteronomy: Becoming Holy People* (Downers Grove, IL: IVP Connect, 2004), 32–26.

15. Bruce M. Metzeger and Michael D. Coogan, eds., *The Oxford Companion to the Bible* (Oxford, UK: Oxford University Press).

16. Stephen Mitchell, *The Book of Job* (San Francisco: North Point Press, 1987), cited in R. T. Pennock, *Tower of Babel* (Cambridge, MA: MIT Press, 1999).

17. Stormie Omartin, *The Power of a Praying Wife* (Eugene, OR: Harvest House, 1997), 81–85.

18. Timothy Keller, *The Reason for God: Belief in an Age of Skepticism* (New York: Penguin, 2008), 170–200.

Whom Am I Living For?

Website References

1. Love me for who I am - A Poem

    expertscolumn.com/content/love-me-who-i-am-poem

Dr. Elizabeth Thambiraj

1 Apr 2012 – … but what make my life worth living for are those people who believe in me after knowing my imperfection. … Love me for who I am - A Poem …

2. Living, Not A Moment Wasted: My Last Poem For Who Knows How …

wwwnotamomentwasted.blogspot.com/ … /my-last-poem-for-who-kno …

18 Apr 2012 – A poem I wrote a while back, kinda to God, that it's not enough to write and talk, but I need to not be a hypocrite and actually live it out. So here …

3. **Morley, Hilda, "It is the *living* who cannot," The *Poetry* Foundation**, www. poetryfoundation.org/poem/182043.

It is the living who cannot / live without the dead, / who wish them / back,

4. John Keats Quotes (Author of The Complete Poems)

www.goodreads.com/author/quotes/11978.John_Keats

John Keats, Bright Star: Love Letters and Poems of John Keats to Fanny … Still, still to hear her tender-taken breath, And so live ever---or else swoon in death. " …

5. The Dash Poem | Living It With Lisa

livingitwithlisa.com/tag/the-dash-poem

There are many today who are reflecting on the loved ones they have lost … on 9/11 and on on any other day. This year has been a year of loss in our family.

6. A Man's A Man For A' That by Robert Burns Classic Famous Poet …

allpoetry.com/opoem/350-Robert-Burns-A-Man-s-A-Man-For-A--That

Is there for honesty poverty / That hings his head, an' a' that; / The coward slave - we pass him by, / We dare be poor for a' that! / For a' that, an' a' that, / Our toils …

7. Christian Living Poems

christian-poems.ochristian.com › Christian Poems

25+ items – A selection of poetry of faith, hope, endurance, and …

Living And Dying - Living for Christ, I die;--how strange, that I, Thus dying, live …

Look Up - Christian, lookup? thy feet may slide; This is a slippery way! Yet One …

Mystery of Relationships through the Lens of Scriptures

8. A Year of Living Poetically: Poetry Memorization Guide, mensaforkids.com/poetry/ MFK-Poetry-all.pdf.

   File Format: PDF/Adobe Acrobat

   property of the originating entities. A Year of Living Poetically: Poetry Memorization Guide. A long time ago, memorizing poetry was par for the course in school.

9. Short Love Poems - "He Loves Me", "love is strange" and other 1 ...

   www.short-love-poem.com/iloveyou.html

   My Love For You - short I Love You poems for singles and married. ... that won't let me live. There's pain in my life only you can relief. I'm so glad it was you ...

10. When Love Begins, Falling in Love Poem

    www.familyfriendpoems.com › Love Poems › Falling in Love Poems

    Rating: 4.6 - 607 votes

    Falling in Love Poem, When Love Begins, Love Poems, This poem is about a ... go back to acting the way he did while we were living together and first married.

Book References

1. "Prayer to Move Your Mountains," *Powerful Prayers for The Spirit-Filled Life* (Nashville, TN: Thomas Nelson, 2000).

2. William R. Miller and Kathleen A. Jackson, *Practical Psychology for Pastors* (Upper Saddle River, NJ: Prentice-Hall, 1995).

3. Jay E. Adams, *The Christian Counselor's Manual: The Practice of Nouthetic Counseling* (Grand Rapids, MI: Zondervan, 1973).

4. John G. Kruis, *Quick Scripture Reference for Counseling* (Grand Rapids, MI: Baker Books), 169–170.

5. David G. Benner and Peter C. Hill, *Baker Encyclopaedia of Psychology and Counseling* (Grand Rapids, MI: Baker Books, 1999).

6. Larry Crabb, *Effective Biblical Counseling: How Caring Christians Can Become Capable Counselors* (Grand Rapids, MI: Zondervan, 1977). 100–104.

Dr. Elizabeth Thambiraj

7.   *The Matthew Henry Study Bible* (Iowa Falls, IA: World Bible Publishing, 1990).

8.   Beth Moore, *David: Seeking a Heart Like His* (Nashville, TN: Life Way Christian Resources, 2010), 206–210.

9.   Jay E. Adams, *Critical Stages of Biblical Counseling: Finishing Well, Breaking Through, Getting Started* (NJ: Zondervan, 2002).

10. Jay E. Adams, *How to Help People Change: The Four-Step Biblical Process* (Grand Rapids, MI: Zondervan, 1986).

11. John F. MacArthur Jr., Wayne A. Mack, and the Master's College Faculty, *Introduction to Biblical Counseling: A Basic Guide to the Principles and Practice of Counseling* (Nashville: Thomas Nelson, 1994).

12. Jay E. Adams, *Lectures on Counseling* (Grand Rapids, MI: Baker Book House, 1978), 192–203.

13. *Women of Destiny Bible: Women Mentoring Women through the Scriptures* (Nashville, TN: Thomas Nelson, 1982).

14. Stephen D. Eyre, *Deuteronomy: Becoming Holy People* (Downers Grove, IL: IVP Connect, 2004), 32–26.

15. Bruce M. Metzeger and Michael D. Coogan, eds., *The Oxford Companion to the Bible* (Oxford, UK: Oxford University Press).

16. Stephen Mitchell, *The Book of Job* (San Francisco: North Point Press, 1987), cited in R. T. Pennock, *Tower of Babel* (Cambridge, MA: MIT Press, 1999).

17. Stormie Omartin, *The Power of a Praying Wife* (Eugene, OR: Harvest House, 1997), 81–85.

18. Timothy Keller. *The Reason for God: Belief in an Age of Skepticism* (New York: Penguin, 2008), 155–175.

How Great Is Our God!

Website References

1.   Psalms 8 Commentary - Matthew Henry Commentary on the …

     www.biblestudytools.com › Psalms 1-75

Mystery of Relationships through the Lens of Scriptures

Read Psalms 8 commentary using Matthew Henry ... Study the bible online using commentary on ... New International Version Bible (NIV) King James ...

2. Psalm 8 - Matthew Henry's Commentary - Bible Commentary

    www.christnotes.org › ... › Matthew Henry's Commentary › Psalm

    Bible commentary about Psalm 8 (Matthew Henry's Commentary).

3. Matthew Henry's Commentary on the Whole Bible [Psalms ...

    www.apostolic-churches.net/bible/mhc/MHC19000.HTM

    Psalm 8; Psalm 9; Psalm 10; Psalm 11; Psalm 12; ... Matthew Henry Bible Commentary; KJV Bible Advanced Search Page; ... Download The Bible Study Tools;

Reference

The Matthew Henry Study Bible (Iowa Falls, IA: World Bible Publishing, 1990), 855–856.

As the Deer Panteth for the Water ...

Website References

1. As The Deer

    www.saintmina-holmdel.org/Songs/songtext.php?title=As ... Deer

    As The Deer. 1-. As the deer pants for the water. So my soul longs after you. You alone are my heart's desire. And I long to worship you. R-. You alone are my ...

2. [PDF] As the Deer Pants; www.justworship.com/praisepoints/asthedeerpants.pdf

    File Format: PDF/Adobe Acrobat - Quick ViewIt was 2003 and the song 'As the Deer Pants' was on my heart and lips. ... ... but whoever drinks the water (living water) I give him will never thirst. Indeed, the ...

3. Psalm 42: Lyrics, Midi, Sheet Music, MP3

    psalmistry.com/lyrics/42.htm

Dr. Elizabeth Thambiraj

AS THE DEER PANTS FOR THE WATER (PSALM 42). 1. As the deer pants for the water, so my soul pants after Thee. How I thirst for living water. How much …

4. As The Deer Pants For The Water song lyrics by Misc Religious

www.lyrics-p.com/ … /misc-religious-as-the-deer-pants-fo … - United States

As The Deer Pants For The Water song lyrics by Misc Religious.

Book References

1. "Prayer to Move Your Mountains," *Powerful Prayers for The Spirit-Filled Life* (Nashville, TN: Thomas Nelson, 2000).

2. William R. Miller and Kathleen A. Jackson, *Practical Psychology for Pastors* (Upper Saddle River, NJ: Prentice-Hall, 1995).

3. Jay E. Adams, *The Christian Counselor's Manual: The Practice of Nouthetic Counseling* (Grand Rapids, MI: Zondervan, 1973).

4. John G. Kruis, *Quick Scripture Reference for Counseling* (Grand Rapids, MI: Baker Books), 169–170.

5. David G. Benner and Peter C. Hill, *Baker Encyclopaedia of Psychology and Counseling* (Grand Rapids, MI: Baker Books, 1999).

6. Larry Crabb, *Effective Biblical Counseling: How Caring Christians Can Become Capable Counselors* (Grand Rapids, MI: Zondervan, 1977), 100–104.

7. *The Matthew Henry Study Bible* (Iowa Falls, IA: World Bible Publishing, 1990).

8. Beth Moore, *David: Seeking a Heart Like His* (Nashville, TN: Life Way Christian Resources, 2010), 206–210.

9. Jay E. Adams, *Critical Stages of Biblical Counseling: Finishing Well, Breaking Through, Getting Started* (NJ: Zondervan, 2002).

10. Jay E. Adams, *How to Help People Change: The Four-Step Biblical Process* (Grand Rapids, MI: Zondervan, 1986).

11. John F. MacArthur Jr., Wayne A. Mack, and the Master's College Faculty, *Introduction to Biblical Counseling: A Basic Guide to the Principles and Practice of Counseling* (Nashville: Thomas Nelson, 1994).

Mystery of Relationships through the Lens of Scriptures

12. Jay E. Adams, *Lectures on Counseling* (Grand Rapids, MI: Baker Book House, 1978), 192–203.

13. *Women of Destiny Bible: Women Mentoring Women through the Scriptures* (Nashville, TN: Thomas Nelson, 1982).

14. Stephen D. Eyre, *Deuteronomy: Becoming Holy People* (Downers Grove, IL: IVP Connect, 2004), 32–26.

Holding Loose ...

Website References

1. The Soul Versus The Spirit

   www.greatbiblestudy.com/soul_spirit.php

   How did demonic spirits vex and possess (control) people in the Bible? It was through their souls (minds, as in mental illness and insanity), and their bodies ... one another with a pure heart fervently: Being born again, not of corruptible seed, ...

2. The Heart and the Mind ~ What the Biblical - Faith Bible Ministries Blog

   faithbibleministries.wordpress.com/ ... /the-heart-and-the-mind-what-t ...

   Jul 6, 2012 – The Heart and the Mind ~ What the Biblical word "Heart' Means ... describe the immaterial part of man: the heart, soul, spirit, and mind. ... The heart is connected with thinking: As a person "thinketh in his heart, so is he" (Prov.

3. Isaiah 45:1 "This is what the LORD says to his anointed, to Cyrus ...

   bible.cc/isaiah/45-1.htm

   Clarke's Commentary on the Bible. Loose the loins of kings "ungird the loins of ... anointed armor be before by Cyrus doors gates hand have him his hold I is kings loins loose ...

4. bible - ChristArt Christian Clip Art Search - page 3

   www.christart.com/search?q=bible&g=1&start=3

   Boy and girl fish holding Bible ... Loose notes next to a Bible

Dr. Elizabeth Thambiraj

5.   Isaiah 33:23 Your rigging hangs loose: The mast is not held secure …

     bible.cc/isaiah/33-23.htm

     New American Standard Bible (©1995) Your tackle hangs slack; It cannot hold …
     "Thy ropes hang loose; they do not hold fast the support of thy mast; they do not
     hold the flag …

6.   The New Bible.com

     https://www.bible.com

     Bible.com is all new! Enjoy a free online Bible from YouVersion. Now, the simple,
     ad-free Bible experience loved by millions is available at Bible.com.

7.   Anger, Wrath, Temper Control, & the Bible

     www.gospelway.com/christianlife/anger.php

     Bible teaching about anger and controlling your temper … but we must take care lest
     we "fly off the handle," lose … needs to be said, but we should control our anger:
     hold …

8.   Images of diagrams of holding loose

     bing.com/images

9.   Holding Too Tightly - In Touch Ministries

     www.intouch.org › Broadcast › Video Archives › Content

     Holding Too Tightly. Sunday, November 27, 2011. God is the Source of every blessing:
     But when we treasure His gifts more than our … NASB Life Principles Bible.

Book References

1.   Ed Murphy, The Handbook for Spiritual Warfare (Nashville, TN: Thomas Nelson,
     1996), 432–436.

2.   Jay E. Adams, *Critical Stages of Biblical Counseling: Finishing Well, Breaking
     Through, Getting Started* (NJ: Zondervan, 2002).

3.   Jay E. Adams, *How to Help People Change: The Four-Step Biblical Process* (Grand
     Rapids, MI: Zondervan, 1986).

Mystery of Relationships through the Lens of Scriptures

4.   John F. MacArthur Jr., Wayne A. Mack, and the Master's College Faculty, *Introduction to Biblical Counseling: A Basic Guide to the Principles and Practice of Counseling* (Nashville: Thomas Nelson, 1994).

5.   Jay E. Adams, *Lectures on Counseling* (Grand Rapids, MI: Baker Book House, 1978), 192–203.

6.   *Women of Destiny Bible: Women Mentoring Women through the Scriptures* (Nashville, TN: Thomas Nelson, 1982).

For Further Reading

1.   Millard J. Erickson, *Christian Theology* (Grand Rapids, MI: Baker Book House, 1985), 947–1002.

2.   R. T. Kendall, *Understanding Theology: Developing a Healthy Church in the 21ˢᵗ Century* (1996), 357–364.

3.   Jay E. Adams, *A Theology of Christian Counseling: More than Redemption* (Grand Rapids, MI: Zondervan, 1979), 249–275.

4.   Louis Berkhof, *Systematic Theology* (Grand Rapids, MI: Eerdmans, 1996), 423–450.

5.   Robert P. Lightner, *Handbook of Evangelical Theology: Historical, Biblical, and Contemporary Survey and Review* (Grand Rapids, MI: Baker Book House, 1986), 527–544.

6.   Charles Ryrie, *Basic Theology* (Chicago: Moody Press, 1999), 374–377.

7.   A. H. Strong, *Systematic Theology* (NJ: Fleming H. Revell, 1907), 869–881.

8.   Wayne Grudem, *Systematic Theology: An Introduction to Biblical Doctrine* (Grand Rapids: Zondervan, 1994), 736–761; 840–850.

9.   Steven W. Waterhouse, *Not by Bread Alone: An Outlined Guide to Bible Doctrine* (Amarillo, TX: Westcliffe Press, 2007), 188–191.

10.   John Theodore Muller, *Christian Dogmatics: A Handbook of Doctrinal Theology for Pastors, Teachers, and Laymen* (St. Louis, MO: Concordia Publishing House, 1934), 384–386.

11.   "Prayer to Move Your Mountains," *Powerful Prayers for The Spirit-Filled Life* (Nashville, TN: Thomas Nelson, 2000).

Dr. Elizabeth Thambiraj

12. John White, *Parables: The Greatest Stories Ever Told* (IL: Intervarsity Press, 1999).

13. *The ESV Study Bible* (Wheaton, IL: Crossway Bibles, 2008).

14. *The Matthew Henry Study Bible* (Iowa Falls, IA: World Bible Publishing, 1990).

Emotional Abuse in a Nutshell

End Notes

1. Focus Helps | Emotional and verbal abuse |

   www.focushelps.ca/article/addictions-abuse/verbal-and-emotional ...

   ... emotional abuse is even more devastating than physical abuse.

   Emotional abuse tears at a person's self-esteem and can greatly impair ... Can we pray for ...

2. Ibid.

3. Ibid.

4. ABUSE - Definition from the KJV Dictionary

   av1611.com/kjbp/kjv-dictionary/abuse.html

   KJV Dictionary Definition: abuse abuse. ... Practicing abuse; offering harsh words, ... Bible Verses by Topic Nave's Topical Bible

5. "Psychological Abuse," *Wikipedia,* en.wikipedia.org/wiki/Emotional_abuse.

   Psychological abuse, also referred to as emotional abuse or mental abuse, is a form of abuse characterized by a person subjecting or exposing another to behavior that ...

6. Emotional Abuse - EQI

   eqi.org/eabuse1.htm

   EQI.org Home. Emotional Abuse. Sexual and physical abuse are just the tip of the abuse iceberg. The bulk of the abuse in the "developed ...

Mystery of Relationships through the Lens of Scriptures

7.   Emotional abuse is Heart and Soul Mutilation

www.joy2meu.com/emotional_abuse.html

Emotional abuse is a devastating, debilitating heart and soul mutilation. The deepest lasting wound with any abuse is the emotional wound - author of Codependence ...

8.   *The Bing Dictionary,* s.v. "codependency,"

co·de·pen·den·cy

[kỏ di péndənssee]

1.   mutual need: the dependence of two people, groups, or organisms on each other, especially when this reinforces mutually harmful behavior patterns

2.   relationship of mutual need: a situation in which a person such as the partner of an alcoholic or a parent of a drug-addicted child needs to feel needed by the other person

9. "Codependency," *Wikipedia,* en.wikipedia.org/wiki/Codependency.

Codependency is defined as a psychological condition or a relationship in which a person is controlled or manipulated by another who is affected with a pathological ...

10.   "Enmeshment," *Wikipedia,* en.wikipedia.org/wiki/Enmeshment.

Family characteristics

Remedies

Enmeshment is a state of cross-generational bonding within a family, whereby a child (normally of the opposite sex) becomes a surrogate spouse for their mother or father.

11.   "Murray Bowen," *Wikipedia,* en.wikipedia.org/wiki/Murray_Bowen.

Biography·

Work

1   Biography; 2 Work. 2.1 Interlocking concepts; 2.2 Differentiation of self; 2.3 Triangles; 2.4 Emotional cutoff; 3 See also; 4 Publications. 4.1 Publications about Bowen

239

Dr. Elizabeth Thambiraj

12. Fruit Of The Spirit

www.spirithome.com/fruits-of-the-spirit.html

What are the fruit that the Spirit grows in you? ... nor rejoice in sin; ... using the Spirit's gifts to grow the Spirit's fruit, ...

Website References

1. Focus Helps | Emotional and verbal abuse |

www.focushelps.ca/article/addictions-abuse/verbal-and-emotional ...

... emotional abuse is even more devastating than physical abuse.

Emotional abuse tears at a person's self-esteem and can greatly impair ... Can we pray for ...

2. Physical, Emotional and Sexual Abuse Articles & Advice ...

www.deborahkingcenter.com/resources/abuse

Physical and Emotional Abuse. Physical abuse is just as damaging to young bodies and souls, and sadly, just as prevalent.

3. Special Prayers, Prayer for Those Affected by Physical ...

1stholistic.com/Spl_prayers/prayer_for-those-affected-by-violence.htm

Special Prayers, Prayer for Those Affected by Physical, Sexual, Political or Emotional Violence. SpecialGifts.com ... We pray for those who have suffered abuse, ...

4. Prayer, Emotional Abuse

www.christianprayercenter.com/prayers/request-196841.html

Submit your prayer requests for other Christians to pray for. ... pharmacy and physical therapy. ... Prayer Request: Emotional Abuse. Prayers for Relationships

5. Abuse, Mental, Physical, Verbal, Emotional, Psychological ...

cyberparent.com/abuse

Mystery of Relationships through the Lens of Scriptures

Emotional, verbal, mental, physical abuse, with abusers and abused in men, women, ...
They often turn into physical abuse. Physical abuse always escalates.

6.   Prayers for Healing: Emotional - National Prayer Bank

nationalprayerbank.com/prayer/healing/emotional

... Prayers for Healing: Emotional | Post prayer requests ... healing from sexual and
emotional abuse, ... Please pray for emotional healing and physical healing.

7.   Emotional Abuse in the Local Church - Focus on the Family

www.focusonthefamily.com › ... › Understanding Emotional Abuse

Is your church a safe place for victims of emotional abuse ... prayer partners and
provide ongoing emotional and ... Cycle of Physical and Emotional Abuse, ...

8.   Emotional Abuse: Signs and Symptoms - Buzzle

www.buzzle.com/articles/emotional-abuse-signs-and-symptoms.html

But, unlike physical abuse, the effects of emotional abuse on mental health are long-
term and ... I believe it also took the help of a Higher power, prayers from ...

9.   Intensive Counseling for Abuse Healing - A Place of Hope

www.aplaceofhope.com/abuse-treatment.html

Emotional abuse; Physical abuse; Sexual abuse; Sexual assault/date rape; Other major
life traumas; Integrative Medicine, Whole Person Care. As you're experiencing a ...

10.   Emotional and Verbal Abuse Within Marriage : Marriage ...

marriagemissions.com/dealing-with-emotional-and-verbal-abuse ...

"Emotional abuse leaves few physical scars. ... He is putting me through so much
abuse and pain. I'm so confused. I pray to God to please give me guidance, ...

11.   This is a War: Emotional Abuse

www.thisisawar.com/AbuseEmotional.htm

Information about the impact of emotional abuse on relationships and on mental
health.

Dr. Elizabeth Thambiraj

12. Enmeshment: What Is Enmeshment? - EzineArticles

    ezinearticles.com › Relationships

    2012-10-29 · The word enmeshment is often used in the world of psychology, therapy and in every day relationships. These could be with family, friends and with intimate ...

13. The Bowen Center - Bowen Theory - Differentiation of Self

    www.thebowencenter.org/pages/conceptds.html

    Murray Bowen; 8 Concepts; Triangles; Differentiation of Self; Nuclear Family Emotional System; Family Projection Process; Multigenerational Transmission Process

Book References

1. Peter Scazzero, *Emotionally Healthy Spirituality* (Thomas Nelson, 2011).

2. I. Goldenberg and H. Goldenberg, *Family Therapy: An Overview* (Pacific Grove, CA: Brookes/Cole Publishing, 2007).

Other References

1. Dan Allender and Tremper Longman III, *Intimate Allies* (Carol Stream, IL: Tyndale House, 1995).

2. I. Goldenberg and H. Goldenberg, *Family Therapy: An Overview* (Pacific Grove, CA: Brookes/Cole Publishing, 2007).

3. R. W. Richardson, *Family Ties That Bind* (Vancouver, BC: International Self-Counsel Press, 1995).

4. Gary Thomas, *Sacred Marriage: What If God Designed Marriage More to Make Us Holy than to Make Us Happy* (Toronto: Harper Collins Canada, 2002).

5. Mary E. DeMuth, *Authentic Parenting in a Postmodern Culture: Practical Help for Shaping Your Children's Hearts, Minds, and Souls* (Eugene, OR: Harvest House Publishers, 2007).

6. William T. Kirwan, *Biblical Concepts for Christian Counseling: A Case for Integrating Psychology and Theology* (Grand Rapids, MI: Baker Book House, 1984).

Mystery of Relationships through the Lens of Scriptures

Recommended Reading & Resources

7. Larry Crabb, *Effective Biblical Counseling: How Caring Christians Can Become Capable Counselors* (Grand Rapids, MI: Zondervan, 1977).

8. Everett L. Worthington Jr., *Hope-Focused Marriage Counseling* (IL: IVP Academic, 2005).

9. Russell Barkley and Arthur Robin, *Your Defiant Teen: 10 Steps to Resolve Conflict and Rebuild Your Relationship* (New York: A division of Guilford Publications, 2008).

10. David Furlong, *Healing Your Family Patterns: How to Access the Past to Heal the Present* (London: Judy Piatkus, 1997).

For Further Reading

1. Millard J. Erickson, *Christian Theology* (Grand Rapids, MI: Baker Book House, 1985), 947–1002.

2. R. T. Kendall, *Understanding Theology: Developing a Healthy Church in the 21st Century* (1996), 357–364.

3. Jay E. Adams, *A Theology of Christian Counseling: More than Redemption* (Grand Rapids, MI: Zondervan, 1979), 249–275.

4. Louis Berkhof, *Systematic Theology* (Grand Rapids, MI: Eerdmans, 1996), 423–450.

5. Robert P. Lightner, *Handbook of Evangelical Theology: Historical, Biblical, and Contemporary Survey and Review* (Grand Rapids, MI: Baker Book House, 1986). 527–544.

6. Charles Ryrie, *Basic Theology* (Chicago: Moody Press, 1999), 374–377.

7. A. H. Strong, *Systematic Theology* (NJ: Fleming H. Revell, 1907). 869–881.

8. Wayne Grudem, *Systematic Theology: An Introduction to Biblical Doctrine* (Grand Rapids: Zondervan, 1994). 736–761; 840–850.

9. Steven W. Waterhouse, *Not by Bread Alone: An Outlined Guide to Bible Doctrine* (Amarillo, TX: Westcliffe Press, 2007). 188–191.

Dr. Elizabeth Thambiraj

10. John Theodore Muller, *Christian Dogmatics: A Handbook of Doctrinal Theology for Pastors, Teachers, and Laymen* (St. Louis, MO: Concordia Publishing House, 1934). 384–386.

11. "Prayer to Move Your Mountains," *Powerful Prayers for The Spirit-Filled Life* (Nashville, TN: Thomas Nelson, 2000).

12. John White, *Parables: The Greatest Stories Ever Told* (IL: Intervarsity Press, 1999).

13. *The ESV Study Bible* (Wheaton, IL: Crossway Bibles, 2008).

14. *The Matthew Henry Study Bible* (Iowa Falls, IA: World Bible Publishing, 1990).

Recommended Further Reading

1. Beverly Engel, The Emotionally Abused Woman: Overcoming Destructive Patterns and Reclaiming Yourself.

2. Beverly Engel, The Emotionally Abusive Relationship: How to Stop Being Abused and How to Stop Abusing.

3. Patricia Evans, *The Verbally Abusive Relationship: How to Recognize It and How to Respond* (Holbrook, MA: Bob Adams, 1992).

4. Stalking the Soul: Emotional Abuse and the Erosion of Identity.

5. Emotional Fitness.

Other References

1. Adapted from the University of Illinois Counseling Center and http://www.bpdcentral. com/resources/abuse/evabuse.shtml.

2. For a depiction of an abuse victim, see Richard Dreyfuss in *Silent Fall,* written by Akiva Goldsman (1994; Morgan Creek Productions, Warner Brothers).

Mystery of Relationships through the Lens of Scriptures

Misplaced Priorities

Website References

1. Misplaced Priority - My Spouse or My Job?

   ezinearticles.com › Relationships › Marriage

   2007-11-16 · My question to you today is what is your priority, your spouse or your job? Your pay check or your spouse's love? Acceptance by your colleagues at work or ...

2. Misplaced priority | Business Standard

   www.business-standard.com › Opinion › Editorial › Editorials

   Indians are taught early that science is only a means to an end. All the bright young people who enter the "science stream" of various schools are told to have their ...

3. Winter cycling misplaced 'priority' | Columnists ...

   www.calgarysun.com/2012/10/08/winter-cycling-misplaced-priority

   The good news is an extra 27 lane kilometres of road will be cleared sooner this winter. The bad news is the city isn't doing it because of increased traffic volume ...

4. Misplaced priority - Sify

   www.sify.com › Finance › Default

   2014-02-16 · Indians are taught early that science is only a means to an end. All the bright young people who enter the science stream of various schools are told to ...

5. A Misplaced Priority - MyDD

   mydd.com/story/2009/9/28/14128/9031

   The White House has announced that the President will travel to Copenhagen on Thursday in an effort to save Chicago's sagging bid to host the 2016 Summer Olympics.

Dr. Elizabeth Thambiraj

Bible Citations

King James Version (1611) - <u>View 1611 Bible Scan</u>

New American Standard Version (1995) - "Scripture taken from the NEW AMERICAN STANDARD BIBLE®, Copyright © 1960,1962,1963,1968,1971,1972,1973,1975,1977,19 95 by The Lockman Foundation. Used by permission."

American Standard Version (1901) – Scripture taken from the American Standard Version 1901 by Thomas Nelson & Sons.

Basic English Bible

Webster's Bible

Weymoth Bible

The World English Bible is based on the American Standard Version of the Holy Bible first published in 1901, the Biblia Hebraica Stutgartensa Old Testament, and the Greek Majority Text New Testament.

Wycliffe Bible Copyright © 2001 by Terence P. Noble.

Young's Literal Translation by Robert Young, 1862, 1887, 1898, author of *The Analytical Concordance to the Bible. Revised Edition.*

Book References

1. Peter Scazzero, *Emotionally Healthy Spirituality* (Thomas Nelson, 2011).

2. I. Goldenberg and H. Goldenberg, *Family Therapy: An Overview* (Pacific Grove, CA: Brookes/Cole Publishing, 2007).

Other References

1. Dan Allender and Tremper Longman III, *Intimate Allies* (Carol Stream, IL: Tyndale House, 1995).

2. I. Goldenberg and H. Goldenberg, *Family Therapy: An Overview* (Pacific Grove, CA: Brookes/Cole Publishing, 2007).

3. R. W. Richardson, *Family Ties That Bind* (Vancouver, BC: International Self-Counsel Press, 1995).

Mystery of Relationships through the Lens of Scriptures

4. Gary Thomas, *Sacred Marriage: What If God Designed Marriage More to Make Us Holy than to Make Us Happy* (Toronto: Harper Collins Canada, 2002).

5. Mary E. DeMuth, *Authentic Parenting in a Postmodern Culture: Practical Help for Shaping Your Children's Hearts, Minds, and Souls* (Eugene, OR: Harvest House Publishers, 2007).

6. William T. Kirwan, *Biblical Concepts for Christian Counseling: A Case for Integrating Psychology and Theology* (Grand Rapids, MI: Baker Book House, 1984).

Recommended Reading & Resources

7. Larry Crabb, *Effective Biblical Counseling: How Caring Christians Can Become Capable Counselors* (Grand Rapids, MI: Zondervan, 1977).

8. Everett L. Worthington Jr., *Hope-Focused Marriage Counseling* (IL: IVP Academic, 2005).

9. Russell Barkley and Arthur Robin, *Your Defiant Teen: 10 Steps to Resolve Conflict and Rebuild Your Relationship* (New York: A division of Guilford Publications, 2008).

10. David Furlong, *Healing Your Family Patterns: How to Access the Past to Heal the Present* (London: Judy Piatkus, 1997).

For Further Reading

1. Millard J. Erickson, *Christian Theology* (Grand Rapids, MI: Baker Book House, 1985), 947–1002.

2. R. T. Kendall, *Understanding Theology: Developing a Healthy Church in the 21st Century* (1996), 357–364.

3   Jay E. Adams, *A Theology of Christian Counseling: More than Redemption* (Grand Rapids, MI: Zondervan, 1979), 249–275.

4. Louis Berkhof, *Systematic Theology* (Grand Rapids, MI: Eerdmans, 1996), 423–450.

5. Robert P. Lightner, *Handbook of Evangelical Theology: Historical, Biblical, and Contemporary Survey and Review* (Grand Rapids, MI: Baker Book House, 1986), 527–544.

6. Charles Ryrie, *Basic Theology* (Chicago: Moody Press, 1999). 374–377.

Dr. Elizabeth Thambiraj

7. A. H. Strong, *Systematic Theology* (NJ: Fleming H. Revell, 1907), 869–881.

8 Wayne Grudem, *Systematic Theology: An Introduction to Biblical Doctrine* (Grand Rapids: Zondervan, 1994), 736–761; 840–850.

9. Steven W. Waterhouse, *Not by Bread Alone: An Outlined Guide to Bible Doctrine* (Amarillo, TX: Westcliffe Press, 2007), 188–191.

10. John Theodore Muller, *Christian Dogmatics: A Handbook of Doctrinal Theology for Pastors, Teachers, and Laymen* (St. Louis, MO: Concordia Publishing House, 1934), 384–386.

11. "Prayer to Move Your Mountains," *Powerful Prayers for The Spirit-Filled Life* (Nashville, TN: Thomas Nelson, 2000).

12. John White, *Parables: The Greatest Stories Ever Told* (IL: Intervarsity Press, 1999).

13. *The ESV Study Bible* (Wheaton, IL: Crossway Bibles, 2008).

14. *The Matthew Henry Study Bible* (Iowa Falls, IA: World Bible Publishing, 1990).

True Love

Website References

1. Definition for Forgiveness - AllAboutGOD.com

   www.allaboutgod.com/definition-for-forgiveness-faq.htm

   Read a definition of forgiveness and thoughts about when to forgive, how to help others forgive, and what to do when you don't feel …

2. Salvation - What is God's Plan of Salvation?

   christianity.about.com/od/conversion/p/salvation.htm

   An Easy Explanation of Biblical Salvation: Biblical salvation is God's way of providing his people deliverance from sin and spiritual death through repentance and faith in Jesus Christ. Jesus, the perfect God-man, came to offer the pure, complete and everlasting sacrif …

3. *Dictionary.com*, s.v. "affection," dictionary.reference.com/browse/Affection.

Mystery of Relationships through the Lens of Scriptures

4. Vocabulary.com, s.v. "anguish," www.vocabulary.com/dictionary/anguish.

    The noun anguish refers to severe physical or emotional pain or distress. A trip to the dentist might cause a cavity-prone person a lot of anguish.

5. *The Free Online Dictionary,* s.v. "suffering," www.thefreedictionary.com/suffering.

    The Scene of Suffering is a destructive or painful action, such as death on the stage, bodily agony, wounds and the like.

6. "Victory," *Wikipedia,* en.wikipedia.org/wiki/Victory.

    Victory (from Latin victoria) is a term, originally applied to warfare, given to success achieved in personal combat, after military operations in general or, by …

7. *Dictionary.com,* s.v. "victory," dictionary.reference.com/browse/victory.

    noun, plural victories. 1. a success or triumph over an enemy in battle or war. 2. an engagement ending in such triumph: American victories in the Pacific were won at …

8. "Contentment," *Wikipedia,* en.wikipedia.org/wiki/Contentment.

    Contentment is the acknowledgement and satisfaction of reaching capacity. The level of capacity reached may be sought after, expected, desired, or simply …

9. What the Bible Says About Contentment

    www.whatsaiththescripture.com/Fellowship/What_Bible_Contentment.html

    Godliness and contentment are indeed rare gems. They are the rarest of gem to be found in man.

10. Daily Bible Study - Song of Solomon 2-4

    www.keyway.ca/htm2008/20080114.htm

    Daily Bible Study. Bible. Discover the amazing truth of the Gospel. Eternal life … a well of living waters" (Song of Solomon 4:15 KJV) ultimately describe? See …

Other References

1. Dan Allender and Tremper Longman III, *Intimate Allies* (Carol Stream, IL: Tyndale House, 1995).

Dr. Elizabeth Thambiraj

2. I. Goldenberg and H. Goldenberg, *Family Therapy: An Overview* (Pacific Grove, CA: Brookes/Cole Publishing, 2007).

3. R. W. Richardson, *Family Ties That Bind* (Vancouver, BC: International Self-Counsel Press, 1995).

4. Gary Thomas, *Sacred Marriage: What If God Designed Marriage More to Make Us Holy than to Make Us Happy* (Toronto: Harper Collins Canada, 2002).

5. Mary E. DeMuth, *Authentic Parenting in a Postmodern Culture: Practical Help for Shaping Your Children's Hearts, Minds, and Souls* (Eugene, OR: Harvest House Publishers, 2007).

6. William T. Kirwan, *Biblical Concepts for Christian Counseling: A Case for Integrating Psychology and Theology* (Grand Rapids, MI: Baker Book House, 1984).

A Scriptural View of Marriage

Website References

1. Nehemiah Chapter 3 - THE STUDY BIBLE

www.thestudybible.org/Nehemiah-3

The book of Nehemiah chapter 3 from the King James Bible Online. The Study Bible. Search keywords in the Bible: Find a specific verse: Chapter ...

Book References

1. Peter Scazzero, *Emotionally Healthy Spirituality* (Thomas Nelson, 2011).

2. I. Goldenberg and H. Goldenberg, *Family Therapy: An Overview* (Pacific Grove, CA: Brookes/Cole Publishing, 2007)

3. *God's Words of Life on Marriage* (Zondervan, 2000).

Other References

1. Dan Allender and Tremper Longman III, *Intimate Allies* (Carol Stream, IL: Tyndale House, 1995).

Mystery of Relationships through the Lens of Scriptures

2. I. Goldenberg and H. Goldenberg, *Family Therapy: An Overview* (Pacific Grove, CA: Brookes/Cole Publishing, 2007).

3. R. W. Richardson, *Family Ties That Bind* (Vancouver, BC: International Self-Counsel Press, 1995).

4. Gary Thomas, *Sacred Marriage: What If God Designed Marriage More to Make Us Holy than to Make Us Happy* (Toronto: Harper Collins Canada, 2002).

5. Mary E. DeMuth, *Authentic Parenting in a Postmodern Culture: Practical Help for Shaping Your Children's Hearts, Minds, and Souls* (Eugene, OR: Harvest House Publishers, 2007).

6. William T. Kirwan, *Biblical Concepts for Christian Counseling: A Case for Integrating Psychology and Theology* (Grand Rapids, MI: Baker Book House, 1984).

Recommended *Reading* & Resources

7. Larry Crabb, *Effective Biblical Counseling: How Caring Christians Can Become Capable Counselors* (Grand Rapids, MI: Zondervan, 1977).

8. Everett L. Worthington Jr., *Hope-Focused Marriage Counseling* (IL: IVP Academic, 2005).

9. Russell Barkley and Arthur Robin, *Your Defiant Teen: 10 Steps to Resolve Conflict and Rebuild Your Relationship* (New York: A division of Guilford Publications, 2008).

10. David Furlong, *Healing Your Family Patterns: How to Access the Past to Heal the Present* (London: Judy Piatkus, 1997).

For Further Reading

1. Millard J. Erickson, *Christian Theology* (Grand Rapids, MI: Baker Book House, 1985), 947–1002.

2. R. T. Kendall, *Understanding Theology: Developing a Healthy Church in the 21st Century* (1996), 357–364.

3. Jay E. Adams, *A Theology of Christian Counseling: More than Redemption* (Grand Rapids, MI: Zondervan, 1979), 249–275.

4. Louis Berkhof, *Systematic Theology* (Grand Rapids, MI: Eerdmans, 1996), 423–450.

Dr. Elizabeth Thambiraj

5. Robert P. Lightner, *Handbook of Evangelical Theology: Historical, Biblical, and Contemporary Survey and Review* (Grand Rapids, MI: Baker Book House, 1986), 527–544.

6. Charles Ryrie, *Basic Theology* (Chicago: Moody Press, 1999), 374–377.

7. A. H. Strong, *Systematic Theology* (NJ: Fleming H. Revell, 1907), 869–881.

8. Wayne Grudem, *Systematic Theology: An Introduction to Biblical Doctrine* (Grand Rapids: Zondervan, 1994), 736–761; 840–850.

9   Steven W. Waterhouse, *Not by Bread Alone: An Outlined Guide to Bible Doctrine* (Amarillo, TX: Westcliffe Press, 2007), 188–191.

10. John Theodore Muller, *Christian Dogmatics: A Handbook of Doctrinal Theology for Pastors, Teachers, and Laymen* (St. Louis, MO: Concordia Publishing House, 1934), 384–386.

11. "Prayer to Move Your Mountains," *Powerful Prayers for The Spirit-Filled Life* (Nashville, TN: Thomas Nelson, 2000).

12. John White, *Parables: The Greatest Stories Ever Told* (IL: Intervarsity Press, 1999).

13. *The ESV Study Bible* (Wheaton, IL: Crossway Bibles, 2008).

14. *The Matthew Henry Study Bible* (Iowa Falls, IA: World Bible Publishing, 1990).

Gender Roles: A Glimpse

Book References

1. Dan Allender and Tremper Longman III, *Intimate Allies* (Carol Stream, IL: Tyndale House, 1995).

2. Jay E. Adams, *Critical Stages of Biblical Counseling: Finishing Well, Breaking Through, Getting Started* (NJ: Zondervan, 2002).

3. Jay E. Adams, *How to Help People Change: The Four-Step Biblical Process* (Grand Rapids, MI: Zondervan, 1986).

4. John F. MacArthur Jr., Wayne A. Mack, and the Master's College Faculty, *Introduction to Biblical Counseling: A Basic Guide to the Principles and Practice of Counseling* (Nashville: Thomas Nelson, 1994).

Mystery of Relationships through the Lens of Scriptures

5.   Jay E. Adams, *Lectures on Counseling* (Grand Rapids, MI: Baker Book House, 1978), 192–203.

6.   *Women of Destiny Bible: Women Mentoring Women through the Scriptures* (Nashville, TN: Thomas Nelson, 1982).

7.   Dan Allender and Tremper Longman III, *Intimate Allies* (Carol Stream, IL: Tyndale House, 1995), 301, 346.

8.   Ibid., 331.

9.   David A. Norris, *Lasting Success: Quality Decisions, Relationships, and Untamed Emotions* (Ames, IA: Alpha Heartland Press, 2003).

Website References

1.   Gender Roles in the Bible | Wanderings Toward Truth …

      williamsofield.wordpress.com/2007/11/02/gender-roles-in-the-bible

      2007-11-02 · When the Bible talks about gender roles, it only talks about them in the context of family and church. … think that from a biblical perspective, …

2.   Gender Roles In A Biblical Perspective For The Orthodox …

      www.orthodoxherald.com/2010/06/12/gender-roles-in-a-biblical …

      Gender Roles In A Biblical Perspective For The Orthodox Christians In The American Context. Written By: Fr. Dr. Jacob Mathew on Jun 12th, 2010 and filed under …

3.   ::: www.2Timothy42.org :: Gender Issues from a Biblical …

      www.2timothy42.org/Resources/essay.php?EssayID=5

      Gender Issues from a Biblical Perspective: A Response to Evangelical Feminism. When dealing with the historical relationships between the church and gender, …

Part III

William T. Kirwan, *Biblical Concepts for Christian Counseling: A Case for Integrating Psychology and Theology* (Grand Rapids, MI: Baker Book House, 1984).

Dr. Elizabeth Thambiraj

Part IV

End Notes

1. Focus Helps | Emotional and verbal abuse |

    www.focushelps.ca/article/addictions-abuse/verbal-and-emotional ...

    ... emotional abuse is even more devastating than physical abuse.

    Emotional abuse tears at a person's self-esteem and can greatly impair ... Can we pray for ...

2. Ibid.

For Further Reading

"The Hardwired Difference between Male and Female Brains Could Explain Why Men Are 'Better at Map Reading,'" *The Independent*, http://www.independent.co.uk/life-style/the-hardwired-difference-between-male-and-female-brains-could-explain-why-men-are-better-at-map-reading-8978248.html. Intuition is thinking without thinking. It's what people call gut feelings.

Book References

1. Peter Scazzero, *Emotionally Healthy Spirituality* (Thomas Nelson, 2011).

2. I. Goldenberg and H. Goldenberg, *Family Therapy: An Overview* (Pacific Grove, CA: Brookes/Cole Publishing, 2007).

3. *God's Words of Life on Marriage* (Zondervan, 2000).

Other References

1. Dan Allender and Tremper Longman III, *Intimate Allies* (Carol Stream, IL: Tyndale House, 1995).

2. I. Goldenberg and H. Goldenberg, *Family Therapy: An Overview* (Pacific Grove, CA: Brookes/Cole Publishing, 2007).

Mystery of Relationships through the Lens of Scriptures

3. R. W. Richardson, *Family Ties That Bind* (Vancouver, BC: International Self-Counsel Press, 1995).

4. Gary Thomas, *Sacred Marriage: What If God Designed Marriage More to Make Us Holy than to Make Us Happy* (Toronto: Harper Collins Canada, 2002).

5. Mary E. DeMuth, *Authentic Parenting in a Postmodern Culture: Practical Help for Shaping Your Children's Hearts, Minds, and Souls* (Eugene, OR: Harvest House Publishers, 2007).

6. William T. Kirwan, *Biblical Concepts for Christian Counseling: A Case for Integrating Psychology and Theology* (Grand Rapids, MI: Baker Book House, 1984).

Recommended Reading & Resources

7. Larry Crabb, *Effective Biblical Counseling: How Caring Christians Can Become Capable Counselors* (Grand Rapids, MI: Zondervan, 1977).

8. Everett L. Worthington Jr., *Hope-Focused Marriage Counseling* (IL: IVP Academic, 2005).

9. Russell Barkley and Arthur Robin, *Your Defiant Teen: 10 Steps to Resolve Conflict and Rebuild Your Relationship* (New York: A division of Guilford Publications, 2008).

10. David Furlong, *Healing Your Family Patterns: How to Access the Past to Heal the Present* (London: Judy Piatkus, 1997).

For Further Reading

1. Millard J. Erickson, *Christian Theology* (Grand Rapids, MI: Baker Book House, 1985), 947–1002.

2. R. T. Kendall, *Understanding Theology: Developing a Healthy Church in the 21st Century* (1996), 357–364.

3. Jay E. Adams, *A Theology of Christian Counseling: More than Redemption* (Grand Rapids, MI: Zondervan, 1979), 249–275.

4. Louis Berkhof, *Systematic Theology* (Grand Rapids, MI: Eerdmans, 1996), 423–450.

Dr. Elizabeth Thambiraj

5. Robert P. Lightner, *Handbook of Evangelical Theology: Historical, Biblical, and Contemporary Survey and Review* (Grand Rapids, MI: Baker Book House, 1986), 527–544.

6. Charles Ryrie, *Basic Theology* (Chicago: Moody Press, 1999), 374–377.

7. A. H. Strong, *Systematic Theology* (NJ: Fleming H. Revell, 1907), 869–881.

8. Wayne Grudem, *Systematic Theology: An Introduction to Biblical Doctrine* (Grand Rapids: Zondervan, 1994), 736–761; 840–850.

9. Steven W. Waterhouse, *Not by Bread Alone: An Outlined Guide to Bible Doctrine* (Amarillo, TX: Westcliffe Press, 2007), 188–191.

10. John Theodore Muller, *Christian Dogmatics: A Handbook of Doctrinal Theology for Pastors, Teachers, and Laymen* (St. Louis, MO: Concordia Publishing House, 1934), 384–386.

11. "Prayer to Move Your Mountains," *Powerful Prayers for The Spirit-Filled Life* (Nashville, TN: Thomas Nelson, 2000).

12. John White, *Parables: The Greatest Stories Ever Told* (IL: Intervarsity Press, 1999).

13. *The ESV Study Bible* (Wheaton, IL: Crossway Bibles, 2008).

14. *The Matthew Henry Study Bible* (Iowa Falls, IA: World Bible Publishing, 1990).

Selected Bibliography

Adams, Jay E. *The Christian Counselor's Manual: The Practice of Nouthetic Counseling.* Grand Rapids, MI: Zondervan, 1973.

———. *Critical Stages of Biblical Counseling: Finishing Well, Breaking Through, Getting Started.* NJ: Zondervan, 2002.

———. *How to Help People Change: The Four-Step Biblical Process.* Grand Rapids, MI: Zondervan, 1986.

———. *Lectures on Counseling.* Grand Rapids, MI: Baker Book House, 1978. 192–203.

Almy, Gary L., *How Christian Is Christian Counseling? The Dangerous Secular Influences That Keep Us from Caring for Souls.* IL: Crossway Books, 2000. 43–51.

Berkhof, Louis. *Systematic Theology.* Grand Rapids, MI: Eerdmans, 1996. 423–450.

Benner, David G., and Peter C. Hill. *Baker Encyclopedia of Psychology and Counseling.* 2nd ed. Grand Rapids, MI: Baker Books, 1999.

Brand, Paul, and Philip Yancey. *Fearfully and Wonderfully Made: A Surgeon Looks at the Human and Spiritual Body.* Zondervan: 1987.

Corey, Gerald. *Theory and Practice of Counseling and Psychotherapy, From the comprehensive Corey Library of Texts and Videos.* Brooks and Cole, Thomas Learning, Stamford: <u>U.S.A@ HYPERLINK "mailto:U.S.A@2001"2001</u>.

Crab, Larry. *Effective Biblical Counseling: How Caring Christians can Become Capable Counselors.* Hammersmith, 1985. 100–104.

Erickson, Millard J. *Christian Theology.* Grand Rapids, MI: Baker Book House, 1985. 947–1002.

Eyre, Stephen D. *Deuteronomy: Becoming Holy People, IVP Connect.* Downers Grove, IL: Intervarsity Press, 2004. 32–26.

The ESV Study Bible. Wheaton, IL: Crossway Bibles, 2008.

Grudem, Wayne. *Systematic Theology: An Introduction to Biblical Doctrine.* Grand Rapids, MI: Zondervan, 1994. 736–761, 840–850.

Jacobson, Michael D. *A Biblical and Medical Overview of How to Care for Your Body and Mind: The Word on Health.* Chicago: Moody Press, 2000.

Dr. Elizabeth Thambiraj

Keller, Timothy. *Counterfeit Gods: The Empty Promises of Money, Sex, and Power, and the Only Hope That Matters.* New York: Penguin, 2009.

——. *The Prodigal God: Recovering the Heart of the Christian Faith.* New York: Penguin, 2008.

——. *The Reason for God: Belief in an Age of Skepticism.* New York: Penguin, 2008. 170–200.

Kendall, R. T. *Understanding Theology: Developing a Healthy Church in the 21st Century.* 1996. 357–364.

Kirwan, William T. *Biblical Concepts for Christian Counseling: A Case for Integrating Psychology and Theology.* Grand Rapids, MI: Baker Book House, 1984.

Lightner, Robert P. *Handbook of Evangelical Theology: Historical, Biblical, and Contemporary Survey and Review.* Grand Rapids, MI: Baker Book House, 1986. 527–544.

MacArthur, John F. Jr., and Wayne A. Mack. The Master's College Faculty. *Introduction to Biblical Counseling: A Basic Guide to the Principles and Practice of Counseling.* Nashville, TN: Thomas Nelson, 1994.

Malgo, Wim. *Biblical Counseling from Twenty-Five Years of the International Ministry by Wim Malgo.* Columbia, SC: Midnight Call, 1979. 9–12.

The Matthew Henry Study Bible: The Best of Matthew Henry's Notes in a Handy One-Volume Reference Bible. Iowa Falls, IA: World Bible Publishing, 1994.

Metzeger, Bruce M., and Michael D. Coogan, eds. *The Oxford Companion to the Bible.* Oxford, UK: Oxford University Press, 1993.

Miller, William R., and Kathleen A. Jackson. *Practical Psychology for Pastors.* NJ: The University of Mexico, Prentice Hall, Upper S le River, 1995. 248–292.

Mitchell, Stephen. *The Book of Job.* North Point Press: San Francisco, 1987. Cited in R. T. Pennock. *Tower of Babel.* Cambridge, MA: MIT Press, 1999.

Moore, Beth. *David: Seeking a Heart Like His.* Nashville, TN: Life Way Christian Resources, 2010. 206–210.

Muller, John Theodore. *Christian Dogmatics: A handbook of Doctrinal Theology for Pastors, Teachers, and Laymen.* St. Louis, MO: Concordia Publishing House, 1934. 384–386.

Norris, David A. *Lasting Success: Quality Decisions, Relationships, and Untamed Emotions.* Ames, IA: Heartland Press, 2003.

258

Mystery of Relationships through the Lens of Scriptures

Omartin, Stormie. *The Power of a Praying Wife.* Eugene, OR: Harvest House Publishers, 1997. 81–85.

Powlison, David. *Seeing with New Eyes: Counseling and Human Condition through the Lens of Scripture.* NJ: P&R Publishing, 2003. 211–223.

"Prayer to Move Your Mountains." *Powerful Prayers for the Spirit-Filled Life.* Nashville: Thomas Nelson, Inc, 2000.

Price, Charles. *Living Truth: Experiencing Christ in You; Journey into the Heart of God.* Toronto.

Ryrie, Charles. *Basic Theology.* Chicago: Moody Press, 1999. 374–377.

Strong, A. H. *Systematic Theology.* NJ: Fleming H. Revell, 1907. 869–881.

VanAtta, Lucibel. *Women Encouraging Women:* Portland, OR: Multnomah, 1987. 129–130.

Waterhouse, Steven W. *Not by Bread Alone: An Outlined Guide to Bible Doctrine.* Amarillo, TX: Westcliffe Press, 2007. 188–191.

White, John. *Parables: The Greatest Stories Ever Told.* IL: Intervarsity Press, 1999.

Women of Destiny Bible: Women Mentoring Women through the Scriptures. Nashville, TN: Thomas Nelson Publishers, 1982.

Suggestions for Further Reading

Access the videos at http://www.bcdasocal.org/.

Below is a list of my forty favorite books on biblical counseling.

- Adams, Jay. *Competent to Counsel: Biblical Counseling.* 1970. The book that started the biblical counseling movement. Jay Adams challenged the concept of Christian psychology/psychiatry with boldly proclaimed truth about the sufficiency of God's Word and His grace as the true solution for the life problems of Christians.
- Adams, Jay. *Theology of Christian Counseling Theology and Counseling.* Jay Adams addresses the topics of counseling with theology.
- Adams, Jay. *Christian Counselor's Manual.* 1973. This work is 475 pages of practical application of scripture to numerous life and counseling issues. This book was the first of its kind and still a beneficial resource.
- Adams, Jay. *Marriage, Divorce, and Remarriage.* Detailed analysis of everything the Bible teaches on each of the three topics. Necessary resource for counseling cases involving marriage, divorce, and remarriage issues.
- Adams, Jay. *The Christian Counselor's Commentary Counseling Commentary.* Adams's own translation is featured in this unique series of commentaries, in which the author relates Bible passages to discipleship and counseling topics.

Dr. Elizabeth Thambiraj

- Adams, Jay. *Christ and Your Problems.* One of the best first-week homework assignments, this is an accurate, readable, practical exposition of 1 Corinthians 10:13.
- Berg, Jim. *Changed into His Image [Sanctification].* Fine, thorough study on the process of biblical change including putting the flesh to death, renewing the mind, and becoming like Christ. Includes useful reproducible study sheets.
- Berg, Jim. *Created for His Glory [Redemption + its Implications].* Another practical and theologically precise book from the long-time dean of students at Bob Jones University. Includes specific studies and tools for use by disciple makers and biblical counselors.
- Bevington, Bob and Jerry Bridges. *The Great Exchange.* This book chronicles the atonement one key verse at a time through Acts and the epistles. Good theology is vital to good counseling and discipleship.
- Bridges, Jerry. *Pursuit of Holiness.* One of the top five discipleship books, useful for strengthening the immature believer's understanding of life's purpose and how to respond to the truth of God's Word.
- Bridges, Jerry. *Respectable Sins [Confront, Overcome Sin].* Describes the despicable nature of sin and the Bible's methods for overcoming sin and comments on specific common sins that must be overcome.
- Bulkley, Ed. *Only God Can Heal the Heart.* 1995. Weaves a fictional tale of psychology, biblical counseling, real-life issues, and some memorable characters with practical teaching on biblical counseling principles.
- Fitzpatrick, Elyse. *Love to Eat, Hate to Eat [Food, Eating].* A well-written, practical, biblical perspective on common

Mystery of Relationships through the Lens of Scriptures

struggles with food, the motives behind them, and the biblical solution to these sins.

- Friessen, Gerry. *Decision Making and the Will of God [Decision Making]*. This extensive book examines the Christian culture's common unbiblical methods of decision making and the Bible's teaching on how to choose when no option is commanded by scripture.

- Ganz, Rich. *Psychobabble [Psychology/Psychiatry]*. This landmark book is Rich Ganz's testimony of how he went from secular psychiatrist to Christian to biblical counselor. Now a pastor, Rich writes clearly and with memorable accounts.

- Halla, Jim. *Pain: The Plight of Fallen Man [Pain]*. Medical Doctor Jim Halla has written the top book on the Bible's counsel for those who suffer from severe or unending pain.

- Harvey, Dave. *When Sinners Say "I Do" [Marriage]*. Pastor Dave Harvey combines theological truths about anthropology, bibliology, and sanctification with the forum of marriage. The result is practical truth for each stage of marriage.

- Hendrickson, Laura. *Autism Spectrum [Autism]*. Medical Doctor Laura Hendrickson uses God's Word and the experience of her ministry to her own son to provide an excellent application of scripture to a specific issue of our time.

- Hendrickson, Laura and Elyse Fitzpatrick. *Will Medicine Stop the Pain? [Pain, Prescription Meds]*. Dr. Hendrickson and Elyse Fitzpatrick discuss real-life issues: depression, anxiety, emotions, and fear. The culture's solution (prescription medications) is contrasted with God's sufficient word.

- Johnston, Wayne and Wayne Mack. *A Christian Growth and Discipleship Manual [Homework]*. Useful studies for

Dr. Elizabeth Thambiraj

discipling and biblical counseling. Each topic is addressed thoroughly. Studies are useful for personal growth, homework assignments, or as resources for topical studies.

- MacArthur, John. *Counseling.* Landmark book that addresses counseling theologically (finding the scriptures as the source for God-honoring counsel) and practically (with Wayne Mack's counseling model).

- MacArthur, John. *Pastoral Ministry.* Practical, challenging book for shepherds striving to please the Master by serving the flock.

- MacArthur, John. *Slave.* Only two translations render *doulos* as "slave." Dr. MacArthur unpacks the truth of this word that most New Testament authors used to describe themselves to point us to biblical views of self and Christ.

- MacArthur, John. *Our Sufficiency in Christ [Bibliology].* 1991. Claims that the Word of God is sufficient for counseling Christians. A bold contrast of the counsel of scripture and the counsel of our culture.

- Mack, Wayne. *Fear Factor [Fear].* Thorough book that is vital for developing a biblical view of fear, anxiety, worry, and the solutions of God's Word for each. Carefully explained examples and application questions.

- Mack, Wayne. *Strengthening Your Marriage [Marriage].* A thorough collection of Bible studies, data-gathering resources, and homework assignments essential for every discipler and biblical counselor.

- Mack, Wayne and Carol Mack. *Sweethearts for a Lifetime [Marriage].* Wayne and Carol Mack use the wisdom derived from years of studying God's Word in regard to marriage to

Mystery of Relationships through the Lens of Scriptures

create a practical, useful book with plenty of precise questions and helpful resources.

- Mack, Wayne. *Homework Manual for Biblical Living Volumes 1 and 2 [Homework]*. Wayne Mack's original collection of biblical counseling homework assignments is essential, especially in the unique and practical data-gathering, log-list, self-rating, and score-card creations.

- Peace, Martha. *The Excellent Wife [Marriage: Wife]*. Brilliant and systematic summary of scripture's teachings for the married Christian woman.

- Powlison, David. *Seeing with New Eyes [Biblical Counseling]*. A foundational and sweeping explanation of how the scriptures address man and counseling.

- Priolo, Lou. *Heart of Anger [Parenting]*. Detailed examination of biblical hamartiology and anthropology in regard to angry children. The book employs real-life examples, practical exposition of scripture, and understandable methods.

- Priolo, Lou. *The Complete Husband [Marriage: Husband]*. Thorough study of the roles and responsibilities of a husband.

- Smith, Robert. *The Christian Counselor's Medical Desk Reference [Medical, Physical]*. Medical Doctor and NANC Board Member Robert Smith explains the body, medicine, psychotropic drugs, physical versus nonphysical problems, depression, fatigue, sexual problems, sleep, and many other current medical issues from God's Word and the perspective of a physician.

- Strauch, Alexander. *Biblical Eldership [Church Leadership]*. A case for eldership that reflects the Word of God. Vital for church leaders.

Dr. Elizabeth Thambiraj

- Tripp, Paul David. *War of Words [Communication].* Solid, useful book addressing communication from God's Word.
- Tripp, Paul David. *Instruments in the Redeemer's Hands [Biblical Counseling].* Love, know, speak, do. This is the author's format for biblical counseling and discipleship. A person-to-person ministry can be enhanced by understanding the biblical principles of this book.
- Tripp, Paul David. *Age of Opportunity [Parenting Teens].* Useful writing about how the Bible addresses common family conflicts and teen problems.
- Wheat, Ed and Gaye Wheat. *Intended for Pleasure [Sex].* Practical, useful, direct, and beneficial explanation of sexual relations physically and in regard to the theology of the Bible. Ed Wheat is a medical doctor and biblical counselor.
- Whitney, Don. *Spiritual Disciplines for the Christian Life [Discipleship].* Southern Baptist Theological Seminary Professor Don Whitney provides fine instruction for ten biblical disciplines taught in God's Word (we disagree on chapter 9). A must for disciplers.
- Younts, Jay. *Everyday Talk [Parenting].* The rare book that addresses Christian parenting with a real, understandable balance of all the tools God gives parents to communicate with, to love, to teach, and to train their children. A good read.

can be obtained at www.ICGtesting.com

01B/3/P